IIOP Complete

Understanding CORBA and Middleware Interoperability

The Addison-Wesley Object Technology Series

Grady Booch, Ivar Jacobson, and James Rumbaugh, Series Editors

For more information check out the series web site [http://www.awl.com /cseng/otseries/] as well as the pages on each book [http://www.awl.com/cseng/I-S-B-N/] (I-S-B-N represents the actual ISBN, including dashes).

David Bellin and Susan Suchman Simone, *The CRC Card Book*, ISBN 0-201-89535-8

Robert V. Binder, *Testing Object-Oriented Systems: Models, Patterns, and Tools*, ISBN 0-201-80938-9

Bob Blakley, *CORBA Security: An Introduction to Safe Computing with Objects*, ISBN 0-201-32565-9

Grady Booch, *Object Solutions: Managing the Object-Oriented Project*, ISBN 0-8053-0594-7

Grady Booch, *Object-Oriented Analysis and Design with Applications, Second Edition*, ISBN 0-8053-5340-2

Grady Booch, James Rumbaugh, and Ivar Jacobson, *The Unified Modeling Language User Guide*, ISBN 0-201-57168-4

Don Box, *Essential COM*, ISBN 0-201-63446-5

Don Box, Keith Brown, Tim Ewald, and Chris Sells, *Effective COM: 50 Ways to Improve Your COM and MTS-based Applications*, ISBN 0-201-37968-6

Alistair Cockburn, *Surviving Object-Oriented Projects: A Manager's Guide*, ISBN 0-201-49834-0

Dave Collins, *Designing Object-Oriented User Interfaces*, ISBN 0-8053-5350-X

Jim Conallen, *Building Web Applications with UML*, ISBN 0-201-61577-0

Bruce Powel Douglass, *Doing Hard Time: Designing and Implementing Embedded Systems with UML*, ISBN 0-201-49837-5

Bruce Powel Douglass, *Real-Time UML, Second Edition: Developing Efficient Objects for Embedded Systems*, ISBN 0-201-65784-8

Desmond F. D'Souza and Alan Cameron Wills, *Objects, Components, and Frameworks with UML: The Catalysis Approach*, ISBN 0-201-31012-0

Martin Fowler, *Analysis Patterns: Reusable Object Models*, ISBN 0-201-89542-0

Martin Fowler, *Refactoring: Improving the Design of Existing Code*, ISBN 0-201-48567-2

Martin Fowler with Kendall Scott, *UML Distilled, Second Edition: Applying the Standard Object Modeling Language*, ISBN 0-201-65783-X

Peter Heinckiens, *Building Scalable Database Applications: Object-Oriented Design, Architectures, and Implementations*, ISBN 0-201-31013-9

Christine Hofmeister, Robert Nord, Soni Dilip, *Applied Software Architecture*, ISBN 0-201-32571-3

Ivar Jacobson, Grady Booch, and James Rumbaugh, *The Unified Software Development Process*, ISBN 0-201-57169-2

Ivar Jacobson, Magnus Christerson, Patrik Jonsson, and Gunnar Overgaard, *Object-Oriented Software Engineering: A Use Case Driven Approach*, ISBN 0-201-54435-0

Ivar Jacobson, Maria Ericsson, and Agneta Jacobson, *The Object Advantage: Business Process Reengineering with Object Technology*, ISBN 0-201-42289-1

Ivar Jacobson, Martin Griss, and Patrik Jonsson, *Software Reuse: Architecture, Process and Organization for Business Success*, ISBN 0-201-92476-5

David Jordan, *C++ Object Databases: Programming with the ODMG Standard*, ISBN 0-201-63488-0

Philippe Kruchten, *The Rational Unified Process: An Introduction*, ISBN 0-201-60459-0

Wilf LaLonde, *Discovering Smalltalk*, ISBN 0-8053-2720-7

Dean Leffingwell and Don Widrig, *Managing Software Requirements: A Unified Approach*, ISBN 0-201-61593-2

Chris Marshall, *Enterprise Modeling with UML: Designing Successful Software through Business Analysis*, ISBN 0-201-43313-3

Lockheed Martin Advanced Concepts Center and Rational Software Corporation, *Succeeding with the Booch and OMT Methods: A Practical Approach*, ISBN 0-8053-2279-5

Thomas Mowbray and William Ruh, *Inside CORBA: Distributed Object Standards and Applications*, ISBN 0-201-89540-4

Bernd Oestereich, *Developing Software with UML: Object-Oriented Analysis and Design in Practice*, ISBN 0-201-39826-5

Meilir Page-Jones, *Fundamentals of Object-Oriented Design in UML*, ISBN 0-201-69946-X

Ira Pohl, *Object-Oriented Programming Using C++, Second Edition*, ISBN 0-201-89550-1

Rob Pooley and Perdita Stevens, *Using UML: Software Engineering with Objects and Components*, ISBN 0-201-36067-5

Terry Quatrani, *Visual Modeling with Rational Rose 2000 and UML*, ISBN 0-201-69961-3

Brent E. Rector and Chris Sells, *ATL Internals*, ISBN 0-201-69589-8

Paul R. Reed, Jr., *Developing Applications with Visual Basic and UML*, ISBN 0-201-61579-7

Doug Rosenberg with Kendall Scott, *Use Case Driven Object Modeling with UML: A Practical Approach*, ISBN 0-201-43289-7

Walker Royce, *Software Project Management: A Unified Framework*, ISBN 0-201-30958-0

William Ruh, Thomas Herron, and Paul Klinker, *IIOP Complete: Middleware Interoperability and Distributed Object Standards*, ISBN 0-201-37925-2

James Rumbaugh, Ivar Jacobson, and Grady Booch, *The Unified Modeling Language Reference Manual*, ISBN 0-201-30998-X

Geri Schneider and Jason P. Winters, *Applying Use Cases: A Practical Guide*, ISBN 0-201-30981-5

Yen-Ping Shan and Ralph H. Earle, *Enterprise Computing with Objects: From Client/Server Environments to the Internet*, ISBN 0-201-32566-7

David N. Smith, *IBM Smalltalk: The Language*, ISBN 0-8053-0908-X

Daniel Tkach, Walter Fang, and Andrew So, *Visual Modeling Technique: Object Technology Using Visual Programming*, ISBN 0-8053-2574-3

Daniel Tkach and Richard Puttick, *Object Technology in Application Development, Second Edition*, ISBN 0-201-49833-2

Jos Warmer and Anneke Kleppe, *The Object Constraint Language: Precise Modeling with UML*, ISBN 0-201-37940-6

IIOP Complete

Understanding CORBA
and Middleware Interoperability

William Ruh
Thomas Herron
Paul Klinker

ADDISON-WESLEY

An imprint of Addison Wesley Longman, Inc.

Reading, Massachusetts • Harlow, England • Menlo Park, California
Berkeley, California • Don Mills, Ontario, • Sydney
Bonn • Amsterdam • Tokyo • Mexico City

The publisher offers discounts on this book when ordered in quantity for special sales. For more information, please contact:

Corporate Government and Special Sales
Addison Wesley Longman, Inc.
One Jacob Way
Reading, Massachusetts 01867
(781) 944-3700

Library of Congress Cataloging-in-Publication Data

IIOP complete: understanding CORBA and Middleware Interoperability
      p.   cm.
    ISBN 0-201-37925-2
    1. Middleware. 2. Object-oriented programming (Computer science)
    3. CORBA (Computer architecture)
    QA76.76.M54I36   1999
    005.2'76—dc21   99–11446
                                                            CIP

ISBN 0-201-37925-2
Text printed on recycled and acid-free paper.
1 2 3 4 5 6 7 8 9 10—ML—03 02 01 00 99
First printing, October 1999

Dedication

To my Mother, who taught me to be honest,
and my wife, Karen, who keeps me honest

To my wife, Kathleen, and my parents, Maryellen and James Herron

To my wife, Linda Wiesman Klinker

Contents

List of Figures and Tables

Foreword

"All beginnings are hard." This maxim, thought by the character David Lurie in Chaim Potok's magnificent work *In the Beginning,* carries through most of Potok's books. The reasoning is simple; it's true on many levels, throughout life. From the activation energy necessary to catalyze a chemical reaction, to the "learning curve" necessary to master a new technology, new beginnings require a commitment to make the necessary leaps of faith to bridge to a new way of thinking and doing. Lurie goes on to say to the reader, "Especially a beginning that you make for yourself. That's the hardest beginning of all."

So, reader, here you sit with a tome which intends to progress you on the road to building distributed solutions for the enterprise, an enterprise which grew organically to include what appears to be every known binary format, programming language, operating system, and network protocol ever known. You haven't a choice; we're all building distributed solutions, never more so than since the Internet caused our supply chains to be more closely connected than ever. In the decade since the foundation of the Object Management Group, I've watched as the distributed system integration problem got somewhat easier to solve, but more importantly, as systems managers, developers, and planners finally recognized the underlying problem itself.

Here's the bad news: distributed systems are hard. Distributed computing introduces new system failure modes, new systems incompatibilities, higher reliance on trusted systems, new concurrency and deadlock problems, and a host of new management issues. That is, as a good friend of mine once put it, distributed computing includes some inherent difficulty, limitations of physics we might say, that only magic can overcome.

Fortunately, there is good news to take with the bad. Even tools that fail to meet the standard of miracles, that bring forth only pebbles from stones, can be of value to you in building integrated systems for the heterogeneous enterprise. Not surprisingly, the cornerstone of the solution has to rest on standards, standards which seek not to impose regularity on the chaos, but rather seek only to get all the elements to agree to speak. In the vernacular of today, some territory must be yielded for peace.

The foundations of distributed computing in the heterogeneous enterprise rest squarely on the Common Object Request Broker Architecture (CORBA) standard. Designed for heterogeneity in all aspects, supporting languages from

1950's COBOL to 1990's Java, CORBA focuses on getting agreement where it counts: at the edges (application programming interfaces) of the brittle systems (both new and legacy) which make up today's real computing world. CORBA implementations from dozens of vendors have been successfully deployed in customs and immigration services, real-time news delivery services, equity and risk trading settings, military early warning surveillance, retail and supply-chain solutions, human genome sequencing systems, discrete and continuous manufacturing lines, and thousands of other uses.

But back to you, reader. To join the ranks of those that have successfully deployed distributed technology in a real system, you're about to apply your own activation energy by reading this book. With its focus on architects, developers, and integrators, including its detailed references and clear overviews, this book will give you the background you need to solve the inherently difficult systems development problems. More important, Mr. Ruh's extensive background and experience in building and directing the construction of large systems, and his keen insight into future trends, will help you sort out the morass of enterprise integration languages and interfaces.

I'm not sure reading systems architecture and programming references is generally considered amusing, but you will find in these pages more than sufficient information to get you past the difficult beginning. Enjoy the journey!

Richard Mark Soley, Ph.D.
Chairman and Chief Executive Officer
Object Management Group, Inc.
Framingham, Massachusetts
January 1999

Preface

The Importance of Middleware and Interoperability

The development of applications in business enterprises has been fundamentally altered by two strong desires. The first is to be able to develop new software as components, thereby allowing their reuse. The second is to be able to create new applications by integrating legacy systems, databases, and components with new packaged or Internet applications in very short time frames. *Middleware* is the name given to a breed of software that allows component technology to be developed and integrated into new applications. The software industry has rushed to fill this need by providing a wide variety of middleware technologies. Much of what has been available is proprietary to a specific vendor, thereby locking a developer into its solution. However, this has been changing through the efforts of groups such as the Object Management Group (OMG) that have provided a forum for the creation of middleware standards.

Most enterprise information systems contain a diversity of technology in their operational systems. Being tied to any single vendor puts an enterprise at a disadvantage because no one can accurately predict the demands that it will have for the next generation of applications. The Internet will be a critical component of every major enterprise in the future, and the nature of its design and usage requires that an organization support diversity.

The Common Object Request Broker Architecture (CORBA) is a standard for distributed object middleware created by the OMG. The Internet Inter-ORB Protocol (IIOP) is one of the standards created by the OMG. IIOP was established to allow interoperability of CORBA middleware and distributed components. It has become widely adopted by many software vendors and embedded into their products.

This book is about the state of middleware technology, focusing on the issue of interoperability. Middleware evolution will continue at an ever increasing pace, with an emphasis on distributed objects and components. Interoperability will be demanded by developers to ease their burdens in integrating together distributed components and applications and IIOP will play an important role in solving this problem.

The IIOP specification is an extremely simple and concise document. However, it is only a description of the standard. By itself, it doesn't aid the reader in acquiring a deeper understanding of the technology. This book is intended to provide the reader with an understanding of the IIOP standard and its usage. It is aimed at readers who currently use or will use technologies that employ IIOP. It can help the network engineer understand the effect of the protocol, the programmer to make better design decisions, and the integrator to help non-object systems integrate with object-based systems.

To thoroughly understand IIOP, one must view it from three perspectives. The first is *technical,* including a treatment of the standard, examples, and considerations related to implementation. The second is *interoperability,* to examine potential configurations in which IIOP can be applied. The third is *business,* to understand how IIOP fits into the marketplace and the level of acceptance it has and might achieve.

The authors have each been involved with object technology from both a system integration and product development perspective. Through these experiences, we have used a variety of competing technologies as well as applied IIOP-based technology to new systems and applications. This book will help the reader develop interoperable solutions using IIOP.

Overview of Contents

Part 1 provides a solid discussion of IIOP and its place in the world. It is aimed at the reader who does not understand middleware and its evolution. Chapter 1 touches on most aspects of IIOP, giving a quick peek at the book's contents. Chapter 2 gives a broad understanding of the current state of middleware technology. At the end of Part 1, the reader should understand the world of middleware, with an emphasis on the CORBA and IIOP standards.

Part 2 is a detailed discussion of the IIOP standard. Chapter 3 describes the OMG standards process that established IIOP. It describes IIOP's message formats, data representations, and transport requirements in Chapters 4 and 5. Chapter 6 explains how several CORBA ORBs have implemented IIOP. All aspects of the standard are addressed in detail, as well as the latest changes to the standard in Chapter 7. These changes will find themselves in the next generation of CORBA-based products.

Part 3 discusses advanced topics related to IIOP. This includes a description in Chapter 8 of the role of security in middleware as well as how it can be accomplished using IIOP. Other topics addressed in Chapters 9 and 10 are how to build interoperable solutions, the fit of IIOP into Java and the Web, and the future of IIOP.

Acknowledgments

The process of writing a book requires a significant amount of support from many people. This support comes in the form of reviews, discussion, encouragement, organization, and coordination. We were fortunate to have support from a wide variety of friends, associates, and other characters. We wish to thank all of them for being there at our moments of need. We especially want to thank Bret Hartman, Barry Horowitz, Frank Maginnis, Raphael Malveaux, John Marsh, Thomas Mowbray, Makoto Oya, Aarthi Prasad, Karen Ruh, Takaaki Shigematsu, Kim Warren, Eric Watson, Julie Vazquez, Robert Vazquez, and Ron Zahavi.

We are extremely proud to be associated with Addison-Wesley and our editor Carter Shanklin. They have provided us two outstanding people in Krysia Bebick and Kristin Erickson who made the process of writing this book a lot easier. The production coordinator, Jacquelyn Doucette, deserves special thanks and has our appreciation for helping produce a quality product. Laura Michaels's copyediting was a work of art by itself.

Special thanks is given to the reviewers of the book whose comments and invaluable insights significantly increased its quality. We specifically want to acknowledge John M. Anderson, Boeing; Dave Curtis; Naci Dai; Fred Hebbel, CTO, SYSNETICS; Glen Jones, Raytheon E-Systems; Dr. Christopher LoPresti; Robert Stodola, SmithKline Beecham Pharmaceuticals R&D; Dave Tropeano; and Alan L. Pope, Quantitative Data Systems, Inc.

Finally, we thank Elizabeth (Liz) May, who organized and coordinated the manuscript among all parties. Her support and efforts on this book were very important to getting it to completion. We thank her for helping to "herd the cats" home!

IIOP and Middleware Basics

An Introduction to IIOP

1.1 The Internet Inter-ORB Protocol

The Internet Inter-ORB Protocol (IIOP), pronounced "eye-op," is the most widely known of the standards from the Object Management Group (OMG). However, despite the name recognition it has achieved, IIOP is not well understood. It is not a self-contained specification. Rather, it is an integral part of the broader Common Object Request Broker Architecture (CORBA) specification, one of the leading middleware solutions for developing integrated enterprise systems.

To understand IIOP, one must look at the evolution of CORBA, from the earliest specifications and products to the next generation of extensions. In this chapter, we provide the reader with an introduction into the Common Object Request Broker Architecture. This context is important to understanding the role of IIOP in addressing interoperability in object-based middleware. In addition, we will give a quick peek into the IIOP standard. This quick peek will cover all of the aspects of IIOP including data representation, messaging and protocol assumptions. We end the chapter by giving a glimpse into the future directions of IIOP as well as providing a roadmap for the rest of the book.

1.1.1 The Common Object Request Broker Architecture

The OMG was established in 1989 to create standards for distributed object computing. One of its aims was to "move software development closer to the age of components." Its standards were intended to allow interoperability of objects, components, and applications in a heterogeneous networked environment. Early efforts resulted in the creation of the Object Management Architecture (OMA) specification. The OMA reference model as it now stands is shown in Figure 1.1.

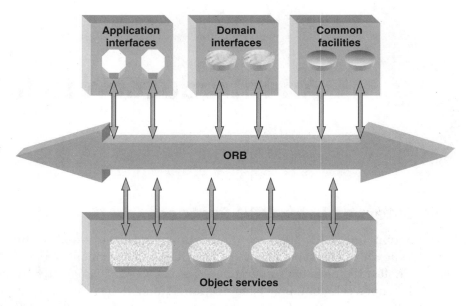

FIGURE 1.1   The OMG's Object Management Architecture

The OMA is a cornerstone of the OMG's standards. It provides a definition of object concepts and terminology, but leaves actual implementation decisions to vendors. This allows a variety of approaches to be taken to build a product. The OMA describes five components, as follows.

1. *Object request broker.* The object request broker (ORB) is the core component of the OMA. It transparently allows requests from the other four components to be transmitted, using standardized interfaces. Interfaces for CORBA objects are defined by the interface definition language (IDL), a programming language-independent specification. The IDL is used to create the visible interface between a client and a server.

2. *Object services.* The object services are the set of system-level services required in order to build robust distributed object systems.

3. *Common facilities.* Beyond system-level services, applications require user-oriented services such as printing and document management. The common facilities address this broad area.

4. *Domain interfaces.* These are predefined interfaces based on a specific industry need in areas such as health care, manufacturing, financial services, and telecommunications.

5. *Application interfaces.* These are the interfaces that are specific to an organization or application and are developed during system construction.

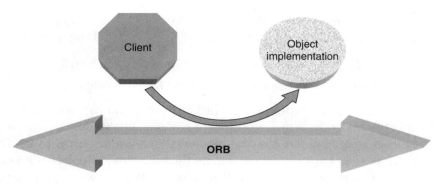

FIGURE 1.2   How CORBA Handles Requests

The OMA specifies a classical abstract object model. According to this model, a client submits a request to an object. A client is an entity that requires a service to be performed outside of its internal definition. An **object,** also called an **object implementation** or **server,** performs one or more services for a client. The request consists of an *operation*—also called a *method*—a target object, and zero or more parameters. The interface is the description of operations supported by the object with the associated request format. IDL is used to define an interface between clients and servers.

CORBA is the standard that specifies a concrete object model based on the OMA's abstract model. Its basic function is to handle requests between clients and object implementations, as shown in Figure 1.2. The ORB handles these requests, either within a single computer or across a network in a transparent fashion.

CORBA has several mechanisms to handle these requests. The client can use the following:

- *IDL stub.* An interface that is completely defined in the IDL and tied to a specific target object
- *Dynamic invocation.* A general interface that is independent of the target object interface

The client also can talk directly to the ORB, but this is used only rarely. The client makes a request by having an object reference, a pointer or address on a network, for an object with a desired service. The client either sends the request through the static IDL stubs or generates the request and sends it through the dynamic invocation. When the request is completed, the client will receive the prescribed results from the object implementation.

The programmer selects which of two types of skeleton interfaces through which the object implementation will receive requests from a client:

- *Static IDL skeleton.* A static interface defined in the IDL
- *Dynamic skeleton.* A general interface for receiving requests

The object implementation may decide to communicate with either the ORB or the object adapter, which the ORB provides, while it is processing a request. The object adapter is the primary method of communication with the ORB and its services. The ORB can provide more than one type of object adapter. Object adapters can provide different mechanisms for the generation and interpretation of object references, the registration of implementations, or security interactions. The programmer builds static and dynamic skeletons on top of the object adapter. The overall structure for requests is shown in Figure 1.3.

The choice of when to use static and when to use dynamic invocations and skeletons is left to the programmer. The tradeoff is performance versus flexibility. A static interface fits a traditional programming model, whereby the interface specification is set during design for the object implementation and is well known to the client. However, dynamic interfaces allow systems to be more flexible to change. For example, as new services are developed or an object is given a choice of services from which to select, a dynamic interface allows clients to generate the interface at runtime. In addition, the object implementation might want to be able to add services without requiring changes to its interface or the code that calls the interface.

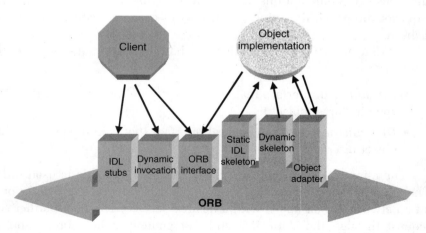

FIGURE 1.3 Available Interfaces for Clients and Object Implementation in CORBA

The choice of implementation for CORBA is left to the vendors, as long as vendors implement the interfaces appropriately. Objects that live within a specific ORB domain are guaranteed interoperability. However, the openness with regard to implementation choice leads to a lack of interoperability between two ORBs. We cover this in more detail next.

1.1.2   ORB Interoperability

The core element of CORBA is the ORB. The first implementations of an ORB based on the CORBA 1.0 standard successfully implemented the specification. However, ORBs were not able to interoperate because the standard did not address interoperability between ORBs from different vendors. Without such interoperability, the long-term commercial viability of CORBA was in question. Companies applying or embedding CORBA into their products would not be assured that their product could work with other products. Interoperability between ORBs was a primary issue to be resolved, beginning with the CORBA 2.0 standard and continuing with CORBA 3.0, the current version.

The General Inter-ORB Protocol (GIOP), pronounced "gee-op," was defined as the mechanism that would facilitate ORB-to-ORB interaction. GIOP is designed to run on top of any connection-oriented transport protocol that meets a minimal set of assumptions. IIOP is a specialization of the GIOP for the TCP/IP protocol. GIOP and IIOP are the heart of ORB interoperability within the CORBA specification.

1.1.3   GIOP and IIOP

The GIOP is intended to provide a protocol that is the lowest level of interoperability between ORBs, as shown in Figure 1.4. It fits above layer four, the transport layer, of the Open Systems Interconnection (OSI) seven-layer model (as is true with almost all higher level protocol implementations). However, it does not fit the traditional definition of layer five of the model. In fact, it provides capabilities that incorporate features of layers five, six, and seven.

GIOP is neutral with regard to underlying transport protocols. This is because a number of goals were strictly adhered to in the design of GIOP:

- Simplicity with regard to definition
- Scalability with regard to size of network
- Low cost with regard to implementation and network support
- Generality with regard to transport support
- Architectural neutrality with regard to ORBs

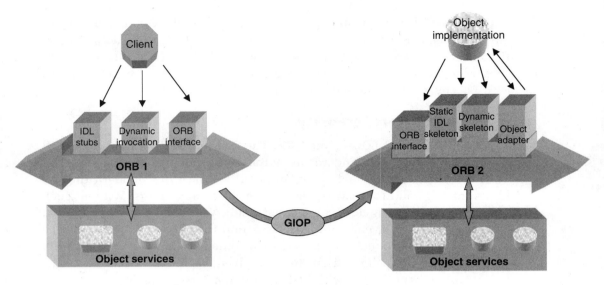

FIGURE 1.4   The Role of GIOP

The success of the GIOP specification in meeting these goals can be seen through the definitions of its three core elements:

- *Common data representation (CDR).* This is a data formatting rule that allows variable byte ordering as well as support for the OMG's IDL.
- *Message formats.* These are eight message formats that support the dynamic location and migration of objects.
- *Transport assumptions.* The GIOP requires a connection-oriented transport that is reliable and can be viewed as a byte stream. Higher-level remote procedure call (RPC) mechanisms are not required.

The specification is compact and meant to serve existing network infrastructures. However, interoperability is not ensured without a specific transport that is supported by all ORB vendors. This is where IIOP comes in. IIOP ensures interoperability on top of the most widely used communications transport platform in use today—TCP/IP—by specifying how the GIOP messages are communicated on a TCP/IP network.

It is important to understand that GIOP and IIOP are an integral part of the CORBA specification and are not separable specifications. An ORB implementation will include both. Because they are intended to provide interoperability between ORBs, they are generally invisible to the programmer or user. ORB-enabled objects, components, and applications benefit from being able to seamlessly connect to each other, independent of the underlying ORB used in each.

1.1.4 ORB Interoperability and IIOP

The GIOP and IIOP came about as an answer to the problems of interoperability. Interoperability requirements, as defined by the OMG, are as follows:

- Ability for two ORBs to interact, insulated from having to have knowledge of implementations
- Support of all CORBA functionality across ORBs
- Preservation of content and semantics of ORB-specific information between ORBs

GIOP and IIOP were intended as only one important element to meeting interoperability requirements by ensuring ORB-to-ORB interoperability. They also enable ORBs to achieve the other two interoperability requirements for achieving higher-level interoperability in CORBA:

- ORB interoperability architecture
- Inter-ORB bridge support

1.1.5 Architecture, Domains, and Bridging

The GIOP/IIOP, interoperability architecture, and inter-ORB bridging support specifications were intended to provide the developer of an ORB flexibility in the solution to implementing interoperability between ORBs. However, the reality has been that the vast majority of commercial implementations implement IIOP as the internal communications protocol, rather than applying inter-ORB bridging. We will discuss the rationale for this choice as we examine this topic.

Does the fact that a single approach has been applied mean the topic is irrelevant? The answer lies in whom the question is directed towards. To the ORB developer, the interoperability architecture seems irrelevant. To the developer of an application, it may also seem irrelevant. However, this area is of enormous interest to the system architect or developer who must manage interoperability across a variety of applications or must build custom infrastructure that is not commercially available (like a real-time ORB). The interoperability architecture can be a useful tool to organizing and structuring their systems or building custom infrastructure.

The system developer uses the ORB interoperability architecture's conventions and compliance points to guide them in developing higher-level interoperability solutions between disparate applications. This architecture is a conceptual framework. Its two most important concepts are:

- the use of domains to define a point at which interoperability must be managed and
- the immediate as well as mediated bridging of ORB domains as the two choices for implementing IIOP/GIOP in the ORB.

A **domain** is a logical grouping based on security, product, application, or any other meaningful characteristic. **Bridging** is a concept from the networking community whereby a translation is made from the internal communication and information structures to those of either the intended recipient or a common transient format.

In the CORBA world a domain has a distinct scope. Within the scope of the domain, the ORB transparently handles interoperability. This is, because common characteristics and rules exist for each domain, usually defined by a vendor. Interoperability is required between different domains with different characteristics or rules via bridging. Domain differences can be administrative, related to such areas as naming or security, as well as technological, related to such areas as protocols or syntax. A common and practical case is the case of a heterogeneous environment having multiple ORBs. In this case, each vendor's ORB is a domain. This would exist if an organization wanted to integrate two applications that were built on two different ORBs. It also is likely that a single vendor's ORB might allow for multiple domains, especially of different administrative types. As an example, a vendor might provide security services. If an organization uses the same vendor's ORB for developing applications, some with the security services and others without, then each application can be viewed as a domain. Finally, it is possible that ORBs from several vendors might natively interoperate and be used within a single domain. This is highly unlikely, however, given the nature of vendors and the implementation choices that make complete interoperability difficult. These concepts are depicted in Figure 1.5.

With bridging means, the ORBs interoperate through a common communications mechanism that might differ from the communications mechanism used within the ORB. The bridge acts as a translator between the two. There are two types of bridges: immediate and mediated. An **immediate bridge** translates directly into the internal form of the other ORB. This works only when the internal structure is well known in advance. A **mediated bridge** can be viewed as a translator in which relevant dialogue between the ORBs is reformed into a lingua franca. The translation is done at both ends of the communication channel. Therefore each ORB is insulated from knowing the specific implementations of another ORB. Immediate and mediated bridges are shown in Figure 1.6.

IIOP is the common language for broad-based, mediated bridging. That is, it is the communications mechanism used by ORBs to communicate with each other. When one ORB is using IIOP as its internal communications mechanism, then immediate bridging is easily realized.

A bridge can be organized by the ORB either as an internal mechanism—**in-line bridging**—or as a separate component outside the ORB—**request-level**

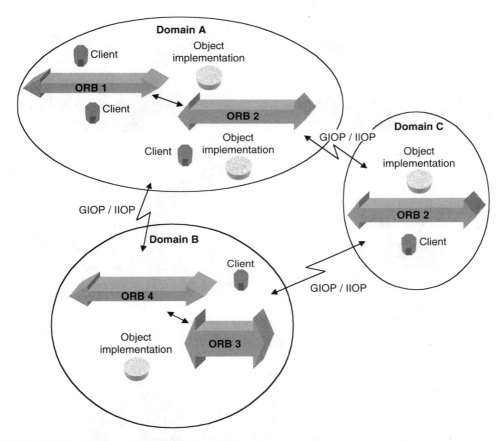

FIGURE 1.5   The Concept of CORBA Domains

bridging. Information communication between domains is handled through these bridges. Specified application programming interfaces (APIs) and conventions enable a developer to construct a bridge. Such bridges can be used to connect to other CORBA domains as well as to non-CORBA systems that have integrated an IIOP-based ORB for communications. Bridging implementation concepts are shown in Figure 1.7.

The interoperability specifications were driven by the need to support a robust, ORB-enabled marketplace The commercial ORB vendors have overwhelmingly chosen to implement native IIOP solutions rather than use bridging. This is because the use of bridges is inefficient and complex in most circumstances. The choice to implement native IIOP is of great benefit to the general purpose user of CORBA technology. However, ORB diversity

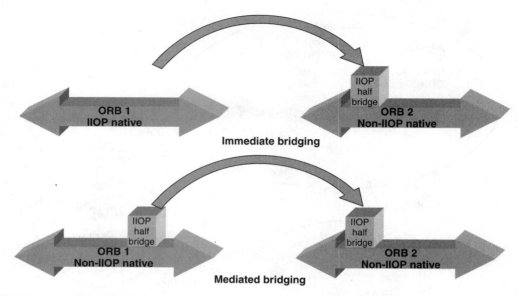

FIGURE 1.6   CORBA Bridging

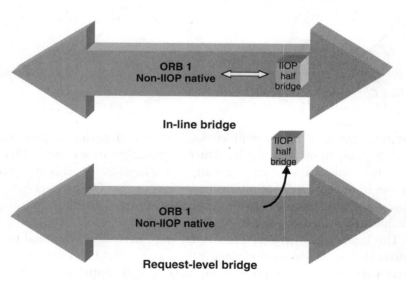

FIGURE 1.7   Implementing Bridges with ORBs

and specialization is already a fact of life. In addition to general purpose ORBs, there are fault-tolerant ORBs, real-time ORBs, and ORBs embedded into products, as well as other specializations. Even within an ORB product line, different partitions of ORBs exist, with different security boundaries, protocol support, and integration with a diversity of external systems that will require various bridging mechanisms. Finally, the actual use of ORBs in large-scale systems is still not fully understood. Scope, lifecycle, and distribution are issues that will be addressed as more mission-critical systems are built. The designers of the interoperability specification took all of this into account as they prepared their initial design, as well as the subsequent several iterations.

1.1.6   Examples of IIOP Usage

Although IIOP was designed to provide interoperability between general purpose ORBs, like any useful technology innovative uses can be found for it. The most common configuration for IIOP, as discussed previously, is the use by an ORB as the native communications mechanism within the ORB. This is shown in Figure 1.8. This allows any other ORB that supports IIOP, either natively or through a bridge, to be connected without significant effort. Examples of innovative use are connecting proprietary, object-based systems to CORBA systems or even integrating embedded systems through IIOP interfaces.

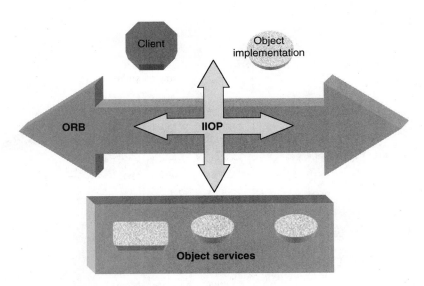

FIGURE 1.8   IIOP Native Implementation

Given the widespread use of TCP/IP networks within organizations and on the Internet, IIOP will allow an ORB to seamlessly fit into existing networks. The types of ORBs that will support this configuration are most likely general purpose. However, ORBs can be optimized for special circumstances. Examples of this are ORBs specialized for real-time processing or for network environments that are not TCP/IP based or ORBs that are embedded into products that use proprietary messaging for internal communications. In each of these examples, the ORB would communicate internally using a specialized communications mechanism. Interoperability would be supported through the use of a IIOP-based half bridge, as shown in Figure 1.9.

Although IIOP has not been completely explored by the original designers, it could be applied to systems or applications that need to communicate with ORB-based objects but do not use an ORB as their primary method of communications. The authors have seen a variety of configurations applied in enterprise systems. In several real-time and fault-tolerant situations, the ORB uses an immediate bridging approach through an in-line bridge to communicate between the real-time or fault-tolerant ORB and the commercial ORB. In addition, pre-existing messaging systems have been integrated with commercial ORB products using a bridging approach with a request-level bridge. As IIOP rises in popularity, more examples of these types of uses can be expected of sophisticated technology organizations.

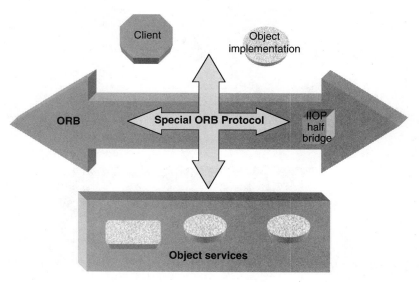

FIGURE 1.9   IIOP Half-Bridge Bridging

1.2   A Quick Peek at IIOP

IIOP is a fairly simple protocol that can be understood very quickly through examination of the CDRs, GIOP messages, and IIOP specialization. The details and the importance of each of these are explored in more detail throughout this book.

1.2.1   Common Data Representation

The CDR is the transfer syntax for communication. It is used to map a CORBA data type into a low-level representation. It supports

- primitive types,
- constructed types,
- pseudo-object types, and
- object references.

The CDR is formatted to be sent in an octet stream. The octet stream can be thought of as an arbitrarily long sequence of 8-bit values.

The primitive types supported include `char` (character), `short`, `long`, `float`, `double`, and `boolean` in various forms (unsigned, wide, and so on). They are specified for both big-endian and little-endian orderings. Alignment is important, with primitive types followed explicitly according to the specification. Constructed types, as well as all of the others, have the same alignment restrictions as the primitives. Structures, unions, arrays, sequences, fixed-point, strings, and enumerated values are supported in constructed types. Pseudo-object types define entities that are neither primitive nor constructed, such as a TypeCode, principal, context, and exception. They represent well-known CORBA classes that are represented in one object and recreated in another. Finally, object references can be encoded into CDR.

1.2.2   GIOP Messages

In its most recent form, GIOP supports eight messages. Figure 1.10 lists these messages and their relationships with the client and server. The arrows show what can originate a message.

Each message must have a GIOP header that identifies the message and its byte ordering. Three messages can originate only from the client:

- Request
- LocateRequest
- CancelRequest

The request object encodes an object invocation from a client to a server. It includes a request header and body in addition to the GIOP message header.

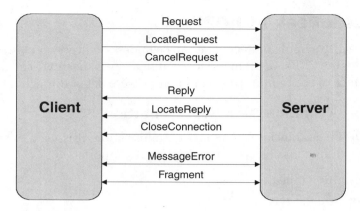

FIGURE 1.10   GIOP Messaging

The client may send a LocateRequest message to obtain additional information from the server. There are three types of information the client wants:

- Is an object reference valid?
- Can the current server receive the request from an object reference?
- What is the address to which to send an object request?

This same information can be obtained from the Request message, but using this type of message imposes additional overhead that the LocateRequest message does not require. The CancelRequest message is sent by a client to a server to terminate a prior request, either a Request or LocateRequest message.

The server is the only entity that can originate these messages:

- Reply
- LocateReply
- CloseConnection

The Reply message is sent by a server to the client if the response expected flag in the Request message is set to `True`. It includes a reply header and body as well as the GIOP message header. The LocateReply message is used to respond to LocateRequest messages. It too has a header and body in addition to the GIOP message header. A CloseConnection message informs a client that it should not expect to receive any further information related to a request. The message contains only the GIOP header and message type.

Clients and servers both support two message types:

- MessageError
- Fragment

A MessageError is sent when a client or server detects an error condition as a result of a message. It has a header and a message type. The Fragment message is used when a Request or Reply is broken into blocks that are sent independently. The initial Request or Reply message indicates that additional segments will be sent. Each additional segment is sent using the Fragment message. A Request, Reply, or Fragment message indicates that further fragments will be sent by including a `True` setting in the fragment flag field. The last Fragment message sets this field to `False`.

1.2.3   Specializing GIOP into IIOP

IIOP enables clients and object implementations to communicate over TCP/IP (Transmission Control Protocol/Internet Protocol). The GIOP specialization into IIOP is required due to the implementation mandated by TCP/IP concepts and in the mapping of high-level objects to low-level protocols.

TCP/IP is a connection-oriented protocol whereby a receiver listens for a request at a specified address from a sender. The address of the receiver is a combination of an IP host address and a TCP port number. The host address is almost always a physical location on the network that represents a network adapter card, while the port number is a logical address that represents the receiver on the host. Multiple receivers may exist on a single host, each with its own port address. The host address is used to find the right computer on the network. The port number is the address at which the software is found.

The sender initiates a request by finding the address for the receiver and requesting a connection. The receiver may accept or reject the connection request. An IIOP implementation requires that a TCP/IP connection be established between the sender and receiver in order for them to communicate GIOP messages and CDR formatted information.

Once a connection is established, GIOP messages may be sent between the sender and receiver. These messages are used to represent interactions between a client and object implementation. Once the request is completed, the TCP/IP connection is closed.

Objects must be able to represent themselves as being accessible through IIOP. The representation is described using the **interoperable object references** (IOR). The IOR is a data structure that is visible and maintained by the ORB. It provides information on type, protocol support, and ORB services available. IORs are not unique to IIOP. They can be set up for any situation in which objects will be accessed across two or more domains. The IIOP IOR's are predefined and shown in Figure 1.11. This is shown in the Interface Definition Language. The IDL is beyond the scope of this book, so some knowledge on the reader's part of programming languages is assumed.

```
module IIOP {                    //IDL extended for version 1.1
  struct Version {
          octet          major;
          octet          minor
  };
  structProfileBody_1_{          //renamed from ProfileBody
          Version          iiop_version;
          string           host;
          unsigned short   port;
          sequence<octet>  object_key;
  };
  struct ProfileBody_1_1{
          Version          iiop_version;
          string           host;
          unsigned short   port;
          sequence<octet>  object_key;

          //Added in 1.1
          sequence <IOP::TaggedComponent>components;
  };
};
```

FIGURE 1.11   IIOP IOR Structure

The IIOP IOR allows an object to identify the version of IIOP supported, the IP host and TCP port numbers, and a unique key to identify the object by the receiving ORB. The unique key is represented as a sequence. A sequence is an indeterminate length array. In addition, IIOP version 1.1 supports the ability to identify components that can be useful in making an invocation to provide pre-processing of a request. As of version 1.1, five components are supported:

- TAG_ORB_TYPE
- TAG_CODE_SETS
- TAG_SEC_NAME
- TAG_ASSOCIATION_OPTIONS
- TAG_GENERIC_SEC_MECH

TAG_ORB_TYPE identifies the kind of ORB used by the object implementation. Specific ORBs are assigned a number by the OMG upon request. The TAG_CODE_SETS identifies the object implementations native char code set,

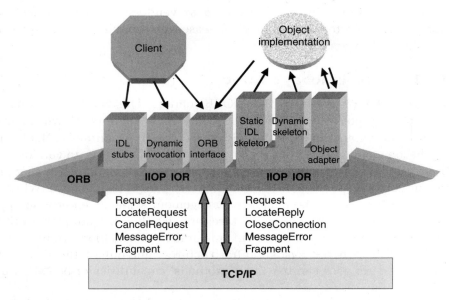

FIGURE 1.12   IIOP in the CORBA Architecture

as well as its conversion code sets. `TAG_SEC_NAME`, `TAG_ASSOCIATION_OPTIONS`, and `TAG_GENERIC_SEC_MECH` are used by the CORBA security services for configuring and managing security between the client and server. They will be discussed in detail in Chapter 8. The OMG allocates component tags so that they will not overlap, creating a situation where a tag has two or more meanings and thereby compromise interoperability.

The core of specializing GIOP into IIOP consists of

- creating the mechanisms to establish a TCP/IP connection and
- the IIOP IOR profiles.

The relationships between clients, object implementations, ORBs, IORs, GIOP messages, and TCP/IP in the CORBA architecture are shown in Figure 1.12.

1.3   The Role of IIOP in Software

IIOP's simplicity allows it to be easily implemented in ORBs that desire to communicate with each other. Its major advantage over similar protocols is its focus on object-based systems. This allows object-based systems, as well as non-object-based systems that have been bridged to an ORB, to communicate with object-based systems.

IIOP has grown in popularity because vendors and users of technology want to be able to migrate to object-based environments while preserving investments in existing technology.

1.3.1   IIOP in Today's World

The earliest adopters of IIOP were ORB vendors. This is not surprising, since IIOP was proposed and standardized by these vendors. However, this by itself is not enough to explain IIOP's rapid rise in prominence. IIOP support has become one of the standard checkbox items that software vendors add to their products. The actual implementations of IIOP use an ORB as a part of the underlying product infrastructure. Vendors selling World Wide Web-enabled (Web) products, database management systems, enterprise applications, and other various infrastructures are also the early adopters of IIOP for integration into their products. This integration allows their products to work with a CORBA-based system infrastructure right out of the box. CORBA objects and services can use these products' capabilities or be called by the products.

The continued success of IIOP also is based in part on the high level of adoption by the Java community. In 1997, OMG and Javasoft announced that Java would support IIOP. Until then, the remote method invocation (RMI) was a non-CORBA ORB used by Java. The support for IIOP meant that a subset of RMI would be supported on top of IIOP. Through this integration, CORBA/IIOP has become a more approachable environment for users. Java users are provided an environment that enables stronger enterprise integration and interoperability with Java applets. Unfortunately, Javasoft has given a mixed message on support for this RMI, leaving users without a clear picture of the future. RMI development and support continues at the same time RMI on top of IIOP is supported. The marketplace as well as Sun Microsystems and Javasoft will determine the fate of the architectural underpinnings for Java.

One of the major competitors to CORBA is Component Object Model (COM) from Microsoft. COM has its own proprietary infrastructure. Gateways between COM and CORBA using IIOP have been developed to allow COM and CORBA objects to interoperate.

IIOP has successfully integrated ORBs, Java, and COM-based systems, thereby allowing different objects to interoperate. It has had several years of use, with some minor modifications to the specification. The specification currently is going through a major modification that will significantly enhance its capabilities. In addition, new competitors are emerging that will need to be dealt with if it is to continue its success.

1.3.2   IIOP in the Future

By the time this book is printed, GIOP and IIOP should have completed a new revision. These modifications relate to new capabilities being specified in the areas of messaging, firewall security, and pass by value.

The messaging changes result from influences from the traditional, message-oriented middleware (MOM) community. CORBA has been primarily a synchronous communication infrastructure, although deferred synchronous is supported. The new CORBA messaging specification provides asynchronous method invocation, time-independent invocation, and quality-of-service capabilities. These require extensions to the GIOP, which in turn require that the messaging service context be specified and that IOR components be routed. The routing changes provide increased efficiency. IIOP will then support time-independence. These changes, once completed, will extend rather than change the existing specifications.

Firewall security changes to GIOP and IIOP were required by the CORBA firewall specification. They were implemented to allow the GIOP and IIOP protocols to pass through a firewall. Due to the complexity of communicating through a firewall, significant changes were required in GIOP and IIOP. These changes occurred in both data elements as well as message formats.

CORBA uses pass by reference, the traditional mechanism, while some important technologies and applications such as Java require pass by value. This latter capability requires that GIOP messages allow values to be passed as part of the message format.

The OMG's CORBA standard is in a constant state of evolution. Changes such as messaging, firewalls and pass by value were in the process of being finalized at the time of writing of this book. All of these changes are described in detail later in this book in Chapter 7.

Following these enhancements, the future growth of IIOP will be heavily tied to its success on the Web and the Internet. The World Wide Web Consortium (W3C), an organization dedicated to improving the Web through the development of protocols and other technologies to ensure interoperability, has been working on a successor to the hypertext transport protocol (HTTP), HTTP-NG ("next generation"). A draft specification has been defined and a pilot implementation completed. This protocol provides similar functionality to IIOP but is not compatible with it. HTTP-NG is new enough that it hasn't become universally accepted or used. Nor has it been around long enough to be considered within the context of a CORBA standard. However, with the weight of the W3C and the Internet community behind it, it must be considered within the context of IIOP's future. We discuss HTTP-NG further in Chapter 9.

1.4   **What You Will Learn from This Book**

The next generation of products, services, and systems will be based on a distributed object model. Most software vendors have evolved or are planning to evolve their products along these lines. The strong interdependence in the marketplace, driven by the desire or organizations to buy products that work together and form an integrated enterprise, requires that vendors have a strategy for interoperability. The OMG provides distributed object technology standards that are a solution for interoperability.

IIOP is a robust architecture, taken in the broadest sense to mean IIOP, GIOP, and interoperability between CORBA and non-CORBA object systems. It was designed from an enterprise perspective, based on real experiences with CORBA implementations. This book will give you a broad perspective of IIOP.

In Chapter 2, we address the wide range of middleware choices that exist in the marketplace. This will allow you to understand the position of CORBA and IIOP with respect to competitive and cooperative technologies. Chapters 3 through 6 discuss the specifics of IIOP, including details of the OMG IIOP standardization process, followed by in-depth discussions of CDR, message protocol patterns, message stream patterns, and object adapter patterns. Chapter 7 deals with the next generation of IIOP based on current proposals for specification enhancement. Chapters 8 through 10 cover special topics such as security, building interoperable solutions, Web and Java integration, and future standardization activities.

Middleware and IIOP

2.1 Enterprises Require Middleware Infrastructure

Enterprise computing systems consist of application processes executing on multiple machines. These application processes fulfill the business needs of the enterprise through the collaborative utilization of services such as data management and algorithmic transformation. **Distribution transparency** is the successful management and use of system functionality across the enterprise. **Middleware** is a class of software developed to meet the needs of distribution transparency. CORBA is a type of middleware.

In this chapter, we provide a perspective for the GIOP/IIOP messaging protocol by examining the broad range of middleware solutions. We discuss the problem that GIOP/IIOP solves and the context for that solution. We begin with middleware issues, requirements, and considerations and then address the major classes of middleware: database access, RPCs, transaction monitors, message-oriented middleware, and distributed object technology.

In the chapter, we also provide a broad perspective on the role of middleware and how different middleware solutions compare and contrast, as well as where CORBA fits into this spectrum. This is intended to provide sufficient background for the reader and not as a complete in-depth evaluation and comparison, which is beyond the scope of the book.

2.1.1 What is the Middleware Infrastructure?

Middleware allows application processes to transparently collaborate across processes and networks despite different system policies, operating systems, programming languages, machine data formats, and networking protocols. In performing this function, it replaces layers five through seven of the OSI model, as shown in Figure 2.1.

Distribution transparency is an expression of middleware engineering requirements. Specific examples of these requirements include:

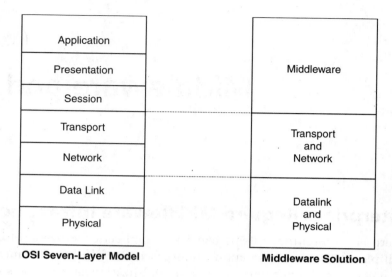

FIGURE 2.1   Middleware in the OSI Seven-Layer Model

- easing the burden of developing distributed applications, typically by providing communication services,
- correcting endpoint domain inconsistencies, and
- providing solutions that are reliable and scalable.

While there is no formal characterization of middleware, in general there are five categories based on significant standards or products in the marketplace. These are:

- *Data Access.* Connectivity to databases
- *Remote Procedure Call (RPC).* Procedure calls between distributed applications
- *Transaction Processing Monitors.* Distributed transaction management
- *Message Oriented Middleware (MOM).* Asynchronous communications between systems
- *Distributed Object Technology.* Object invocations between distributed applications

Each of these classes of middleware reduces the complexity of building certain classes of distributed systems. It is interesting to note that the order also implies the evolution of this technology. Data access and RPC middleware arrived first on the scene, followed by transaction processing monitors and

MOM middleware. Distributed object technology is the latest category of middleware, this is the class where CORBA fits. As you will see, this category in general, and CORBA specifically, is based on the best attributes of each of the other categories. CORBA, in particular, supports most of the features and attributes of all the other classes with the underpinning of GIOP/IIOP, the only real interoperable solution for middleware available.

All middleware requires an underlying transparent and associated network protocol as a base on which to build. The datalink and physical layers are typically hidden from the middleware by the transport and network layers. Therefore, they are relatively unimportant to middleware design.

2.1.2   The Importance of the Transport and Network Layer

The transport layer provides a constrained set of functionality within the context of layered communication middleware. It eases the burden of network communication programming for middleware developers. Its purpose is to deliver messages between a pair of network address endpoints, called ports. It is the encapsulation of the details of network layer messaging.

The transport and network layer provides two types of communication: virtual circuit and datagram. **Virtual circuit** communication is known as *connection-oriented* and **datagram communication** as *connectionless.*

Connection-oriented communication requires that a virtual circuit be established between the communication initiator and the target before messages can be exchanged. Connection-oriented messaging is analogous to a telephone communication, whereby connection establishment precedes any conversation. This type of messaging is best suited for applications that require reliability in communication.

Connectionless transport communication is much like using the postal service. A message is addressed and posted to the transport layer. Message delivery occurs without the active participation of the initiator.

Communicating endpoints that utilize these communication mechanisms must assume the roles of server and client. A **server** is a process that is responsible for establishing a communication endpoint and then listening for and accepting incoming requests. Servers passively accept and respond to messages sent by clients. A **client** is a process responsible for initiating communications with a server.

A stream interface is utilized to simplify and coordinate message exchange; servers and clients utilize that stream interface for communicating messages. This interface consists of two operations: send and receive. Data is sent using the send operation and retrieved using the receive operation. The data sent is buffered at the receiver. This buffered send operation simplifies the coordination of data delivery and retrieval by permitting asynchronous retrieval of delivered message data. Message sending is subsequently decoupled from message retrieval.

The transport protocol communicates messages of any size through the services of the network protocol. It accepts and delivers data in the form of *streams,* while the network protocol accepts and delivers data in the form of *packets.* To use the network protocol, the transport must convert message streams into packets and provide them to the network protocol for routing. The transport layer at the target endpoint subsequently accepts packets and collates them into a message stream. The most popular transport mechanism is TCP (and its related protocol UDP), while IP is the most popular network protocol.

A programmer that uses the transport as the mechanism for developing distributed applications will find that they must develop an immense amount of code, coupled with a high level of expertise related to the intricacies of networking. Middleware emerged as a result of this complexity.

2.2   Middleware Requirements

Middleware technology provides an improved technology for the developer to build distributed applications. It provides the ability to focus on the semantics of the integration, rather than the mechanics. In order to achieve these benefits, middleware products must strive to support the following software engineering characteristics:

- Simplicity
- Portability
- Adaptability
- Scalability
- Maturity
- Interoperability
- Reliability

While it can be argued all software needs to strive to have these characteristics, they are at the core of any successful middleware. This is due to the system orientation of middleware. These characteristics are what any organization requires in their systems and therefore out of their middleware. However, these characteristics are at too high a level and must be translated into a set of requirements that are meaningful to middleware. These requirements are described in detail in the following sections.

2.2.1   Ease of Use

Middleware primarily provides easy-to-use connectivity to enterprise services. It reduces the burden and development time of application programs. At a minimum, it should shield application developers from low-level network programming detail. Ideally it should create and manage the semantics of the interaction between a client and server.

2.2.2   Application to Middleware Integration

A desirable feature of middleware is the seamless integration of the application with middleware messaging facilities. Transparent connectivity is required to translate the application programming environment into middleware messages.

2.2.3   Messaging Model Integration

Middleware encapsulates the details of the transport layer communication and adds functionality such as message and connection management. Middleware typically provides at least one of the following messaging models:

- Request-reply
- Send-and-forget
- Publish-and-subscribe

Request-reply is a two-way middleware messaging protocol that is best suited for tightly coupled client-server applications. Request-reply communication is natively two-way and blocking because service consumers cannot continue without an immediate reply from a service provider. Request-reply messaging is categorized as synchronous, since the participants synchronize, or coordinate, messaging.

Send-and-forget, or asynchronous message-passing, is a one-way middleware messaging protocol. Asynchronous messaging protocols do not require simultaneous, coordinated participation. Asynchronous messaging protocols are used by such applications as electronic mail and group multicast. Send-and-forget communication is natively one-way and nonsimultaneous because message senders do not require an immediate reply. The sender is usually aware of who the receiver is. This pattern is most appropriate to batch mode, unacknowledged messaging, and unilateral control types of applications.

Publish-and-subscribe also is an asynchronous messaging protocol. Its pattern is most appropriate to event-driven, data feed, and content-push types of applications. Subscribers register for a type of message or event that might be sent. The difference with send-and-forget is the sender or publisher does not need to be aware of who the registered subscribers of the message will be. Publish-and-subscribe communication is natively one-way and nonsimulta-neous because publishers do not require knowledge about or a response from subscribers.

A large proportion of messaging in a distributed environment utilizes syn-chronous request-reply messaging. Service applications that process input data and return results can be considered well suited to it. With synchronous mes-saging, clients and servers exchange request and reply messages. The client transmits a request message and blocks it until it receives a reply message, which implies the successful delivery of the request message. These delivery assurances reduce the failure mode control processing requirements of soft-ware that use synchronous messaging.

Some forms of applications do not require request-reply semantics. For example, an email application delivers a one-way message to a target address. Message reply may occur later or not at all. Asynchronous messaging, send-and-forget or publish-and-subscribe, does not require server response and does not block client processing.

Most middleware has typically provided a single variant of these messag-ing models. The current trend is to support all of these forms in middleware products. Middleware software must rectify differences between the messaging models of system components in order to provide distribution transparency.

2.2.4 Endpoint Binding Transparency

To establish a connection or deliver a message, the transport layer requires net-work endpoint information. Distribution transparency requires that the middle-ware layer abstract the mapping of application layer software components from the physical network endpoints. References or binding handles provide a mech-anism for encapsulating a physical network endpoint with a system-level name.

2.2.5 Availability and Reliability

Distributed software systems must provide for the notification of and con-trolled recovery in situations involving network hardware failure and software exceptions. Servers must be available to provide services whenever clients request them. When a server is down, so is the business that it supports. How-ever, servers can be unavailable for many reasons, including problems with the

- server platform hardware,
- server platform software,
- networking, or
- application server.

In the later case, the code for the server and the code for the middleware that supports its execution must be hardened. Its reliability must approach that of the operating system on which it runs. Obviously, it must be thoroughly tested. When failures do occur, a server must be able to quickly recover and restart itself. Recovery should recapture as much user work as possible, and data must be left in a consistent state as well. If a server platform will be down for an extended time, the application might be restarted on a different platform.

2.2.6 Distributed Transaction Properties

Distributed environments require synchronization and coordination services for the concurrent update of enterprise resources such as files and databases. The integrity of distributed enterprise information resources must be preserved by logically grouping information updates into a unit that fails or succeeds as a unit.

In cases in which multiple, heterogeneous databases are accessed, developers may use transaction processing monitors. In multi-tier environments, a transaction monitor approach is required. This is due to the level of support required to effectively manage access and update to multiple heterogeneous databases, mainframe integration and supporting resource managers other than databases such as a message queue.

2.2.7 Scalability and Load Balancing

As the number of users in a distributed system increases, limited system resources are consumed and bottlenecks result. To relieve these, resources might be duplicated or routing controls might be provided that direct traffic to the least used system resource. Ensuring that system resources are balanced for efficiency is essential. Middleware scalability may be defined as the efficient utilization of critical physical resources.

2.2.8 Security

Security within a distributed system requires the application of a suite of middleware control and transformation services. The security services performed by middleware are defined and controlled by a security policy. Typically, separate groups will establish different security policies. In addition, every middleware product will provide its own set of security services. These inconsistencies result in multiple security policy and technology domains. Thus two communicating endpoints could belong to separate security policy domains.

2.2.9 Binding Information Name Spaces

To obtain the services of a distributed system, a client first must obtain a binding handle or reference. Successfully locating the correct reference requires that a naming policy be established that ensures that each reference name has a unique representation. Inconsistencies result in multiple referencing domains. The ability to integrate across multiple name spaces and ensure consistency is required.

2.3   Interoperability Design Issues

Distribution transparency problems exist in almost every aspect of building and operating information systems. For example, the build environments of two application processes might differ as a result of separate design and implementation decisions. Build environment dependencies are selected to achieve a desired set of characteristics or optimizations, such as efficiency, evolvability, modularity, or simplicity. Examples of such dependencies are programming languages, operating systems, procedure call signatures, and syntaxes. Differences in these dependencies adversely affect communications and are difficult to correct.

The operational environments of two application processes might also have different administrative priorities. Examples of operational environment dependencies are control characteristics or optimizations such as location, transaction, scalability, error recovery, and security transparency. As in build environments, differences in dependencies adversely affect communication and are difficult to correct.

Three critical issues impact middleware interoperability and require careful consideration:

- Many different transport level networking protocols exist and are being used in distributed environments. Examples include TCP/IP, Apple's Appletalk, Digital Equipment Corporation's (now a part of Compaq) DECnet, and IBM's SNA. Interface and connection management rules and other implicit dependencies might differ for each; each networking protocol is its own domain. Since two communicating endpoints could belong to separate transport protocol domains, distribution transparencies require that these inconsistencies be corrected.

- A middleware product can be built using different messaging models as described in Section 2.2.3. It can be anticipated that any organization will employ several products in their systems. As a result, multiple messaging domains, one for each type of messaging model supported, are unable to interoperate unless corrected.

- The semantics of the interactions are the final area that must be addressed to achieve real interoperability. Message formats and data representations are two of the most important areas that must be addressed. Furthermore, correctly characterizing the semantics of the middleware within the scope of the interaction decreases the complexity of interoperability.

Any credible interoperability solution for middleware needs to address all three of these concerns.

2.4 Addressing Middleware Interoperability

Domains provide a view of a system as being organized into common spheres of concern. It is at the intersection of these domains that interoperability is most important to manage. These spheres of concern may be administrative related to organizational structure or business function. They may almost be technical related to system construction, such as different middleware products. In order to connect domains together, distribution transparency requires that protocol differences between domains be resolved. The resolution of protocol differences may be through dynamic or static agreement. An example of a dynamic protocol resolution is a bridge. A bridge corrects protocol differences at domain boundaries as the system is executing. An example of a static protocol resolution is a standard that resolves protocol differences by eliminating them. A standard leads to a better solution. Bridges are more complex and inefficient. However, standards require reaching a consensus that often is politically or technically impossible. Four areas that must be considered in a solution are:

- Data transfer representation
- Message formats
- Data representation
- Semantic representation

2.4.1 Data Transfer Representation

The transport layer carries data between network endpoints. Data streams sent between endpoints are unformatted and may be of unlimited size. Prearranged formats are required to convert a data stream into a message that can be understood by both the sender and the receiver. A tightly coordinated message format and data transfer syntax represents a standardized protocol, or a shared technical domain. Typically, every middleware product will establish its own canonical message format and data transfer syntax. These inconsistencies produce multiple message formatting domains. Since two communicating endpoints could belong to separate message syntax domains, distribution transparencies require that these inconsistencies be corrected.

2.4.2 Data Representation

A distributed system consists of heterogeneous hardware platforms such as Sun SPARC or Intel *x*86 PC. Each hardware platform represents the memory image of its atomic types, such as character data, in a format unique to the platform. The two most popular data representations are known as big endian and little endian. We will address this topic in more detail in Chapter 4.

In order for communication to be effective between platforms the data representations must be converted. Typically, every middleware product will establish its own data image translation mechanism. These inconsistencies produce multiple data translation domains. Since two communicating endpoints could belong to separate data translation domains, distribution transparencies require that these inconsistencies be corrected.

2.4.3   Message Formats

The logical format of an on-the-wire message typically consists of header information and payload. The message header provides receivers with information about message routing and payload, while the payload typically consists of data that has been flattened for streamed transmission across the network. Different middleware approaches use different message framing arrangements that are incompatible. Since two communicating endpoints could belong to separate message framing domains, distribution transparencies require that these inconsistencies be corrected.

2.4.4   Semantic Representation

Even if a message is properly formatted and its data representations compatible with the receiver's expectations, additional processing or incorrect actions may result due to a mismatch on the semantics. It is difficult to merge together similar classes of middleware, it is extraordinary to deal with interoperability across categories of middleware.

2.5   Comparing and Contrasting Middleware

Middleware can be broken into five different classes:

- Database Access
- Remote Procedure Call
- Transaction Processing Monitors
- Message-Oriented
- Distributed Objects

Each of these were created to solve the problem of connecting together software that is distributed on a computer network. However, each has developed at a different pace, with different areas of emphasis and giving the developer different results. The issue of interoperability is also different for each class. Although each faces the four different challenges discussed in section 2.4, they each emphasize only one or two of these problems in their solutions.

In the next five sections, each class of middleware will be discussed in terms of its characteristics, interoperability concerns, and messaging models. Each section concludes with strengths and weaknesses. By comparing and contrasting the different middleware, it should help to understand the role of IIOP and how it fits into the world of middleware and interoperability. Furthermore, it will clarify the types of problems that distributed object technology in general and CORBA with IIOP specifically are best suited to address.

2.6   Database Access Middleware

Before networking became popular, corporate information systems resided on a single mainframe. This mainframe provided a complete solution to the needs of enterprise information technology. Environmental pressures, including the need for responsiveness, flexibility, and diverse functionality, forced a paradigm shift from centralized systems to distributed client-server architectures. Early client-server architectures focused on providing connectivity to distributed relational databases. This form of middleware became known as **database access middleware,** which may be considered one of the most popular, widespread, and mature forms of middleware.

2.6.1   Characteristics

Database access middleware primarily provides easy-to-use connectivity to database servers. It also reduces the burden and development time of application programs; at a minimum, it shields application developers from low-level network programming detail. Experience with database middleware has resulted in the evolution of a number of rapid application development (RAD) tools. These RAD tools reduce the complexity and development time of database access applications. They include an interactive development environment (IDE) that integrates end-to-end distributed application development. Some also have been integrated with object-oriented analysis and design tools.

Implementations of database access middleware must address scalability limitations. For example, acceptable data transfer and network bandwidth characteristics might be obtained only by shifting the physical location of presentation, data access, and business logic code across client, server, or third-tier machines.

Many database access middleware implementations use a two-tier architecture. Architectures of this type place the physical location of presentation, data access, and business logic code on client machines. However, excessive network traffic and data transfers might occur with this architecture because all algorithmic processing of the data occurs at the client. By contrast, a three-tier architecture places data access and business logic code on a third-tier host rather than the client or the database server machine. This third-tier host centralizes business logic and control processing of the database data, thereby reducing network resource consumption.

2.6.2   Interoperability

Interoperability is focused on interactions between the data access middleware and the databases. Interoperability between different middleware does not exist. The industry has settled on the Standard Query Language (SQL) as the standard syntax of query and control messages of relational databases. This language enables application code to utilize heterogeneous databases. Although SQL provides the solution to standardizing database message syntax, proprietary extensions called **stored procedures** have subsequently become a barrier to interoperability. A stored procedure bundles SQL statements and procedures statements.

Microsoft, among others, has promulgated ODBC as an API to abstract access to heterogeneous relational databases. ODBC allows the client runtime to issue messages to the database gateway. The gateway then translates the message into a format appropriate to the target database.

2.6.3   Strengths and Weaknesses

Database access middleware has several strengths, as follows.

- *Ease of use.* RAD tools provide excellent support for producing software on time and under budget. The speed and ease of use of these tools might outweigh the weaknesses of data access middleware development.

- *Standardization of database interfaces.* The interface standard ODBC resolves the protocol differences between database proprietary dependencies. It has become a de facto interface standard for heterogeneous database access. Standards such as ODBC provide a significant contribution to middleware distribution transparency.

However, database access middleware also has its weaknesses, particularly limitations in the following areas.

- *Programming model limitations.* RAD tools provide a limited framework for distributed application development, although they do provide good single-use application solutions. Many RAD tools generate middleware code in their own proprietary Fourth Generation Language (4GL). These languages often reduce the complexity of programming at the expense of being tied to a single vendor for support.

- *Tight coupling.* Many two-tier database access approaches result in a tight coupling between client and server. Applications developed under this approach result in proprietary stovepipe systems. These systems are brittle to change and unfit for heterogeneous complex environments.

- *Messaging model limitations.* Database access middleware is primarily synchronous. Furthermore, the problem space it addresses is limited to a small (but important) class of problems.

2.7   Remote Procedure Calls

While database access middleware is specialized to database access, RPCs provide a more general approach to middleware. The notion of remote procedures has been around since the mid-1970s. Much theoretical writing on the subject resulted in RPC research implementations such as the Courier Project in 1979 and the Cedar Project in 1984. Like local procedure calling, RPCs transfer data and control to separate logical service units. The RPC messaging model enjoyed a degree of popularity due to its similarity with traditional application procedure calling.

2.7.1   Characteristics

RPCs provide distributed procedure calling that mimics the semantics of local procedure calling. The primary difference between a normal procedure call and the use of an RPC is that the communications occur across a network. This is accomplished through the use of stubs that exist between the client and server and act on behalf of each. The client makes a call to the client stub. The client stub handles the communications to the server stub, including the passing of arguments and managing data representation.

Open Network Computing (ONC) and Distributed Computing Environment (DCE) are the most widely supported RPC middleware. ONC was developed by Sun Microsystems and was one of the first commercial implementations. The Open Software Foundation, now called The Open Group, developed the DCE standard.

The elements of RPC middleware consist of a language compiler and runtime libraries. Client and server stubs are generated when an interface definition is passed through the compiler. The interface definition is usually expressed through an interface definition language. The output of the compiler is used by the client and server applications and supported by the runtime libraries.

2.7.2   Messaging Executive and Transport Layer Interfacing

The basic RPC is a synchronous, request-reply mechanism, just like a normal procedure call. This means that the client is blocked until the server responds to the call. However, RPC middleware has been enhanced to include the ability for asynchronous operation through the use of techniques such as lightweight processes or threads. This asynchronous behavior is still managed within the context of a request-reply.

There are three types of RPC message exchange protocols:

- request
- request-reply
- request-reply-acknowledge

Requests can be idempotent, meaning they can be initiated more than once or at-most-once. Idempotents are used in situations where the server does not maintain state information or state is not affected by multiple requests. At-most-once guarantees that duplicate requests will be detected and handled appropriately. For example, sending multiple requests for a light switch to be in the on position will not affect it if it is already in the on position. However, sending an increment request to a counter multiple times will result in multiple increments unless the counter can identify duplicate requests.

Requests can be either point-to-point or broadcast. In point-to-point mode the request is sent to a specific server. Broadcast requests can be sent to a set of servers or to all servers available on a network. Both ONC and DCE support idempotent as well as at-most-once requests. In addition, both can perform requests in either point-to-point or broadcast mode.

There are three potential reply options. The first option is without a reply. The client is requesting the server to perform an action but requires no further information. The second option returns a reply. In the final configuration the client acknowledges the reply was received.

These capabilities can be implemented using either connection-oriented or connectionless transport mechanisms. The use of a connection-oriented transport layer can lead to the consumption of significant resource consumption including network bandwidth, socket connections, and machine processes. Use of connectionless protocols could lead to problems with integrity and reliability. ONC and DCE provide the user with choices of transport protocols. One of the features of ONC is transport independence while DCE is oriented around the use of TCP and UDP.

2.7.3   Messaging Executive and Endpoint Binding Transparency

In order for RPC middleware to provide messaging it must interface with a transport layer. The transport layer requires network endpoint information. Different techniques that can be applied include references and binding handles.

DCE offers a number of endpoint binding mechanisms. However, in ONC no network wide binding service is available. ONC clients must explicitly specify the host location of desired remote services. A port mapper is provided to provide a list of port numbers for every server registered at its host location. Used in conjunction with a naming service this approximates binding transparency.

2.7.4   IDL Interoperability

IDLs capture metadata about procedures provided by a server. The metadata includes the names of the procedures and the type declarations of procedure parameters. Parameters are tagged as input, output, or input/output.

IDL techniques provide seamless integration of an application-layer environment with middleware messaging facilities. They provide application-to-middleware interfacing. The interface code is generated by a compiler using IDL interface contract specifications. These specifications are written in an abstract notation by the server application programmer.

Compilers can generate interface code for multiple programming languages. Application-to-middleware layer interface code is called **client stub** and **server stub.** A client stub represents the server procedure in the client programming environment. It creates a transport layer request message, in which it places packaged argument data, and blocks application-layer execution until a reply message is received from the server. A server stub obtains the request message, extracts the argument data, and invokes the remote procedure. It creates a transport-layer reply message, in which it places packaged return data. The client stub receives the reply message, extracts the data, and returns control and data to the application layer. This technique permits RPC communication between clients and servers that have different programming language environments.

The IDL compilers used in OSF DCE and SUN ONC generate bridge code for the C programming language. Third-party products provide support for a variety of languages for both DCE and ONC.

An important part of interface definitions are the definitions of data representations. The Sun ONC/External Data Representation (XDR) notation was originally intended to represent data but was extended to included the definition of programs. It supports the definition of constants, structures, enumerated types, unions, and programs. The DCE IDL notation was designed with a C language syntax. It supports more data types and has more options than ONC/XDR.

2.7.5   Data Transfer Representation Interoperability

RPCs reduce the burden of development by utilizing IDL techniques to seamlessly integrate application procedure calls with request-reply messages. In addition, IDL compilers generate bridge routines, called **stubs** and **skeletons.** These translate message data into a canonical form that is appropriate for cross-platform messaging and according to a set of encoding rules with which clients and servers must comply. Different RPC approaches such ONC and DCE use different data transfer rules.

The transfer syntax standards utilized by ONC and DCE include ONC/XDR and DCE/Network Data Representation (NDR), respectively. Both provide the rules for packing and aligning RPC message payload data bytes used in on-the-wire message transmission. They allow client and server development environments to have different programming language, operating system, and hardware platform environments. The payload data includes IDL-defined procedure argument, return, and context values. The syntaxes differ largely because of the different IDL-specified data types. Specifically, DCE IDL defines types such as pipe, array, pointer, and context handle data types that are not defined in ONC IDL. The ONC/XDR notation supports the definition of structures, enumerated types, unions, programs, and primitives.

2.7.6   Data Representation Interoperability

RPC IDL skeletons and stubs flatten potentially complex programming language data into a selected format that is appropriate for messaging. In addition, stub and skeleton routines convert the memory images of data into endian format appropriate to the target hardware platform.

DCE uses a "receiver-makes-right" policy for data image endian translation. This policy provides that messages be sent with endian information attached. Message receivers are responsible for performing endian translation, if required. Sun ONC/XDR standardizes on the big-endian format for data transmission. Conversion to and from big endian must occur for machines that do not support big endian.

2.7.7   Message Format Interoperability

The logical format of an on-the-wire RPC message typically consists of header information and payload. The message header provides receivers with information about message routing and payload, while the payload typically consists of procedure argument data that has been flattened for streamed transmission across the network. Different RPC approaches use different message framing arrangements, which are incompatible. For example, DCE and ONC's message framing techniques are not compatible, although they may be bridged.

2.7.8   Strengths and Weaknesses

The strengths of RPC middleware include the following:

- *Ease of use.* RPCs provide excellent integration of procedural based applications. They reduce the complexity by insulating the developer from operating system and network programming details.

- *Portability.* IDL compilers provide a greater degree of efficiency for porting applications than do other forms of middleware. In addition, location transparency is supported by a number of different implementations.

- *Robustness.* RPC solutions have been commercially available since the 1980's. They have been successfully applied to a variety of problems. They are suitable for application in certain types of mission critical applications that require scalability, fault tolerance, and reliability.

The weaknesses of RPC middleware include the following:

- *Inflexible to change.* RPC middleware is tightly coupled to an application at the time of development. It assumes a static relationship between client and server at runtime.

- *Programming model limitations.* RPC technology was being defined at a time when object oriented concepts were just beginning to emerge. As a result it is based heavily on procedure oriented languages.

- *Message model limitations.* RPC technology is synchronous in nature and therefore only applicable to a request/response oriented application. It does not easily support event driven or control applications due to the nature of a procedure call.

2.8   Transaction Processing Monitors

Information system organizations, driven by rapidly changing business environments, adopted distributed client-server systems on UNIX and NT machines with database access and RPC middleware to increase the flexibility of their information systems. Early systems consisted of a two-tier architecture; these were data-centric. Communication consisted of database proprietary SQL syntax and client request messages with status and data server responses. Managed environment issues, such as reliability, scalability, security, and availability, were database environment issues.

However, two-tier architectures were unacceptably inefficient. Subsequent evaluation of alternative physical architectures revealed the superiority of the three-tier architecture. This exhibited improved scalability, evolvability, and portability over the two-tier architecture. However, these advantages were offset by several unresolved, managed environment requirements. In particular, transactions, scalability, and security issues remained unsupported, deficiencies that certain types of applications, in particular mission-critical applications, could not accept. **Mission-critical applications** are a category of enterprise computing that is intended to support highly vital business functionality. Systems considered mission critical must be highly robust, available, and secure. Mainframes have provided this level of system support since the 1970s, the first being IBM's Customer Interface Control System (CICS).

Transaction processing (TP) monitors provide support for mission-critical requirements for three-tier distributed architectures. Products such as BEA's Tuxedo, Transarc's Encina, and Microsoft's MTS were developed to support mission-critical applications on nonmainframe platforms. TP monitors extend middleware core messaging functionality to meet the needs of mission-critical applications.

2.8.1   Characteristics

Data integrity is essential to mission-critical applications. TP monitors preserve the integrity of distributed enterprise information resources such as databases, files, and message queues. The term *transaction* is used to define a group of changes that either succeed together or do not occur at all. TP monitors assure the integrity of information resources by coordinating and controlling distributed resource updates.

TP monitors also can resolve a number of managed environment issues, including the following.

- Ensure that a single logical unit (atomic) of actions taken on a set of data are consistently applied.
- Restore/rollback the state of data that was inconsistently acted on due to network or application failure.
- Provide functionality for large numbers of simultaneous users without performance degradation.
- Provide authorized and audited access to data.
- Optionally provide application development tools, including database interfaces, system administration, and load balancing.

TP monitors provide scalability by multiplexing numerous client connections and interactions with information resources. They schedule and prioritize multiple information requests and generally provide multiple instances to respond to load. They also provide reliability by supporting rollback, failover, auto restart, centralized management, error logging, and replication to eliminate single points of failure.

TP monitors extend the capabilities of middleware from program to program and program to data messaging to managed environment issues such as transactional integrity, reliability, scalability, and security. TP monitors ease development and reduce development time by insulating developers from providing an infrastructure to deal with such issues as scalability, security, reliability, and transactional integrity. For example, Microsoft estimates that MTS reduces multi-tier development time from 30 to 40 percent. The result is shorter development time, less complex programming, and easier deployment and integration. Further, they help isolate business logic from presentation logic and persistent storage logic.

Code portability between different TP monitors and information resource products comes from the distributed transaction processing (DTP) standard. Defined by X/Open Ltd., a UNIX standards consortium, DTP defines the architecture for coordinating the concurrent sharing of transactional information services.

The DTP model defines the programming interfaces, and the interactions for implementing a distributed two-phase commit protocol. Three components are defined:

- Transactional applications (APs)
- Transaction managers (TMs)
- Resource managers (RMs)

In addition, three interfaces are defined:

- The AP to RM interface (RM)
- The AP to TM interface (TX)
- The TM and RM interface (XA)

The XA interface is the most critical and widely supported. It defines the interface that transaction managers and resource managers use to perform the two-phase transaction commit protocol and to do transactional recovery. For example, it is used for all interaction between Tuxedo and Oracle's Database. It is a critical industry standard because TP monitor and resource manager (database) vendors must support it. The XA interface is not used by transactional applications.

The other DTP interfaces, including RM and TX, are used by transactional applications. Database or TP monitor vendors do not support the RM and TX interfaces as closely as the XA interface. For example, Microsoft MTS supports the XA interface but exposes OLE and ODBC interfaces to transactional applications.

2.8.2 Messaging Executive and the Messaging Model

TP monitors use different messaging mechanisms. Some TP monitor products bundle other messaging mechanisms, while others provide their own proprietary approaches. For example, Encina and Tuxedo use the Open Group's DCE RPC and MTS uses MSRPC. MSRPC is a derivative of the DCE RPC. Tuxedo has been integrated by BEA with OMG object-oriented middleware to form their object transaction monitor product. Encina has already been integrated into the IONA ORBIX CORBA middleware.

2.8.3 Interoperability

TP monitors that bundle RPC middleware messaging mechanisms use the interoperability capabilities of those environments. For example, Encina and Tuxedo use Open Group's DCE RPC, while MTS uses DCOM MSRPC. These environments provide robust interoperability solutions for large enterprise environments. Interoperability standards for TP monitors have primarily focused on access from a transaction manager to the resource manager (typically a relational database). Interoperability between TP monitors is non-existent. However, due to the nature of TP monitors it is rare that interoperability is required at this level.

2.8.4 Strengths and Weaknesses

TP monitors have strengths as well as weaknesses. Its strengths include the following.

- *Mission critical features.* TP monitor middleware focuses on supporting managed environment requirements for mission critical applications. This includes support for transactional data integrity, scalability, reliability, and security. Most also provide excellent support for the other middleware requirements such as core messaging and interoperability. In addition, they provide transparency of operating system, programming language, transport layer, and server endpoint location.

- *Hide transactional complexity.* TP monitors insulate developers from dealing with issues such as transactional two-phase commit, security, process and thread management, and database connection management. Their support for the X/Open DTP standard interfaces allow code reuse between different TP monitor and database vendors. The result is shorter development time, less complex programming, and easier deployment and integration.

- *Robust messaging model.* TP monitors can act in either a synchronous or asynchronous manner. This gives the developer the ability to select the best approach for integrating together software.

The weaknesses of a TP monitor are:

- *Complexity of applying.* The most significant weakness of TP monitors is that they are too complex and thus require extensive support and have a steep learning curve. So they might not be appropriate for many applications or environments. Many environments might be better supported by the transactional support provided by a single database.
- *Limited applicability.* TP monitors are appropriate for a limited set of problems.

2.9   Message-Oriented Middleware (MOM)

Client-server messaging generally follows a synchronous communication pattern. Synchronous communication requires two things:

- Availability of both network endpoints that are participating in the communication
- Bilateral application-level participation in message exchange in order to ensure reliability

Message-oriented middleware (MOM), however, provides a degree of freedom over synchronous messaging. It requires the following:

- Availability of *one* of the network endpoints that are participating in the communication
- Unilateral application-level participation in message exchange

2.9.1   Characteristics

As mentioned earlier in the chapter, synchronous communication is characterized by the active, and simultaneous participation of two interacting programs. Similar to telephone communication, initiators obtain a connection with a target by obtaining and using the target's connection address. Subsequent communication occurs through the exchange of request and reply messages.

Asynchronous communication is more like using the post office. The initiator directs an addressed message to a local agent. Middleware then moves the message from the iniator to the local agent of the target address. The target subsequently retrieves the message from its local agent. Asynchronous communication does not require the simultaneous participation of initiator and target. Because of the nature of this interaction, the delivery of messages can be greatly improved using a technique known as store and forward. This technique can be applied to any MOM messaging model. It ensures that messages are saved until they have been properly moved and stored at the next node between endpoints.

Many applications do not require the bilateral participation in message exchange. Examples include notification-driven applications and single-threaded applications that cannot afford the overhead of waiting for synchronous replies. Message-oriented middleware offers an alternative to RPC communication that is more appropriate for these types of applications.

2.9.2 Messaging Executive and the Messaging Model

In general, MOM uses two specialized types of asynchronous communication:

- Message queuing
- Publish-and-subscribe

Message queuing requires unilateral, application-level participation in message communication and the availability of only one of the network endpoints that are participating in the communication. A source application program places a message on the local queue. Middleware then moves the message from the source queue to the target queue. The target application program subsequently retrieves the message from its local queue. Message queuing may be memory- or disk-based, with immediate or delayed delivery. Also, queue managers provide quality of service options, including

- reliable delivery with no message loss,
- guaranteed delivery with immediate or delayed delivery, and
- assured delivery with nonduplicative message delivery.

Like message queing, publish-and-subscribe requires unilateral, application-level participation in message communication. However, it differs in that applications participate as subscribers or publishers. Subscribers register to channels to be sent messages regarding a subject of interest; publishers send subject-tagged messages to channels. Channels decouple publishers and subscribers and subsequently broadcast messages to registered subscribers. Participants are shielded from the implementation dependencies of other publisher or subscriber participants.

2.9.3 Messaging Executive and Endpoint Binding Transparency

Subject channels provide location transparency between clients and servers. Both are shielded from the physical network address dependencies. This is accomplished through the use of an intermediary such as a queue or a subscription service. A queue is used to buffer a message until the server is ready for transmission. Typically, a unique queue is required for each type of interaction between each server. For example, if a client were to send out a purchase order and change address information for customers there would need to be a queue setup for handling both of these exchanges for every server. If there were ten servers that required both of these sets of information there would be twenty queues required. A subscription service would allow servers to register interest in types of information such as change of address and be notified when a client announced to the subscription service that an address had been changed. In this case there would be no need to set up large groups of queues to manage interactions.

2.9.4   Interoperability

There exist no standards for MOM technology other than those created by the market place such as IBM's MQSeries and Microsoft's MSMQ. This has lead to the situation where bridging is required between each of the products in order to achieve interoperability. An interesting side note is that standards are being established in the distributed object middleware area for MOM. This includes standards for JAVA and CORBA. These standards have only recently been adopted and it is expected that in the later part of 1999 MOM products will emerge based on these standards. However, these standards only apply to the interfaces and not to the transmission or implementation of the services or underlying messaging capability.

2.9.5   Strengths and Weaknesses

Like other middleware options, MOM has its strengths and weaknesses. Following are its primary strengths.

- *Eliminates endpoint dependencies.* MOM extends a degree of freedom over synchronous messaging by eliminating the dependency on requiring the target endpoint to simultaneously participate in a communication. Although RPC messaging more closely approximates a procedural programming paradigm, not all applications can use this pattern. For example, communication in event-driven applications is typically asynchronous.

- *Ease of use.* MOM provides a very simple set of operations upon which to implement a solution.

- *Guaranteed delivery.* Through a store-and-forward approach to messaging, MOM technology provides robust communication over unreliable transports. This is because the message will be continuously forwarded until delivery is acknowledged.

MOM's weaknesses include the following.

- *Programming model.* MOM is criticized for exposing a low level of abstraction that does not map to any programming model. Since most applications adhere to a procedural programming model, MOM technology would be unnatural for them.

- *Lack of standards.* Interoperability among MOM products is limited at best and not available in many cases. Applications are nonportable between MOM products because no standards exist.

- *Messaging model.* MOM solutions are all based upon an asynchronous model that is appropriate for very loosely coupled integrations. However, it cannot be used when a tighter integration model is required such as for creating distributed applications. It is primarily useful for data distribution and multi-step workflows between applications.

2.10 Distributed Object Middleware

Distributed object middleware (DOM) such as CORBA and DCOM combines to varying degrees the functionality of all the previously described middleware with object-oriented concepts to extend the benefits of object-oriented software engineering to distributed computing.

DOM is layered between the application and the transport layer. The application software relies on it to abstract the details of communication across a network or across process boundaries. The transport layer relies on it to create and manage messages, typecheck and translate message data, and provide network endpoint information.

The OMG has promulgated CORBA as the middleware interface specification for the generation of object-oriented application software. The OMG middleware approach establishes an architecture that enables application processes to communicate with one another no matter where they are located or who has designed them. CORBA specifications derive from commercially available object technology. The CORBA 2.0 specification defined the protocol for transport layer messaging. It also defined the GIOP message, the CDR, and the IIOP endpoint mapping protocols to interoperate across the transport layer. IIOP extends the endpoint addressing beyond that of RPC.

DCOM is a DOM product developed by Microsoft to extend the messaging capabilities of its COM product. COM provides communication between object linking and embedding (OLE) document components within the same computer. DCOM provides a slight modification of DCE RPC called *object remote procedure calling* (ORPC) to support remote object messaging. Initially, DCOM supported communication only between Intel-based platforms. Work by Software AG extends it to other platforms.

2.10.1   Ease of Use Characteristics

DOM is an advancement over other middleware because it reduces development burden and total cost of ownership of distributed enterprise systems. As mentioned in the previous section, the advantage of object technology derives from its maintainability, reusability, evolvability, and ability to overcome complexity. The modularity of distributed objects allows complex systems to be decomposed into comprehensible units.

Beyond the use of an object model, ease of use in DOM is accomplished through the integration of a variety of high level services such as naming, transactions and security that reduce the burden of development.

2.10.2   Application Integration Characteristics

DOM is the natural evolution of RPC communication to object-oriented languages and systems. Like RPCs, it uses IDL to define a messaging contract between two network endpoints. The IDL generates application to middleware layer code, which is generated by IDL compilers in accordance with the interface defined for the target object. The code is generated for both the client and server environments. It handles all details of packaging and unpackaging argument data from the message streams exchanged between client and servers. For client bridge code, DCOM uses the term *proxy,* while CORBA uses the term *stub.* On the server side, DCOM uses the term *stub,* while CORBA uses the term *skeleton.*

The interaction between the application and middleware layer in the CORBA and DCOM environments is very similar, but there still are significant differences. Communication cannot begin until a network connection is obtained for the target object. Network connections, called *bindings,* identify a target object to a client. Within the binding establishment phase, both environments abstract connection establishment and object activation. Once a binding to the target object is obtained, invocation against operations on the target object is possible. Operation invocation involves the exchange of input and output argument data and the handling of error conditions. CORBA and DCOM differ in the tactical details of obtaining a binding to the target and of operation invocation across an interface contract.

Clients in CORBA and DCOM environments obtain a binding to target objects in different ways. Even the term used for an object binding differs in each. In CORBA, bindings are called *object references* and in DCOM, *interface pointers.* There is no bind operation in the CORBA standard. However, vendors provide operations that activate a server and provide object references to a client. By contrast, in the DCOM environment, clients invoke the static CoCreateInstance() operation, passing identifiers for the implementation class and the interface. However, this is only one approach that can be applied in DCOM. For example, through the use of monikers the same effect can be generated.

Servers are required to be registered by both CORBA and DCOM. This stores an association between the interface and the servers path name. In CORBA the implementation repository holds this information while the registry is used in DCOM.

CORBA and DCOM do not interact identically across IDL interface boundaries primarily because the grammars and syntaxes of Microsoft IDL and OMG IDL are different. Microsoft IDL (MIDL) is based on the DCE IDL. This IDL allows definitions of interfaces, types, operations, and constants. Microsoft extensions to the DCE IDL include new keywords for handling object references, string bindings, reference counting, path resolution, new object creation, and object activation. By contrast, the OMG IDL allows the definition of modules, interfaces, types, operations, constants, and exceptions. In addition, several differences exist in the basic primitive data types supported. MIDL's support of pipes and pointers are not supported in OMG IDL, and OMG's any type is not supported by MIDL. In a general sense, MIDL is based on the C programming language, whereas the OMG IDL is based on C++.

The application layer is also affected by how CORBA and DCOM perform exception handling. The CORBA IDL explicitly supports C++ style exceptions. A set of CORBA system exceptions are defined for network, connection, and parameter exchange conditions. By contrast, all DCOM methods return a 32-bit error code called an HRESULT. Tools are provided to convert HRESULTs into object-oriented programming language exceptions.

Another difference involves multiple inheritance. In CORBA, multiple inheritance is captured in the IDL definitions without restrictions on use. Multiple inheritance in the DCOM environment is accomplished by using an aggregation mechanism. DCOM clients must use the canonical QueryInterface operation to switch between interfaces. Separate interface identifiers and interface pointers are associated with each interface that an object may have. The multiple inheritance restriction in the DCOM environment is related to the DCOM object model. This model requires a standard memory layout or virtual function table for each interface. It allows the integration of binary components that possibly were written in different programming languages, such as C++, Java, and Visual Basic. Since an inherited interface might have been written in any of these languages, it may be integrated only by providing its own virtual function table. Through this approach, each interface has its own separate level of indirection. Traversal between interfaces is explicit and exposed in DCOM clients.

2.10.3   Adaptability and Modularity Characteristics

Use of the principle of modularity and encapsulation inherent to object-oriented software engineering provides a significant advantage for the design and construction of complex enterprise systems. Objects reduce the complexity of system design by allowing a system to be decomposed into cohesive, comprehensible service units. At their most basic level, objects are data types that contain attributes and methods. The methods, or procedures, perform algorithmic transformations or simple accesses to the attribute data. In CORBA and DCOM, a client invokes a method on a remote object's interface. The interface, defined in an IDL, provides a programming language-independent contract between the client and server by mapping to the programming language used in the client and server environments. The interface contract encapsulates, or hides, the implementation details of the target object; the only information exposed to the client is the interface. The separation of interface from implementation reduces the dependencies between the client and server environments. In addition, multiple implementations of the interface may be provided without affecting the client. The interface methods allow the user to manipulate the data and perform specific tasks in a well-defined manner; only clients that have pointers to these object interfaces can invoke these methods.

2.10.4   Security Characteristics

DCOM security is based on NT operating system security, which is based on administered domains that contain user and group accounts. Every NT account has an associated SID (security ID). Authentication into a domain results in a set of tokens that provide user and group privileges in the system. Authorization to use a DCOM object is implemented using ACLs associated with the target object. By contrast, the OMG has specified a much more wide-ranging set of security services for CORBA-based systems. It defines interfaces for providing confidentiality, authentication, authorization, audit, and nonrepudiation.

2.10.5   Transaction Characteristics

DOM provides support for enterprise-level information systems. An essential function required in these systems is the transactional integrity of corporation information resources. CORBA and DCOM distributed object middleware solutions support this requirement. CORBA's support for object transactions is provided through the Object Transaction Service (OTS), while DCOM's support is through the Microsoft Transaction Server (MTS). Both services provide information integrity in transaction-oriented processing.

2.10.6   Messaging Executive and the Messaging Model

Both CORBA and DCOM use a client-server style of communication. This communication is characterized as the integration of application procedure calling with middleware layer synchronous and asynchronous messaging. RPCs abstract the application layer from details of network endpoints, hardware platforms, operating systems, platform data representations, and the transport layer.

OMG GIOP/IIOP and DCOM ORPC messaging are similar in how they use transport communication protocols and support multiple underlying transport protocols, including TCP/IP. They also are similar in their support of multiple outstanding requests to multiple objects over the same connection and of fragmentation of messages for the efficient exchange of large-sized messages. However, DCOM has significantly more restrictions on the wire protocol. It is tied to the underlying RPC structure that is provided by Microsoft and is based on the DCE RPC standard. The DCOM specification deals with many implementation details and limitations. An example is the pinging protocol that is used to garbage collect remote object references. CORBA's GIOP and IIOP standards provide a significant degree of flexiblity. Because of the rules of the OMG the specification do not deal with implementation details or limitations other than the specification of TCP/IP as the underlying transport for IIOP.

2.10.7   Messaging Executive and Independent
Address Spaces

DOM client and object servers may reside in separate platforms and address spaces. These servers can share data only through the methods arguments specified in the IDL contract. The semantics of parameter passing are deep pass-by-copy for data arguments in both CORBA and DCOM environments. The semantics of parameter passing for objects are pass-by-reference and pass-by-value for both CORBA and DCOM.

2.10.8   Messaging Executive and Independent Failure

Compared to local procedure calling, distributed messaging faces a number of additional failure modes. The types of system exceptions include server and client crashes, network communication link failure, security exceptions, and server connection exhaustion. CORBA and DCOM support exceptions through different mechanisms. CORBA supports C++ style exceptions, while DCOM provides a 32-bit error code through HRESULT. CORBA provides a set of system exceptions defined for network, connection, and parameter exchange conditions, while DCOM defines a set of system error codes.

2.10.9   Messaging Executive and Server Binding

Server binding is the acquisition of server network endpoint information. This information includes, at a minimum, the network address of the target server and is required by the transport layer in order to establish a connection or transmit a message. Server binding preferably is dynamic, since the network address, typically the host and port numbers of the target server, is subject to change. Other binding information can be transport layer preferences, the security quality of protection policy, the data transfer syntax policy, and other data. This information might be necessary to resolve the optional or noncanonical aspects of the communication protocol.

Both DCOM and CORBA ORBs maintain binding information and provide binding completion services. DCOM uses an interface pointer as a container for binding information. DCOM interface pointers are the result of the binding completion process and contain the complete network address of the target object. CORBA uses an object reference as a container for binding information. The reference contains network address information that is statically complete or that requires binding completion at runtime. It also contains tagged information such as GIOP/IIOP protocol data or security policy data and may contain transient information.

2.10.10   Messaging Executive and Binding Information Metadata

To assist the binding process, clients in distributed object systems may provide additional identification information regarding the target object they want to use. This global binding metadata may include data on quality of service, interface type, and object instance name.

CORBA uses string names to identify object instances, a set of reference data to identify interfaces, and a set of properties to identify quality of service information. Object instance names are used in conjunction with directory services. Interface reference data is used in conjunction with interface repository services. Quality of service information is used in conjunction with trading services.

DCOM uses **globally unique identifiers** (GUID). A GUID provides uniqueness in time and space by including host and timestamp information. GUIDs are used in the DCOM environment for globally unique interface and implementation class identification.

2.10.11   Interoperability

Hardware platforms that represent and address data in different ways represent separate technical domains. Effective data transfer between two different technical domains requires that any inconsistencies be corrected. CORBA and DCOM provide data transmission interoperability by translating client or server data from their local data representations to a shared data transfer syntax format and then back to the endpoints data representation. A transfer syntax is a set of encoding rules used for the network transmission of data and the conversion to and from different local data representations. The CORBA 2.0 GIOP protocol has established the CDR as its data transfer syntax. For the DCOM environment, it is Network Data Representation (NDR). It is interesting to note that CDR is a subset of NDR.

2.10.12   Strengths and Weaknesses

DOM has several strengths as follows.

- *Standardization.* Since its inception, OMG has leveraged the diverse contributions of its members. Those members contribute broad experience in the research and production of large-scale, object-oriented distributed computing and the OMG legitimately boasts having the world's largest consortium of members. The OMG is the only meaningful standards effort for middleware in existence today. This gives DOM and CORBA a significant edge over all other classes of middleware. Microsoft, through the sheer size of their customer base, makes DCOM a de facto standard.

- *Programming model support.* Most new application development is done using object-oriented languages like Java and C++. DOM technology is the only middleware that naturally integrates with these modern development environments as well as legacy systems and older programming models.

- *Ease of use.* DOM technology provides the largest set of support services. Naming, trading, and transaction services are all integral parts of DOM. The best of Data Access, RPC, TP monitor and MOM middleware have been utilized in CORBA and to a lesser degree in DCOM. These services are integrated together to make it easy to apply them.

- *Flexibility.* DOM technology can be used across a broad spectrum of problems including distributed applications, transaction processing, and system integration.

- *Robust messaging model.* DOM can act in either a synchronous or asynchronous manner. This gives the developer the ability to select the best approach for integrating software. Furthermore, the only standards related to asynchronous messaging exist in the DOM community as defined by OMG as well as the Java community.

- *Eliminates endpoint dependency.* When using the asynchronous messaging capabilities or through other mechanisms such as event services the developer can eliminate endpoint dependency.
- *Interoperability.* GIOP and IIOP are the only standards that exist in middleware for guaranteeing interoperability between middleware products.

However, DOM also has its weaknesses, particularly limitations in the following area:

- *Robustness.* DOM technology has not been available for as long as other middleware technology. As a result the robustness has not been tested and enhanced to the same degree. This is a maturity issue that becomes smaller every year and should disappear in the near future.
- *Complexity.* DOM technology requires more extensive knowledge due to the breadth of capability. However, this is tempered by the fact that not all of the capabilities are required to get started with simple applications. An additional area of complexity is the requirement to use IDL to define interfaces requiring additional knowledge by the developer.

2.11 Middleware and Interoperability: Critical to the Enterprise

In this chapter, we provided a context for the GIOP/IIOP messaging protocol by describing the general problem that middleware solves, providing distribution transparency. We discussed how CORBA and other competitive technologies are designed to solve this problem and the strengths and weaknesses of each solution.

DOM is the result of years of middleware evolution. However, its capabilities are not fully understood in the marketplace where it is generally thought of as a technology for developing new applications using a synchronous method of communication. However, it has most of the features of the other four classes of middleware. As DOM products mature this view will change.

Interoperability has not been a major concern for the other classes of middleware until recently. As middleware becomes more important to the enterprise the lack of interoperability standards will constrain their usefulness. CORBA is the only middleware standard that has fully addressed the issues related to interoperability of middleware.

Following are the main points of the chapter.

- Until the advent of middleware technology, mainframe computing provided the predominant form of enterprise information system technology. Mainframe systems remain popular because of their reliability, scalability, transactional integrity, and security for mission-critical applications and data management. Their weaknesses include inflexibility.

- Middleware technology developed as an alternative to mainframe computing to provide greater adaptability as well as to reduce complexity of programming distributed applications.

- Middleware is slowly evolving, acquiring mainframe characteristics such as reliability, scalability, transactional integrity, and security for mission-critical applications.

- DOM is the next generation evolution of middleware technology. It competes with message-oriented middleware as the predominant form of enterprise computing technology.

- CORBA is the only middleware solution that provides interoperability among different vendors solutions.

- GIOP/IIOP is the specification for a messaging protocol for ensuring interoperability among distributed object middleware.

GIOP and IIOP Standards

The Process of Creating
the IIOP Standard

3.1   The OMG Process

The OMG is a non-profit organization that is dedicated to setting standards related
to distributed object technology. Any company, organization or individual has the
right to join OMG and participate in the setting of standards as long as they comply with the established rules. The result is a self-selecting group that comes
together to create an OMG standard with different experiences, biases, and desires.

In this chapter, we examine the processes and surrounding atmospherics,
which resulted in the specifications for the GIOP/IIOP messaging protocol. We
will review the situation prior to the standard, the requirements that drove the
process, the solutions proposed, and the subsequent outcome of the process.

This chapter may leave the reader with the impression that the process that
led to the GIOP/IIOP specification was very disciplined and orderly. The reality was quite different. The reality included significant technical debate as a
group and among individuals, political maneuvering some of which has been
described as Machiavellian, personal desires and business pressures that often
conflicted with achieving "the best answer."

The GIOP/IIOP standard is the result of a consensus building activity that
led to a successful specification. As you read through this book it is important
to understand that the standard was a result of serious technical debate and
discussion from the best minds available on this topic combined with compromise and concessions in order to achieve a final solution.

3.2   Setting the Stage for Standardization

The CORBA specifications define the mechanisms to register and access distributed objects. CORBA 1.1, published in December 1991, gave the first guidance

relating to ORB interoperability. CORBA 1.1 defined interoperability and the organization of multiple ORBs, including the definition and an approach for reference embedding interoperability using gateways. Reference embedding assumes that two ORBs differ only in object reference representations. Application clients in ORB 1 are able to utilize object implementations from ORB 2 when object references from ORB 2 are embedded into object references appropriate for ORB 1.

Protocol translation gateways would be used when two ORBs differed in many ways, such as object reference representation and message stream formats. They would accept all inter-ORB references. They also would correct differences, forward requests and replies between clients, and target object implementations.

The CORBA 1.1 specifications did not include low-level protocol requirements for the interoperation of CORBA ORB products from different vendors. The interoperability specifications in CORBA 1.1 were not practical solutions. Reference embedding and protocol translation gateways were not developed as solutions because they are difficult to build and produce inefficient communication between ORBs. The OMG recognized this problem and began work in 1992 examining alternative solutions. This included a variety of technical meetings including an OMG sponsored workshop on ORB interoperabilitiy as well as a Request for Information (RFI) where alternative approaches were examined. The information gathered from these was used as the basis for creating the Request for Proposal (RFP).

In October 1993, the OMG broadcast an RFP entitled "Object Request Broker 2.0 Extensions Interoperability and Initialization Request for Proposals." Responses to the RFP were submitted to the OMG in March 1994 and presented at the OMG meeting in April 1994. The responses to the RFP formed the universe of possibilities for an interoperability specification. It was this set of responses that led to the IIOP specification after a series of interactions.

3.3 CORBA 2.0 Interoperability Considerations

Members of the OMG working on the interoperability problem struggled with achieving consensus regarding the following:

- Scope of interoperability requirements
- ORB functionality and services
- Standardized interoperability
- Interoperability gateway or bridges

These were the formal issues that were being wrestled with by the group. However, there was one additional issue that was being dealt with that had equal influence on the final solution. This was the conflict between the DCE community and its opponents. The issue was whether to use DCE as the core of an interoperability solution for CORBA. This issue colored the debate on every issue that was addressed.

The RFP issued in October 1993 included the following evaluation criteria, defining the features of a successful submission:

- Ability for two vendors' ORBs to interoperate without each having prior knowledge of the other's implementation (with possible decreased performance)
- Ability to support all ORB functionality
- Ability to preserve the content and semantics of ORB-specific information across ORB boundaries (for example, security)

The most difficult decision faced by the group was the scope of interoperability. At one end of the spectrum is minimally scoped interoperability that simply requires successful two-way communications. At the other end is broadly scoped interoperability that requires all aspects of distribution transparency are handled.

The group spent a considerable amount of time exploring this issue. They came up with recommendations for both a minimal and broad approach. They cautioned that solutions for minimally scoped interoperability should be evolvable to full distribution transparency, the middleware goal of eliminating all protocol differences that restrict interoperability.

They also recommended that broad solutions for interoperability should depend on a layered model of ORB services. In addition to the concept of a layered architecture the concept of domains were introduced. Domains are a way of grouping together elements of a system that support distribution transparency. A domain would support a common set of administrative and technical protocols. Each domain would have an ORB service from the layered architecture that would correct a specific domain protocol barrier that affected interoperability.

During the CORBA 2.0 RFP process, end users often expressed a desire for an "out-of-the-box" interoperability requirement. Such interoperability demands that a native standardized communication protocol exists among ORB products; end users would not need to correct differences between two ORB products. Contributors who feared negative end-user opinion preferred "out-of-the-box" interoperability provided by standardization approaches.

After significant debate on which approach to adopt, a minimalist approach to the problem was agreed to by the group. The idea of a layered model was pushed aside due to the extent of the technical issues that existed and the significant time required to reach consensus. The boundaries of the problem were subsequently reduced from distribution transparency to simple successful internetworking. However, a compromise was reached between contributing vendors asserting that bridge solutions were valuable and should be retained as a part of the specification.

3.4 The CORBA 2.0 Solution

The final compromise that was reached in developing the interoperability specification was to support both a DCE and non-DCE solution as a part of the specification. This compromise was reached after it became clear that there would not be consensus on a single solution. The recommendation to the OMG architecture board specified a general interoperability solution, the GIOP/IIDP protocols. A DCE proposal was recommended as an optional "environment-specific" profile. A major point of contention that resulted from this compromise was how to allow diverse messaging approaches to a simple, reliable, message exchange standard, while retaining the efficiencies of such a standard. Contributors who feared the infeasibility of a single messaging standard preferred interoperability bridge solutions. Accommodations were made to the specification to deal with these concerns.

The conflict between the two groups had a tremendous impact on the final outcome of the interoperability standards. One of the major reasons that may have helped GIOP/IIOP prevail was because the constructs were defined in IDL as opposed to DCE which define message headers in terms of physical bit-wise layouts. This made it easier for the OMG community to understand. One interesting aspect of the GIOP/IIOP standard that resulted due to the DCE conflict was the definition of the CDR. The original plan was for it to be based on the variable byte-order version of XDR. It was decided to replace XDR with a subset of NDR in the hopes of reaching consensus with the DCE submitters. By the time it was obvious there would be no compromise it was too late to revert to the XDR solution.

As a final note, while there were many accommodations made to support DCE software, vendors have ignored them. IIOP has emerged as the dominant interoperability specification.

3.5 The Challenges and Benefits of Consensus

The OMG provides a unique forum for the design of standards related to distributed object technology. This chapter gave the reader a glimpse into the process used to create the IIOP specifications as well as some of the issues that were addressed prior to achieving consensus.

The main points of this chapter include the following.

- The CORBA 2.0 process focused on providing interoperability among CORBA middleware products to fix a severe deficiency in the original specification.

- Interoperability differences can be resolved through either a general specification or bridging approach.

- Contributors to the CORBA 2.0 process realized that they could not resolve all of the technical and administrative interoperability issues. They agreed to focus on resolving technical messaging differences using a minimalist approach. However, they would accommodate the desires of the pro-DCE contingent.

- The success of IIOP has completely overshadowed the accommodations that were made. However, the influence of DCE on IIOP can be seen in the specification.

General Inter-ORB Protocol

4.1 Introduction to GIOP

In this chapter, we provide the details of the GIOP messaging protocol. We describe GIOP's approach to interobject communication and cover the fundamentals of GIOP's transfer syntax and transport protocol requirements. We also discuss the CDR in detail, including byte alignment, byte ordering, and on-the-wire mappings of data types. We end by showing the set of messages that GIOP uses to pass data and give examples of message streams.

The GIOP specification has three primary parts:

- Transfer syntax
- Message formats
- Transport layers assumptions

The transfer syntax defines a common way to represent data in a CORBA invocation. The formal mapping for data types is the CDR (Common Data Representation) definition. The GIOP is a vehicle for passing the data that has been defined with the CDR. It specifies eight messages that (in theory) have enough functionality that they can be used to solve any distributed problem. The GIOP further specifies its requirements for a transport layer. It needs certain things from a transport layer that must be met before it will work. Each of these topics is covered in greater detail throughout the chapter. We start with the basics, the CDR, which gives agents a shared language. It is from this that all higher-order functionality derives.

4.2 The CDR

The transfer of information requires a common syntax. Otherwise, when two parties communicate, the data in the exchange is guaranteed to be understandable only by the issuing party. The data might be aligned differently, have different byte ordering, or be language-specific. An example is a pointer. What does a pointer to memory mean to a receiver on a completely different machine? The answer is nothing, unless it has been transformed into a form that the receiver can understand. All of this must be taken into account before an agent issues data to another agent. In other words, rules need to be defined to allow agents to understand the data they receive.

Generally, this is handled by defining a neutral, bicanonical, on-the-wire representation of the data. CORBA has done this with its CDR transfer syntax specification. The OMG defined the CDR so that it supports the following features:

- *Variable byte addressing.* The sender does not have to do byte swapping to ensure that the data is in the correct order for the receivers; the receiver is responsible for doing this. This allows the decoupling of knowledge about architecture—the sender does not have to know what kind of machine is on the receiving end of its messages. Usually, the less the client and server have to know about each other, the better.

- *Data alignment.* All data is aligned on its natural boundaries within a GIOP message. CDR defines alignment policies only for primitive types, but all complex types can be broken down into the constituent simple types. Aligning data allows for more efficient handling by machine architectures that enforce data alignment in memory.

- *Complete IDL mapping.* All data types available in the IDL are represented in the CDR. This complete mapping means that IDL developers do not have to worry about marshalling any of their own data types.

We cover CDR in more detail in this chapter, including its design and use.

4.3   Object Addressing

An object is addressed via an **object reference.** The CORBA specification defines an object reference as "an object name that reliably denotes a particular object." An object reference provides a distributed handle to an implementation. This handle acts as a proxy for the object implementation, thereby allowing disparate systems, which might be written in different languages and running on different platforms, to use the object implementation. Whenever an operation is invoked on a object reference, that reference will always communicate with the same implementation. An implementation, however, may be denoted by multiple, distinct references.

When invoking on an object reference, the client should have no notion of the locality of the object implementation. The implementation might reside on the caller's machine or on a remote machine. It might be using one ORB or many. The fundamental ORB interoperability requirement is to allow clients to use object references to invoke operations on objects in other ORBs.

4.4 Marshalling

Differences exist in the byte ordering of words on different machine architectures. These architectural inconsistencies result in multiple machine data addressing domains. Specifically, different architectures have different views of the most and least significant bytes. How are arguments transmitted across machine boundaries if the machines address data differently? Since there are differences in the word byte ordering between domains, the data must undergo some sort of transformation process before transmission. Sending the data as is would cause erroneous results if the sender and receiver had different byte ordering.

Most machines are byte-addressed and provide access for bytes (8 bits), halfwords (16 bits), words (32 bits), and double words (64 bits). Typically, there are two ways that a machine orders bytes within words: big endian and little endian. Big-endian architectures put the byte that is addressed at x...x00 at the most significant end of the word, whereas little-endian architectures put that byte at the least significant end of the word. The address of a datum is the address of the most significant byte in big-endian addressing and the least significant byte in little-endian addressing. For example, the memory representation of sequential bytes is 0x12 0x34 0x56 0x78 on a big-endian machine, while the representation of those same sequential bytes on a little-endian machine is 0x78 0x56 0x34 0x12. The terms *little endian* and *big endian* are an analogy drawn by Cohen from *Gulliver's Travels,* in which the islands of Lilliput and Blefescu feuded over which end of an egg to crack, the little end or the big end. For multibyte data, endian ordering determines which is the most significant byte. Intel *x*86-based computers and some RISC chips, such as the Alpha, use little-endian byte ordering, while many RISC-based UNIX chips, for example Sun's Sparc chip, use big-endian byte ordering. Imagine the result if a UNIX machine passed a long to an Intel *x*86 machine without first converting it to little endian.

It is easy to see how endian-ness can become an issue. It is not uncommon to have different domains of byte ordering, for example a network consisting of a number of Windows NT clients communicating with objects on a Solaris server. The clients are little endian and the server is big endian, so data translation must occur. GIOP provides for this by tagging the message with a flag to indicate endianness and then allowing the sender to send the message in its native endian-ness. We cover later in this chapter more on why CORBA's creators chose this method.

GIOP specifies primitive data types for big-endian and little-endian orderings. Table 4.1 lists these.

Table 4.1 Primitive Types in GIOP

Type	Description
boolean	An 8-bit value with the range [0, 1].
char	An 8-bit value with a mapping into the ISO Latin-1 8859.1 character set.
octet	An 8-bit value in the range [0–255] that is not marshalled during transmission.
short	A 16-bit integer with the range $[-2^{15}, 2^{15} - 1]$.
unsigned short	A 16-bit integer with the range $[0, 2^{16} - 1]$.
wchar	An 8-bit, 16-bit, or 32-bit value that represents international character data.
long	A 32-bit integer with the range $[-2^{31}, 2^{31} - 1]$.
unsigned long	A 32-bit integer with the range $[0, 2^{32} - 1]$.
long long	A 64-bit integer with the range $[-2^{63}, 2^{63} - 1]$.
unsigned long long	A 64-bit integer with the range $[0, 2^{64} - 1]$.
float	A 32-bit value conforming to the ANSI/IEEE 754-1985 floating-point standard.
double	A 64-bit value conforming to the ANSI/IEEE 754-1985 double-precision floating-point standard.
long double	An 128-bit value conforming to the ANSI/IEEE 754-1985 double-precision floating-point standard.

The more complex types, such as structures, are built from the primitive types. Primitive data types are encoded in multiples of octets. This means that data types always use the same number of octets to represent their values. We go into more detail on the reasons behind this later in the chapter. For now, refer to Table 4.2 for the number of octets required to represent each primitive type.

Figure 4.1 shows the layout of the short and unsigned short types. For big-endian shorts, the most significant byte is located at octet 0 and the least significant at octet 1. For little-endian shorts, the reverse is true. In the following several figures, MSB means the most significant byte and LSB means the least significant byte.

Figure 4.2 shows the layout of the long and unsigned long types. For big-endian longs, the most significant byte is located at octet 0 and the least significant at octet 3. For little-endian longs, the reverse is true.

Table 4.2 Octets for Primitive Types

Types	Size (in octets)
boolean, octet, char	1
short, unsigned short	2
long, unsigned long, float	4
long long, unsigned long long, double	8
long double	16

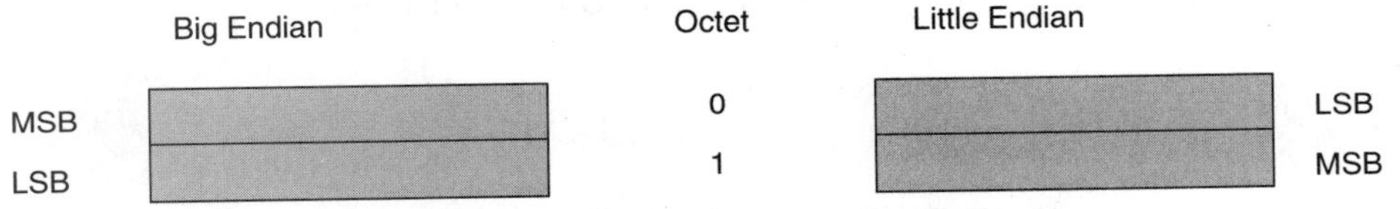

FIGURE 4.1 Layout of Short and Unsigned Short Types

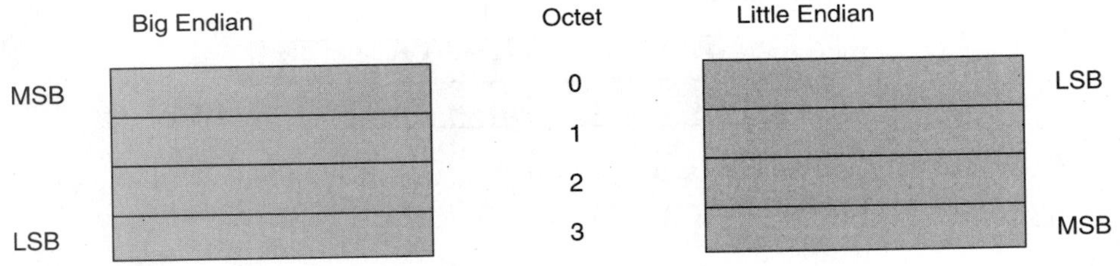

FIGURE 4.2 Layout of Long and Unsigned Long Types

Figure 4.3 shows the layout of the long long and unsigned long long types. For big-endian long longs, the most significant byte is located at octet 0 and the least significant at octet 7. For little-endian long longs, the reverse is true.

Figure 4.4 shows the layout of the float types. For big-endian floats, the most significant byte is located at octet 0 and the least significant at octet 3. For little-endian floats, the most significant byte is located at octet 3 and the least significant at octet 0.

Figure 4.5 shows the layout of the double types. For big-endian double-numbers, the most significant byte is located at octet 0 and the least significant at octet 7. For little-endian double-numbers, the reverse is true.

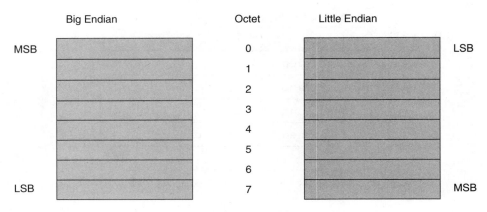

FIGURE 4.3   Layout of `Long Long` and `Unsigned Long Long` Types

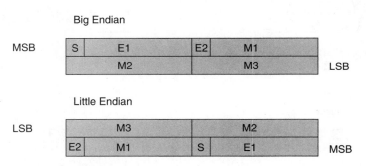

FIGURE 4.4   Layout of `Float` Type

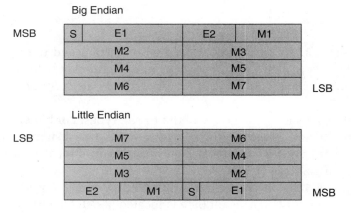

FIGURE 4.5   Layout of `Double` Type

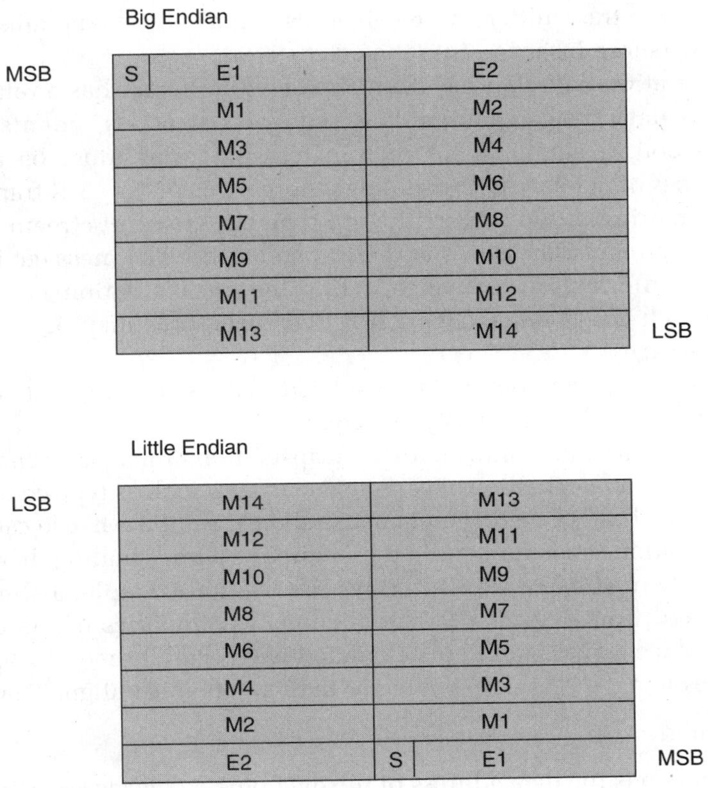

Big Endian

Little Endian

FIGURE 4.6   Layout of `Long Double` Types

Figure 4.6 shows the layout of the `long double` types. For big-endian `long double`, the most significant byte is located at octet 0 and the least significant at octet 15. For little-endian `long double`, the reverse is true.

4.5   The CDR and Streams

When a client invokes a distributed operation on a server, it transfers the operation data it is sending to the server as an **octet stream.** The CORBA specification defines an octet stream as "an abstract notion that typically corresponds to a memory buffer that is to be sent to another process or machine over some IPC mechanism or network transport." An octet is an 8-bit value that undergoes no marshalling, either by the client or by the server. An octet stream is a sequence of these octets that is arbitrarily long and that has a well-defined beginning. An octet does not undergo conversion from one byte order to

another; the transmitter and receiver leave it as is. All data must undergo marshalling before insertion into the octet stream.

Operation data that has been streamed no longer has a relationship to its
original data type; it is simply a sequence of octets. For its content to be
understood, a standard set of transforming rules must be applied to the
sequences of octets. CORBA defines these rules in the CDR transfer syntax for
the formatting of the OMG IDL data types in the octet stream. There are two
kinds of streams: messages and encapsulations. The **message** is GIOP's basic
unit for information exchange, while the encapsulation is an octet stream
into which the marshalling of IDL data structures may occur separate from
any message.

The representation of encapsulated data structures occurs as an octet
sequence; in IDL, the data type `sequence<octet>` allows a marshalled octet
sequence to be added into another encapsulation or message. The encapsulation
allows the premarshalling of complex constants such as type codes, thereby saving the overhead of having them marshalled at runtime. It also can contain other
encapsulations and can handle these without unmarshalling them.

Octets in streams are like arrays in C++; for example, a stream of n octets
is indexed from 0 to $n - 1$. The alignment boundaries of the data contained
within the encapsulation are calculated with octet indices. In some machines,
accesses to a data type that is larger than a byte must align. That is,

$a \bmod n = 0,$

where a is the byte address of the data type being accessed and n is the size
of the data type in bytes. In GIOP, n is restricted to 8 bytes. Any data type that
is larger than 8 bytes, such as a `long double` (16 bytes), is aligned as an 8-byte
data type.

Hardware uses the concept of byte alignment to improve the efficiency of
operations. Misalignment causes hardware complications, since the alignment
of memory typically occurs on a word boundary. Misaligned memory accesses
take multiple aligned memory references. For example, when an access occurs
to a misaligned word in a system with a 32-bit-wide bus to memory, two
accesses are required to get the word. Even if a machine allows misaligned
accesses, programs with aligned access will run faster.

The CDR protocol uses variable alignment and byte ordering—this can
inhibit the ability to optimize for speed. In addition, complex data types might
have their own memory alignment rules that are more complex than with a
fixed alignment. For example, structure alignment might occur such that members match the alignment of the strictest member.

When a GIOP message is received, the data is contained in an encapsulation (an octet stream). To be useful to the receiver, the data needs to be

extracted from the encapsulation. But the data is of different sizes, so how do you index it correctly? The answer is twofold. First, like types are always the same sizes regardless of their values, and second, all data alignment occurs based on type. When data is encoded in a stream, it is encoded as its size, not just with the amount of bytes needed to represent the information. For example, a `long` that contains the value 9 could be represented with 1 byte, 0x09. But it is not. It is represented with 4 bytes: 0x00 0x00 0x00 0x09. If primitive types were not of a fixed size, but varied depending on their content, they would be impossible to read without a tag that associated them to their type. A tag would require at a minimum, one extra byte for each value in the stream. Suppose, a stream consisted of a number of types and the representation of the values required a space of $n - 2$ or less where n is the size in octets, padding bytes for alignment are ignored. Using the tag byte would take less space. Single-byte data types such as `boolean` and `char` always take more space to represent using a tag byte, and no data type will always take less space. Added to the dubious space-saving characteristics of using a tag byte, is the cost of reading and interpreting the byte. Instead, the representation of the values for every type is with the number of bytes of that type, whether or not they are needed to express the value.

The alignment of all primitive data types occurs on their natural boundaries, where an alignment boundary is the size of the primitive datum in octets. In the CDR, the size of a primitive data is n, where

$$n \in \{1, 2, 4, 8\}.$$

Therefore a primitive datum of size n must start at an index in a stream that is a multiple of n. For example, if an unaligned big-endian stream contains the following types and values (expressed in decimal), in order:

boolean = True, long = 132, short = 56, char = Q, long long = 234,663

then its encoding in a stream (in hexidecimal) is as follows:

Value –	0x01	0x00	0x00	0x00	0x84	0x00	0x38	0x51	0x00	0x00
Address –	0	1	2	3	4	5	6	7	8	9

0x00	0x00	0x00	0x03	0x94	0xA7
10	11	12	13	14	15

It is possible to extract from this unaligned stream the values based on the size of the data type. For example, the first value is a `boolean`, so its size is 1 byte. Therefore only the first octet is read when looking for the `boolean`. The next value is a `long`, a 4-byte value, so reading the next four octets yields the value

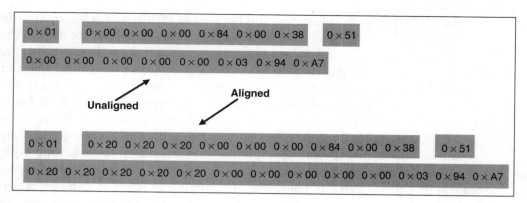

FIGURE 4.7 Comparison of Boolean and Char Padding

of the long. Immediately following it is a 2-byte short, a 1-byte character, and finally an 8-byte long long. Although all of the information is represented and is retrievable from the stream as is, it still must be aligned. Following is the same stream but aligned according to the CDR alignment rules. It uses a blank space, 0x20 in ASCII, for the padding bytes. The CDR does not specify the padding byte value. For convenience, the same padding value is used in these examples that Visibroker uses.

```
Value -     0x01 0x20 0x20 0x20 0x00 0x00 0x00 0x84 0x00 0x38 0x51

Address - 0   1    2    3    4    5    6    7    8    9    10

0x20 0x20 0x20 0x20 0x20 0x00 0x00 0x00 0x00 0x00 0x03 0x94 0xA7

11   12   13   14   15   16   17   18   19   20   21   22   23
```

Notice that the aligned stream is much longer. This seems to be counterintuitive—why add extra information to the call? More data to transfer means decreased performance. The designers of the specification believed that an easier programming model and a well-ordered stream were worth the performance penalty. Figure 4.7 shows the two streams side-by-side and compares them.

Notice that in the figure, the boolean (the first byte in both streams) and the char (the last byte of the first line, in both streams) have no padding bytes in front of them. This is because, as discussed earlier, chars and booleans, which are single-byte values, are aligned at any address. The short did not need alignment, since it naturally fell on an alignment boundary. Only the long and the long long values had to be aligned. The long required three padding bytes and the long long required five.

Table 4.3 shows the octet on which a value is aligned. The alignment of complex data types (constructed from the IDL) is based on their primitive types.

Table 4.3 Primitive Type Octet Alignment

Primitive Type	Octet Alignment
char	1
wchar	1, 2, 4 depending on code set
octet	1
short	2
unsigned short	2
long	4
unsigned long	4
long long	8
unsigned long long	8
float	4
double	8
long double	8
Boolean	1
enum	4

4.5.1 Primitive Types

The encoding of characters, booleans, octets, and integer types is straight-forward. Floating-points are more complex and are encoded as follows:

4.5.1.1 Float

A float is a 4-byte value whose most significant bit is the sign bit. Following the sign bit are 8 bits that represent the exponent. The remaining 23 bits are for the mantissa. The float is encoded as an ANSI/IEEE 754-1985 floating-point number. To calculate a float value from the `float`'s CDR encoding, look at the sign bit. If it is 0, the value is greater than zero. If it is a 1, then the value is a negative number. The exponent is calculated with the formula

$$-1^{sign} \times 2^{n-127}+1 \times m,$$

where n is the exponent, *sign* is the value of the sign bit, and m is the value of the fractional mantissa.

4.5.1.2 Double

A `double` is a double-precision floating-point number. It is an 8-byte value whose most significant bit is the sign bit. Following the sign bit are 11 bits that represent the exponent. The remaining 52 bits are for the mantissa. A `double` is encoded using the ANSI/IEEE 754-1985 "IEEE Standard for Binary Floating-Point Arithmetic." The exponent is calculated with the following formula:

$$-1^{sign} \times 2^{n-1023}+1 \times m,$$

where n is the exponent, *sign* is the value of the sign bit, and m is the value of the fractional mantissa.

4.5.1.3 Long Double

A `long double` is a double precision floating-point number. It is a 16-byte value whose most significant bit is the sign bit. Following the sign bit are 15 bits that represent the exponent. The remaining 112 bits are for the mantissa. A `long double` is encoded using the ANSI/IEEE 754-1985 "IEEE Standard for Binary Floating-Point Arithmetic." The exponent is calculated with the following formula:

$$-1^{sign} \times 2^{n-16383}+1 \times m,$$

where n is the exponent, *sign* is the value of the sign bit, and m is the value of the fractional mantissa.

4.5.2 Complex Types

The encoding of complex types is as follows.

4.5.2.1 Struct

The encoding of the components of a structure, `struct`, occur in the same order that they were declared in the IDL and is determined by the type. For example, a structure, `my_struct`, is defined as follows.

```
struct my_struct {
            long x;
            short y;
            long z;
    };
```

The encoding of `my_struct` looks like the following big-endian stream if all of the elements have the value of 1:

```
0x00 0x00 0x00 0x01 0x00 x01 0x20 0x20 0x00 0x00 0x00 0x01
```

The elements within a structure must still undergo alignment.

4.5.2.2   Union

The encoding of a union starts with the discriminant tag of the type specified in the union declaration. This is followed by the encoding (based on its type) of the selected member. Following is a union defined in the IDL. Each vehicle type in the example has characteristics associated with it that other vehicles might not. For example, only trucks have beds, so it is appropriate that if the vehicle is a truck, the bed length should be specified.

```
enum VehicleType { car, truck, minivan, SUV };
union SpecialInfo switch (VehicleType) {
      case car:boolean hatchback;
      case truck:float bed_length;
      case minivan:short seats;
      case SUV:boolean four_wheel_drive;
};
```

First, create a union and use the car discriminator. Then indicate the vehicle by setting the hatchback flag to True. The union would be encoded as follows:

```
0x00 0x00 0x00 0x00 0x01
```

The first 4 bytes are the long value of zero, which indicates a discriminant tag of car. The next byte is a boolean with the value of True, thereby indicating that the vehicle is a hatchback. Next, create a union and use the minivan discriminator, and set the number of seats to be 7 (a short). The union would be encoded in big endian as follows:

```
0x00 0x00 0x00 0x02 0x00 0x07
```

The first 4 bytes are the long value of 2, which indicates a discriminant tag of minivan. The next 2 bytes are the short, indicating the number of seats, 7.

4.5.2.3   Array

An array's encoding is the encoding of its elements in a sequence. The type of the elements in the array determines their encoding. No encoding of the length of the array occurs, since array lengths are fixed in the IDL. For multi-dimensional arrays, the ordering of the elements is done so that the index of the first dimension is the slowest to change, while the index of the last dimension is the quickest. In the following array of two strings:

```
const long OccupantBound = 2;
typedef string occupants[OccupantBound];
```

adding two people to the array of occupants, Bob and Alice yields the following stream:

```
0x00  0x00  0x00  0x04  0x42  0x6f  0x62  0x00  0x00  0x00  0x00
0x06  0x41  0x6c  0x69  0x63  0x65
```

The flattened array of strings has four components. The first 4 bytes are the size of the first string. In this case, the first string, which is the next 4 bytes, is the name "Bob" with a null byte terminator. The next 4 bytes are the size of the second string, 6 bytes. Following the size, again, is the actual string itself, "Alice" with a null byte terminator. Notice that there is no overall size or number of entries at the head of the stream. As previously noted, the size of arrays is fixed in the IDL, so the receiver knows how big the array will be.

4.5.2.4   Sequence

The encoding of a sequence starts with its length, encoded as an `unsigned long`. The elements of the sequence follow, encoded as their type. In the following is defined and created an unbounded sequence of `longs`:

```
typedef sequence <long> longSeq;
longSeq mySeq;
```

setting the length to 5, and filling it with the values 1 through 5 produces the following big-endian stream:

```
0x00 0x00 0x00 0x05 0x00 0x00 0x00 0x01 0x00 0x00 0x00 0x02
0x00 0x00 0x00 0x03 0x00 0x00 0x00 0x04 0x00 0x00 0x00 0x05
```

The first 4 bytes are the length of the sequence, an `unsigned long`. The following 20 bytes are the values 1 through 5 put into the sequence. Changing the sequence's element types to a `short` results in a big-endian stream that looks like this:

```
0x00 0x00 0x00 0x05 0x00 0x01 0x00 0x02 0x00 0x03 0x00 0x04 0x00 0x05
```

Here, the sequence is much shorter, almost half the original size. When data is being sent across the network, performance is especially important. Care should be taken when choosing the types to hold the data being passed.

4.5.2.5   Enum

An enumerated type, enum, is encoded as an `unsigned long`. Each identifier in an enum has a numeric value associated with it. The values start at zero for the first identifier and increase by 1 for each subsequent identifier. It is these values that are encoded. For example, in a set of cars defined as an enum:

```
enum cars { Probe, Mustang, Viper, Prowler, Corvette };
```

adding a Probe in a stream, changes its encoding to:

```
0x00 0x00 0x00 0x00
```

Remember, the enum's encoding is an unsigned long. Adding a Prowler to a big-endian stream also takes 4 bytes:

```
0x00 0x00 0x00 0x03
```

4.5.2.6   String

A string's encoding starts with an unsigned long to indicate the length of the string. The string's length includes the terminating null, not just the content. Then the string value is encoded. This value is a sequence of octets with a terminating null and can be either in single or multibyte form. For example, in the big-endian encoding of the string "Sports cars":

```
0x00 0x00 0x00 0x0C 0x53 0x70 0x6F 0x72 0x74 0x73 0x20 0x63
0x61 0x72 0x73 0x00
```

The first 4 bytes are the length, 0x0C, which is the value 12 in decimal. Following it are the 12 bytes containing the string's value, ending with the terminating null. The encoding of every variable-length type in CDR begins with its length so that the GIOP message buffer may be navigated quickly (for example, parsed without actually unpacking the contents) without examining every byte looking for a null terminatior. The null terminatior was added to the string to allow string handling routines to operate directly on the marshalled buffer. For example, standard string routines in C and C++, such as strcpy ( ) and strcmp ( ), rely on the null terminator.

4.5.2.7   Wide String

For characters and wide characters to be exchanged between a sender and a receiver, they must either share a common character set or the character set must at some point, be converted to the one the receiver is using. In order for character sets to be transmitted, stored, etc. they are mapped to bit or numeric representation called code sets. Some examples of code sets include ASCII, ISO 8859-1, and EBCDIC. Western languages such as English, French, German, or Spanish can be coded using an 8-bit (byte) character set. If these were the only languages in existence, an 8-bit code set would be sufficient. Other languages exist however and some of these, because of the characters in their language, require 16- and 32- bit code sets. These languages include Japanese and

Chinese. A new standard for all languages is Unicode, a 16-bit encoding. Code sets are covered in more detail in Chapter 5.

A wide string's encoding starts with an `wstring` to indicate the length of the wide string and a terminating null, followed by the individual wide characters and a terminating null. The terminating null for wide strings is a wide `wchar`. The string itself may be octets or unsigned integers. The type is determined by the transfer syntax for `wchar`. In the encoding of the string "Sports cars":

```
0x00 0x00 0x00 0x18 0x00 0x53 0x00 0x70 0x00 0x6F 0x00 0x72
0x00 0x74 0x00 0x73 0x00 0x20 0x00 0x63 0x00 0x61 0x00 0x72
0x00 0x73 0x00 0x00 ·
```

the first 4 bytes are the length, `0x18`, which is the value 24 in decimal. Following it are the 24 bytes containing the string's value, "Sports cars," ending with the terminating null.

4.5.3   Intermediate Byte Ordering

Since we know that machines have different byte orderings, the question then becomes which byte ordering is used to represent the data, little endian or big endian? Since converting the data to an intermediate form reduces performance, GIOP uses the byte ordering of the sender. If the byte ordering of the receiver is different, it will convert it to that ordering. There is a good reason for not forcing the sender to convert to the receiver's byte ordering, it reduces coupling between sender and receiver. The sender and receiver of messages do not need to know what each other's architectures are.

Most CORBA calls occur over more than one machine, a client machine and a server machine. If GIOP used an intermediate data format, which it does not, it would go something like the following. If we had a sender (a) and receiver (b) who have different byte orderings, then any data passed between the two will have to be converted to the receiving end's byte order. Suppose the sending machine converts its data from format F_a to F_i, where F_i is the intermediate format. After conversion, the client passes the data as F_i to the server. The server receives the data and converts it from F_i to F_b. This results in one more conversion than is necessary. If the sender and receiver share the same byte order, the receiver must convert F_i formatted data back to F_a to use it, resulting in two conversions when none were necessary. For this reason an intermediate byte order is not used, it adds overhead and is unnecessary.

The representation of the byte order of the parameters in a GIOP message is a flag in the message header. The recipient of a message translates the byte ordering to one they understand as necessary. No byte ordering translation may be needed if going from machine *A* to machine *B,* where *A* and *B* are the same architecture. For example, if a Windows NT (x86 architecture) machine is sending to another Windows NT machine, the sender and receiver would both be passing data in little-endian format. Therefore neither side would need to convert received data.

A flag in the message header represents the byte ordering of the message. The flag indicates that the encapsulated data is either big endian or little endian. The flag not only indicates the data byte ordering, but all elements after the byte order flag, including the message size (which is a long). Everything before the byte order flag in the message header is a byte value so there are not byte ordering issues for this part of the message.

4.6   TypeCodes in CDR

How does one describe arbitrarily complex IDL type structures at runtime? After seeing how types are encoded, is there a way to describe data canonically across ORBs and hosts? There are cases when types must be checked dynamically, as in the case when a CORBA any type is received as an operation parameter or return data. The contents of a CORBA any type must be examined if details as to the type are a necessity. To make this examination easier, CORBA uses the notion of a TypeCode since they allow data to be self-describing.

TypeCodes are objects that describe data. They are often used to determine the type of object that has been packed into a CORBA any type. This is possible because a CORBA any type contains a value and a TypeCode. The value holds the data for the any, while the TypeCode describes the type of that value. For example, if your server was expecting an any whose value contains a short or a long and cannot handle any other types, it can check the TypeCode of the any. If the TypeCode indicates the value of the any is not a short or a long, your application can ignore the any rather than trying to extract the value that it does not understand.

TypeCodes may be both simple and recursive. TypeCodes for constructed types such as structures are constructed when you compile the IDL. Since constructed types can contain other types, they may be recursive. For example, a structure containing a short and a long will have a TypeCode containing the TypeCodes for the short and long. The structure below:

```
struct my_struct {
        long x;
        short y;
        long z;
    };
```

when compiled using the VisiBroker 3.3 C++ compiler would generate in its client stub (available to both client and server):

```
CORBA::TypeCode_ptr _tc_my_struct_get() {
    static CORBA::StructMember __tc__tc_my_struct[] = {
      CORBA::StructMember(
        "x",
        CORBA::_tc_long_get(),
        CORBA::IDLType::_nil() ),
      CORBA::StructMember(
        "y",
        CORBA::_tc_short_get(),
        CORBA::IDLType::_nil() ),
      CORBA::StructMember(
        "z",
        CORBA::_tc_long_get(),
        CORBA::IDLType::_nil() )
    };

    static CORBA::TypeCode _s_tc__tc_my_struct (
      CORBA::tk_struct,
      "IDL:my_struct:1.0",
      "my_struct",
      CORBA::StructMemberSeq (
        3, 3,
        __tc__tc_my_struct),
      1);
      return &_s_tc__tc_my_struct;
}
```

The above code is used to provide TypeCode information. With this information generated, you can pass data of the type my_struct within a CORBA::Any. From the above code, you can see that when a structure TypeCode is created, it creates a sequence of TypeCodes for its members. Therefore four TypeCodes are involved in this structure: one for the structure itself; and three for the structure's members.

A TypeCode consists of a kind and a sequence of parameters. TypeCodes have a kind called TCKind which describes the type of data, for example if the data is a long the TCKind for it would be tk_long. The TCKind is an enumeration (4 octets in size). Following the kind are zero or more parameter values. The parameters vary depending on the TCKind.

There are three types of parameter lists in the encoding of a TypeCode:

- An empty parameter list, where only the enumerated value of TCKind is encoded.
- A simple parameter list where the enumerated value of TCKind is encoded first, followed by the value(s) of the parameters.
- A complex parameter list where the enumerated value of TCKind is encoded first, followed by the octet sequence that contains the encapsulated marshalled parameters.

Table 4.4 lists the TCKind, its corresponding enumeration value, the parameter type list, and the parameters if any.

4.6.1 Object Reference TypeCode

The TypeCode of an object reference, tk_objref, has, like all complex types, the repositoryID as the first parameter. This identifier is the Interface Repository RepositoryID. The second parameter is the interface name. For this TypeCode, as well as that for exceptions, tk_except, the repositoryID is required. It is optional for the TypeCodes of structures (tk_struct), unions (tk_union), enumerations (tk_enum), and aliases (tk_alias). If it is not used, an empty string appears in its place in the stream.

The name parameter in tk_objref is neither specified nor significant in GIOP. No assumptions about type equivalence should be made, based on the name. Structural information, such as the repositoryID or the TypeCode, that indicates an array's element type is significant and should be used. The lack of specification for name parameters in TypeCodes also applies to structures (tk_struct), unions (tk_union), enumerations (tk_enum), aliases (tk_alias), and exceptions (tk_except). It also holds for the member names in the TypeCodes for structures, unions, enumerations, and exceptions. If a name or member name is unspecified, then the encoding is done as an empty string.

4.6.2 Structure TypeCode

The TypeCode of a structure, tk_struct, optionally has the repositoryID as the first parameter. The next parameter is the name of the structure as defined in the IDL. Next, for each element in the structure, there are two parameters, one is the element's name and the second its TypeCode.

4.6.3 Union TypeCode

The TypeCode of a union, tk_union, optionally has the repositoryID as the first parameter. Then follows the parameters for the union name and the TypeCode of the discriminator. Next comes a long that indicates which type in the sequence describes the union's default case. The long is a negative number if a union has no default case. Finally, the parameters for each element in the union

Table 4.4 TypeCode TCKinds

TCKind	Enum Value	Type	Parameters
tk_null	0	Empty	None
tk_void	1	Empty	None
tk_short	2	Empty	None
tk_long	3	Empty	None
tk_longlong	23	Empty	None
tk_ushort	4	Empty	None
tk_ulong	5	Empty	None
tk_ulonglong	24	Empty	None
tk_fixed	28	Simple	ushort(digits), short(scale)
tk_float	6	Empty	None
tk_double	7	Empty	None
tk_longdouble	25	Empty	None
tk_Boolean	8	Empty	None
tk_char	9	Empty	None
tk_wchar	26	Empty	None
tk_octet	10	Empty	None
tk_any	11	Empty	None
tk_TypeCode	12	Empty	None
tk_Principal	13	Empty	None
tk_objref	14	Complex	string (repositoryID), string (name)
tk_struct	15	Complex	string (repositoryID), string (name), ulong (count) {string (member name), TypeCode (member type)}
tk_union	16	Complex	string (repositoryID), string(name), TypeCode (discriminant type), long (default used), ulong (count) discriminant type (label value), string (member name), TypeCode (member type)}
tk_enum	17	Complex	string (repositoryID), string (name), ulong (count) {string (member name)}

Table 4.4   Continued

TCKind	Enum Value	Type	Parameters
tk_string	18	Simple	ulong (max length)
tk_wstring	27	Simple	ulong (max length or zero if unbounded)
tk_sequence	19	Complex	TypeCode (element type), ulong (max length)
tk_array	20	Complex	TypeCode (element type), ulong (length)
tk_alias	21	Complex	string (repositoryID), string (name), TypeCode
tk_except	22	Complex	string (repositoryID), string (name), ulong (count) {string (member name), TypeCode (member type)}
None	0xffffffff	Simple	long (indirection)

are encoded. Each element has three parameters to describe it: the label value, the member name (string), and the member type described by its TypeCode.

4.6.4   Enumeration TypeCode

The TypeCode of an enumeration, tk_enum, optionally has the repositoryID as the first parameter. The next parameter is the name of the enumeration, obtained from its IDL definition. Following that is a count of the number of enumeration constants and then each enum constant.

4.6.5   Sequence TypeCode

The TypeCode of a sequence, tk_sequence, has a TypeCode for the element type and a long that indicates the length of the sequence as its parameter.

4.6.6   Array TypeCode

The TypeCode of an array, tk_array, starts with a TypeCode that indicates the type of the array elements. Next are *n* parameters of type long, where *n* is the number of dimensions of the array.

4.6.7   Alias TypeCode

The TypeCode of an alias, tk_alias, optionally has the repositoryID as the first parameter.

4.6.8   Exception TypeCode

The TypeCode of an exception, `tk_except`, has the repositoryID as the first parameter. The next parameter is the name of the exception as defined in the IDL. Following that, for each member in the exception, are two parameters, one is the member's name and the second its `TypeCode`.

4.6.9   Indirection

If an IDL data type indirectly contains an instance of itself, then the TypeCode representation of that data type must also contain an indirection. This kind of indirection allows the reduction in size of the encoding (unions with many cases sharing the same value). To prevent the same information from being encoded over and over again, CDR provides a constrained indirection to the original TypeCode encoding. The indirection is a numeric octet offset within the scope of the top level TypeCode that points to the TypeCode's TCKind value.

Indirected TypeCodes do not exist on their own but within some other TypeCode. The indirection is always nested within a TypeCode that is at the highest level in the stream. The encoding of the first reference to a TypeCode uses the normal encoding rules. The encoding of any subsequent references within the scope uses indirection, so that duplicate TypeCodes are not repeated. Indirections may span encapsulation boundries so that it is possible for them to have different byte orderings. The byte orderings are determined by the byte order flag at the beginning of the encapsulation.

If the TypeCode is recursive, the encoding of the second instance of a Type-Code begins before the encoding of the first instance is finished. Since it is always the first reference to an indirected TypeCode that is encoded the offset values will always be negative, so that it points pack to the original TypeCode encoding. The indirection encoding is a TypeCode where the value of TCKind is $2^{32} - 1$ (0xFFFFFFFF). The only parameter of the indirection TypeCode is the offset in octets, which is a `long`. No offsets must be −4 since it would point back to its own the indirection. The offset follows directly after the indirection encoding and is in two's complement form.

Using the indirection example in the CORBA specification, we have the structure `foo`, which contains a member `bar`. The member `bar` is an unbounded sequence of `foo` structures. From this example, we can see a structure containing itself that will cause indirection in its TypeCode.

```
struct foo {
  string tag ;
  sequence <foo> bar ;
}
```

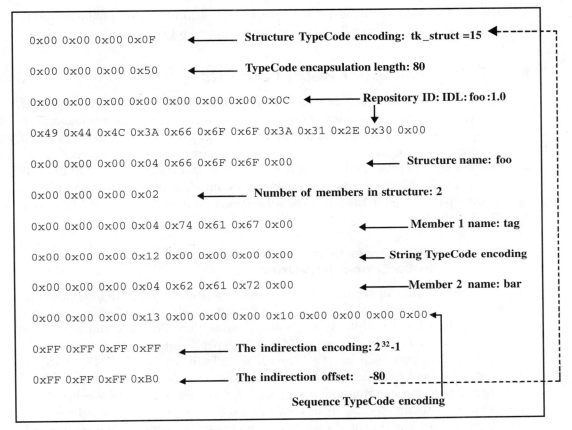

FIGURE 4.8 Structure Foo TypeCode Encoding

If we look at the encoding of the TypeCode for the structure foo, in Figure 4.8, it will become easier to understand indirection.

This encapsulation was passed in a CORBA operation, to describe a CORBA::Any that contains a foo structure. Since the foo structure contains as a member, a sequence of foo structures, the TypeCodes will be recursive. In order for the TypeCode encapsulation to not be infinitely long with circular references, indirection is used. The offset is −80 (in two's complement) which points back to the top of the foo structure TypeCode. The arrow shows how the indirection points back to the foo TypeCode encoding. From this example, it should be fairly easy to see the benefits of indirection.

As mentioned previously, there are two kinds of streams, messages and encapsulations. Encapsulation streams have already been discussed. Next, we cover messaging streams. When messaging is discussed, it is sufficient to describe a client as the agent that opens a connection and originates requests and a server as an agent that accepts connections and receives requests.

4.7 GIOP's Transport Requirements

The design of GIOP does not rely on a specific transport protocol. Instead, it allows the use of a wide range of transport protocols. This section concentrates, however, on TCP/IP because of its popularity and its specification as the baseline transport protocol for GIOP. Probably the best reason to look at it, however, is that this is a book on IIOP, and it is GIOP over TCP/IP that makes IIOP. GIOP fits naturally into TCP/IP because it makes several assumptions about its transport layer. These are discussed in the following subsections, along with a description of how TCP/IP meets them.

4.7.1 GIOP Depends on Its Transport to Be Connection-Oriented

As is shown later in section 4.9, GIOP uses connection IDs to map requests to replies in communications between clients and servers. The definition and lifetime of these IDs is within the scope of the connection. Once the connection terminates, the IDs are no longer valid. GIOP depends on a reliable, connection-oriented transport such as TCP. Thus IIOP is built on TCP. TCP/IP transmits information as a sequence of datagrams. The datagram does not require acknowledgement. It carries information sufficient for routing it from the sender to the receiver, without relying on any earlier exchanges between the sender and receiver. It appears to GIOP that there is a connection between the sender and receiver, but TCP/IP transmits each datagram individually through the network.

When a GIOP message is too large for TCP to send in one datagram, TCP breaks it into multiple datagrams. It treats each datagram as completely separate from any other sent in a related message. For example, a GIOP message that contains a 3,500-byte image encoded as an octet sequence could be broken up into seven 500-octet datagrams (ignoring the GIOP header). IP would then send each of these datagrams to the other end. When the datagrams are in transit, the network doesn't know that there is any connection between them, so datagram five could arrive before datagram four. It is the TCP layer's responsibility to reorder the packets at the receiver's end and combine them so that GIOP receives them as a complete message.

4.7.2 The Transport Protocol Is Reliable

GIOP does not have the facilities to check for packet ordering, bad packets, lost packets, or duplicate packets. These tasks are the responsibility of the transport layer. The TCP layer supports this requirement. It is responsible for guaranteeing that a message gets from the client to the server and vice versa.

4.7.3   The Transport Layer Can Be Viewed as a Stream of Bytes

There can be no arbitrary message size limitations enforced. The transport protocol may not require GIOP to fragment or byte-align the data. One of the TCP layer's responsibilities is to break up large messages into transmittable datagrams. This relieves GIOP from having to do this. This responsibility can be problematic, however. It requires GIOP to send an entire message to the transport layer at once, and it is the transport layer that must break up the message into datagrams. This usually means that the entire message must be loaded into memory and sent at once. Imagine that a message contains a 1GB binary value (say an MPEG movie clip) encoded as a sequence of octets. It would be extremely inefficient, if it is even possible, to load the entire message into memory. Even if one could do this, two issues remain to consider.

- If the transmission medium is low bandwidth, it will take the receiver a significant period to receive it. This causes the server to consume a large amount of resources to hold the message in buffer for hours.
- The receiving application might not have the same capacity that the client application has (for example it has less memory or disk space) and so will be unable to deal with the message as a single, large unit.

As is shown later in Section 4.12.8, the newest version of GIOP, 1.1, allows messages to be fragmented. The GIOP layer, rather than the TCP layer, handles these fragmented messages, thereby allowing the sender to fragment the message into smaller messages that both it and the receiver can handle. Note, the TCP layer will still break up the fragments into packets if needed.

4.7.4   The Transport Layer Must Notify of a Connection Loss

When a disorderly connection loss occurs, for example if a client crashes or the network goes down, the transport layer must give the server some reasonable notification of this event. A server can be multithreaded so that it handles many client connections at once. Connections are limited in number due to resource limitations, so each connection can be quite valuable. Sometimes, a client that has obtained a connection with a server develops a problem and can no longer communicate with the server. The server should immediately drop the connection to free it up for another client. Absent notification of a connection loss, the server would have to enforce a client polling or timeout mechanism, either of which is less efficient and harder to program.

4.7.5   Connection Initiation Model

The transport layer's model for initiating connections has a mapping onto the general connection model of TCP/IP. The server is not the connection initiator. Instead it waits, prepared to accept a request from a client to connect. In TCP/IP terms, it *listens for connections.* A client must know the address of the server before it can initiate a connection. An address in TCP/IP terms is the host IP address and the port on which the server is listening. Once it has the address, the client can attempt to connect by sending a connection request to the address. The listening server may accept the request or reject it, for example, for security reasons. If the server accepts the request, it forms a new, unique connection with the client. Open connections may be closed by either the client or the server. A candidate transport, any transport on which GIOP might be implemented, might not directly support this specific connection model. It is only necessary that the transport's model supports a mapping onto this view. Specifically, the server publishes a known network address in an IOR, which the client uses when initiating a connection.

4.8   OSI and GIOP

To understand the relationship that GIOP, IIOP, and TCP/IP share, you can view them in the context of protocol layers. These layers' relationships can be mapped in a manner similar to the OSI reference model.

4.8.1   The OSI Model

The OSI reference model, shown in Figure 4.9, depicts the different layers of protocols generally needed for building and using computer networks. The

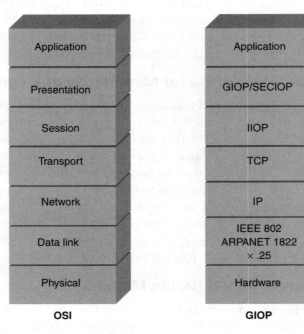

FIGURE 4.9   OSI and GIOP Layered Models

protocol stack starts with hardware at the lowest level and works its way up, adding layers of abstraction until it reaches the application. The layers of abstractions allow the subdivision of network responsibilities into separate components. Communication occurs only between like layers. For example, suppose two applications are running on different machines and are communicating via IIOP—this communication is handled in the application layer. Then the application layers of the machines will communicate with each other, as will the network layers. Layers are an engineering tool that break up a complex problem like networking into manageable pieces. The general responsibilities of the layers are as follows.

- *Physical layer.* This layer provides services for raw bit streams. It handles the physical interfaces between devices and manages how the passing of bits occurs between interfaces. It establishes the physical connection at the level of network cards and cables.

- *Data link layer.* This layer adds a level of reliability to the physical layer via error detection and control. When two systems are directly connected, the data link layer provides enough control and error correction that the higher layers do not need to concern themselves with it. In the case of a connectionless system such as the Internet, where many data links exist together, error control must happen at a higher level. Link encryption also occurs at this layer.

- *Network layer.* This layer is responsible for handling data transmission and switching across a network. When end systems communicate, the data might pass between one or more intermediate nodes. This layer handles the routing of the data through the nodes by adding routing information to the message. The standard interface to this layer is the destination address (for example, the receiving end system) of the data.

- *Transport layer.* Data exchanged between end systems might arrive corrupted, out of sequence, not at all, or multiple times. It is this layer's responsibility to correct such problems by reordering the data, dropping multiple arrivals, or requesting retransmission. The amount of error handling in this layer depends on the services provided by the network layer. If the network layer is datagram-based, such as IP, the transport layer is responsible for a considerable amount of error handling. If the network layer is a virtual circuit, the amount of error handling needed is minimal.

- *Session layer.* This layer is responsible for the reliable delivery of data from the lower layers. The lower layers do not establish protocols of application interaction, however; that is the session layer's responsibility. This layer also dictates the dialogue discipline, either full- or half-duplex, between applications. It also provides the grouping of data and some data recovery. This layer may also do some security work (for example, authentication of nodes).

- *Presentation layer.* This layer prepares information for the application layer. When two applications communicate, they must share a common syntax. In a heterogeneous network, any two applications could have a large number of architectural differences. For example, byte ordering might differ from one machine to another or the primitive data types might have different sizes. Applications might be written in different languages, for example one application is written C++ and another in Smalltalk, so the data structures they are passing to each other have different formats. All of these things require the translation of messages into syntax that the receiver understands. Also, the data that is received might be compressed or encrypted, even in a homogeneous network. It is this layer's responsibility to transform that data and present it to the application layer in a format that the layer can understand.

- *Application layer.* This layer provides the programmatic access to the lower layers. It defines how the user accesses the network.

4.8.2   The GIOP Model

The mapping of the TCP/IP protocol suite and GIOP/IIOP to the OSI stack is not exact. Its primary purpose is to explain the necessity and role of each component in allowing two applications to communication via CORBA. The two lowest layers are not covered here, as are not pertinent to the discussion.

When a group of networked computers is accessible to/from the Internet, it exists within a subnetwork (for example, a local area network, or LAN). Subnetworks connect to other subnetworks via routers. It is the composite of these subnetworks, connected through routers, that make up the Internet. This is depicted in Figure 4.10. When a computer communicates with another computer within its own subnetwork, it uses a network access protocol, for example token ring. The computer also communicates to machines outside of the subnetwork by using the same protocol and communicating with a router.

The basis of the TCP/IP network model is a large number of independent networks connected together by gateways. This is the "catenet model." When a client invokes an operation on a CORBA object, the message's datagrams might pass through a dozen different networks before reaching the server.

The routing needed to accomplish this is invisible to GIOP. All GIOP needs, for the client to access the server (object), is a valid connection. The TCP layer, however, needs to know more than the Internet address, since there might be multiple connections between the client and server. To handle multiple connections, the TCP layer adds a header in front of each datagram that contains source and destination *port numbers* and *sequence numbers.*

The TCP layer uses port numbers to keep track of the different connections. Suppose three different people are transferring files. Your TCP layer might allo-

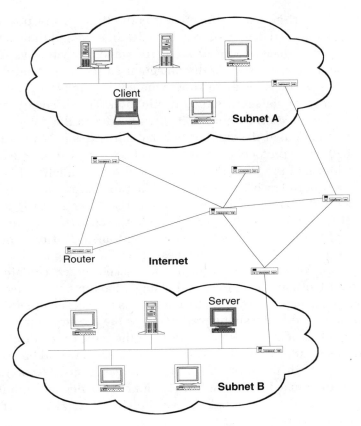

FIGURE 4.10   Routing between Subnetworks

cate port numbers 1000, 1001, and 1002 to these transfers. When one system, for example a client sending a request, is sending a datagram, the number assumed by TCP becomes the "source" port number, since the client is the source of the datagram. Of course, the TCP layer at the other end, acting on behalf of the server receiving the request, has assigned a port number of its own for the conversation. The client's TCP layer must know the port number used by the server end. It puts the server's port number in the "destination" port field. When the server replies to the client's request, thereby sending a datagram back to the client, the TCP layer reverses the source and destination port numbers. This is done because the server is now the source and the client is the destination.

Each transmitted datagram has a sequence number. This number allows the other end to order the datagrams in the correct order. By checking the sequence numbers, the receiver can also guarantee that it has not missed any datagrams.

The TCP layer sends each of these datagrams to the IP layer, passing each the Internet address of the receiver's computer. This is all the IP layer needs in order to deliver the datagram, since it is the IP layer's responsibility for finding a route for the datagram to reach its destination and then actually getting it there. When a datagram reaches an intermediate gateway, such as another router, the gateway forwards the datagram closer to its final destination (one can hope). For the gateway to know where it is going to forward the datagram, it must know the datagram's final destination. The IP layer provides gateways with this information by adding its own header to the datagram. That header includes source and destination Internet addresses (32-bit addresses, such as 128.6.4.194), the protocol number, and a checksum. The source Internet address is the address of the sender's machine, and the destination Internet address is the address of the receiver's machine. The protocol number tells the IP layer at the other end to send the datagram to the TCP layer, since TCP is not the only protocol to use IP. The IP layer then uses the checksum to verify that no corruption of the IP header took place during transit. If it did not check for corrupted headers, it could send the message to the wrong place.

When a router receives a datagram packet, which contains a destination address, it looks at the address and, using a lookup table, determines where to forward the datagram packet. It then forwards the packet either to another router or to a subnetwork. If a subnetwork receives the forwarded packet, the packet is sent to the host machine whose address is the same as the destination process.

At this point, a brief discussion of IP addresses would be useful. You likely are familiar with the form of Internet address `http://www.xxx.xxx`. This maps to an actual Internet address, a four octet decimal number, with each octet separated by a decimal, for example 123.123.123.123. There are three classes of Internet addresses:

- A, which is reserved for use by large networks. The values of the first octet of these addresses range from 1.0.0.0 through 126.0.0.0.
- B, which are reserved for large organizations. The first two octets of these addresses range from 128.1.0.0 through 191.254.0.0. The last two octets are used for host addresses. This allows organizations to have up to 64,156 hosts, or computers, in a network.
- C, which are used for small organizations and users. The first three octets of these addresses range from 192.1.1.0 through 223.254.254.0. This gives class C networks a maximum of 254 hosts.

In the IP address standard, octets with the value of all ones or 255 are used for broadcasting. Broadcasting is used when a sender either wants to talk to every host on the network, or it does not know who it wants to talk to, or it does not know on which specific host the recipient is located. For the latter reason, at least one ORB vendor uses broadcasting for ORB location. For example, to broadcast a message to a Class C network, you would use the Internet address, replacing the host number, the last octet, with the value 255. To send a message to all of the machines on the network 207.123.142.x, a class C network, you would use 207.123.142.255.

A datagram packet that the router sends to a machine's IP layer might be segmented, so the IP layer will buffer the segments until all have arrived. Once they have arrived, the layer reconstructs the datagram and passes it to the TCP layer.

For successful delivery of a datagram to a machine, the machine must have a unique IP address. Simply having the machine's address, however, is insufficient for client-server communications, since data is delivered not just to a machine, but also to a process. Each process therefore must have a unique identifier relative to the host. This unique ID, which is the process's address, is a *port*. It is the TCP layer's responsibility, being a host-to-host protocol, to deliver the data to the correct process. Ports and IP addresses are combined to form a unique address, called a **socket.** Sockets provide a programmatic interface to TCP/IP.

4.9   What Is a Connection

The transmission of data might occur from one process to another without prior coordination and planning. This kind of data transfer is called *connectionless.* Connectionless data transfer is intended for exchanging single packets of information. Generally, a connectionless service is the lowest level of service; at that level, one gives up some reliability in exchange for performance. In a connectionless system, a datagram packet is expendable. If a router detects an error in a packet (say, the checksum is not correct), it can discard the packet without any concern for a successful transmission. The packet can be sent again and again until it is received correctly. Connectionless service allows datagrams to send to multiple hosts, either by broadcasting to all hosts in a network or by multicasting to a group of related hosts.

When a network task requires lengthy exchanges of data, such as in a typical client-server interaction in CORBA, establishing a connection is preferred, both for performance and reliability. Three basic phases occur in a connection:

1. The connection is established.
2. The data is transferred.
3. The connection is terminated.

The transport layer provides a channel for the exchange of data between components in a system. Connection-oriented transports provide two, actively interacting components with a bidirectional stream. The stream coordinates the sending and receiving of data. In addition, connection-oriented protocols define the roles of acceptor and connector. In connection-oriented transports, streams consist of multiple sequenced packets.

In order for a CORBA client to use resources on a remote object, a connection to that object must be established. To open a connection to an object, a client must first obtain the object's object reference. A naming or trading service provides this capability by storing object references, along with information describing them. Object references may also be converted to a string by using the `object_to_string` operation on the ORB. The string form of the object reference can then be stored for use later. To use an object reference that is in string form, it is converted using the `string_to_object` operation also found on the ORB. If an object reference is obtained by these various means, it is typically not until the first invocation that the client issues the connection request. Some ORB vendors will reuse connections. This means that if the object a client wishes to invoke on is in a server that the client already has a connection to, that connection will be used when the client invokes on that new object.

Some ORB vendors provide additional mechanisms to obtain object references. Borland's VisiBroker and Iona's Orbix provide this with their proprietary `bind` commands. The `bind` operation typically can setup a connection to a generic object with the specified interface or to a named instance of the specified interface. The `bind` operation may either establish the connection when it is called, or wait until the first invocation on the bound object, depending on how the vendor wishes to implement it.

CORBA is a set of software libraries, executables, and interaction rules. The set of libraries, along with a daemon process running in the domain, constitutes the ORB, although specific implementations might vary. The ORB daemon is responsible for finding the object implementation pointed to by an object reference and establishing a connection between the holder of the object reference—the client process—and the holder of the object implementation—the server process. The client and the server may reside in the same process.

GIOP defines the agents in a connection as client and server, where the client initiates the connection and sends requests over it. The server uses the connection to reply to the client. Under this definition, GIOP connections are asymmetrical in that clients send only `Request`, `LocateRequest`, `CancelRequest`, `Fragment`, and `MessageError` messages over the connection. Servers send only `Reply`, `LocateReply`, `CloseConnection`, `Fragment`, and `MessageError` messages over the connection. Recall from section 1.2.2 that these are GIOP messages and are the only ones allowed to be sent over GIOP connections. Obviously, a server may act as a client of some other server, in which case it may issue client-only messages. The messages sent by the server, however, are over a new client connection, not its existing server connection. In GIOP 1.1 and GIOP 1.0 connections are asymmetrical to simplify connection closure. It provides a client with some certainty as to which requests were processed and which were not without requiring a two-way handshake on closure.

CORBA objects support a number of different connection durations, both short-lived and long-lived. During a short-lived connection, a client may open a connection for a single request and close it immediately after completion. During longer-lived connections a large number of request and replies may flow between client and server, over the lifetime of the connection. Unlike a short-lived single request connection, in a longer-lived connection a situation may arise where the client has multiple outstanding requests to the server. When the server replies to these requests there must be a way to determine which replies go with which requests. **RequestIDs** provide the means to do this. A requestID must unambiguously associate a reply with a request within the scope and lifetime of a connection. It may be reused if there is no possibility that the previous request using the ID might still have a pending reply. Note that the cancellation of a request does not guarantee that no reply will be sent. It is the client's responsibility to generate and assign requestIDs, and they must be unique among both Request and LocateRequest messages.

Such IDs allows GIOP support in two more critical areas: request multiplexing and overlapping requests. GIOP allows multiple clients to share a connection. A client may be multithreaded, whereby each thread is performing a call to the same server at the same time (either to the same or different objects). Rather than have each call be on a separate connection, the threads may share the connection. The use of a unique requestID allows the target of the request and the corresponding reply to be identified. Since GIOP does not dictate the relative ordering of requests or replies, requests may be asynchronous and arrive at any time. RequestIDs allow related messages to be identified.

4.10 Closing a Connection

A connection can be closed via an *orderly shutdown* or an *abortive disconnect.* An orderly shutdown is done by the server when it reliably sends a CloseConnection message. The client, too, may perform an orderly shutdown on a connection. In this case, there might be pending requests to one or more servers. When the client closes the connections, the server simply cancels any outstanding requests from the client. A server may shutdown a connection once it issues a CloseConnection message reliably. Any pending requests by clients will not be processed. TCP provides reliable delivery of the last message sent during a connection closing, but not all transport protocols provide this level of reliability however. Therefore additional handshaking must be provided to guarantee that both ends of the connection understand the arrangement of any outstanding GIOP requests so a connection is not closed until communication is complete.

If a client detects a connection closure, but has not received a CloseConnection message, the client should assume an abortive disconnect has occurred, and treat the condition as an error. Since the connection no longer exists, the pending requests should be notified by the client with a COMM_FAILURE exception, with its completion status value set to COMPLETED_MAYBE.

4.11 Details on GIOP Messages

Once a connection is established, the client and the server may begin sending GIOP messages across it. Recall from Section 1.2.2, that their are eight types of GIOP messages. These are listed in Table 4.5, along with who may issue them, their values, and in which versions of GIOP they are available. These messages are, in theory, sufficient to accomplish the most complex of distributed tasks. They fall into two categories:

- Administrative
- Object invocation

Administrative messages are

- LocateRequest and LocateReply, used to find objects so that they can use them
- CancelRequest and CloseConnection, used to handle requests that are taking too long to execute or that are no longer desired
- MessageError, sued for error handling

Object invocation messages are Request, Reply, and Fragment, which are used to request an operation on an object and to allow the object to reply.

Each of these messages is covered in detail in upcoming sections.

Table 4.5   GIOP Messages

Message Type	Issuer	Enum Value	GIOP Versions
Request	Client	0	1.0, 1.1
Reply	Server	1	1.0, 1.1
CancelRequest	Client	2	1.0, 1.1
LocateRequest	Client	3	1.0, 1.1
LocateReply	Server	4	1.0, 1.1
CloseConnection	Server	5	1.0, 1.1
MessageError	Both	6	1.0, 1.1
Fragment	Both	7	1.1

4.11.1   GIOP Message Header

When a message is sent from a client to a server or vice versa, information must be transmitted so that the receiver understands what the message is, for which object it is intended, and what to do with it. To this end, GIOP defines a message header that contains such crucial information. This includes the protocol of the message, the version of GIOP used and the message's type, byte ordering, and size.

Figure 4.11 shows the layout of the message header under the two versions of GIOP. The layout aligns all of the types naturally, so no padding bytes are needed. The header breaks down as follows.

- The first 4 bytes are the magic number, which indicates the protocol. For GIOP messages, this contains the value GIOP.
- The next 2 bytes are two octets that contain the major and minor version numbers, in that order.
- The next byte indicates the byte order in version 1.0. In version 1.1, it was changed to a flags field so as to include other flags. Byte order is only one flag setting in version 1.1.
- The next byte is the message type—Request, Reply, and so on.
- The last 4 bytes are an `unsigned long` containing the size of the message.

The GIOP message header is sent on every GIOP message that flows to and from clients and servers. After each message header is another header that is specific to the message type. This *specific* message header is indicated to the recipient by the primary GIOP message header.

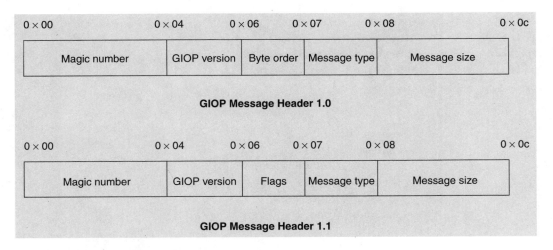

FIGURE 4.11   GIOP Message Headers

Following is the exact definition of the GIOP message header. All GIOP messages begin with the following IDL-defined header:

```
module GIOP { // IDL extended for version 1.1
struct Version {
        octet major;
        octet minor;
};

#ifndef GIOP_1_1
// GIOP 1.0
enum MsgType_1_0 {
// Renamed from MsgType
        Request, Reply, CancelRequest, LocateRequest,
LocateReply,
        CloseConnection, MessageError
};
    #else
    // GIOP 1.1
    enum MsgType_1_1 {
        Request, Reply, CancelRequest, LocateRequest,
LocateReply,
        CloseConnection, MessageError, Fragment // GIOP 1.1
addition
    };
    #endif

    // GIOP 1.0
    struct MessageHeader_1_0 { // Renamed from MessageHeader
        char magic [4];
        Version GIOP_version;
        boolean byte_order;
        octet message_type;
        unsigned long message_size;
    };

    // GIOP 1.1
    struct MessageHeader_1_1 {
        char magic [4];
        Version GIOP_version;
        octet flags; // GIOP 1.1 change
        octet message_type;
        unsigned long message_size;
    };
};
```

The sender of a message places a message header at the beginning of every GIOP message it sends. The first 8 bytes of the header are independent of byte ordering so that the receiver can determine the byte ordering without having readability problems. If the byte ordering flag itself could have different orderings, developing ORBs or using interceptors could cause quite a headache. The next sections discuss the parts of the message header in more detail.

4.11.1.1   Magic Value

The ORB uses the magic value to identify GIOP messages. This value always contains the value "GIOP" in all uppercase letters and encoded in ISO Latin-1 (8859.1). As is shown later in section 8.4.3, SECIOP also has a 4-byte magic value.

4.11.1.2   GIOP Version

There currently are two versions of the GIOP protocol, 1.0 and 1.1. The major GIOP version number of the current CORBA core specification is 1 and the minor versions are 0 and 1. These values are encoded as octets in the `GIOP :: Version` structure. The `GIOP_version` member of the request message header contains the version number of the GIOP protocol that the message uses. The version number applies to GIOP's CDR and message formats (transport-independent elements). The GIOP version number and IIOP version number have the same structure, but they are not equivalent.

4.11.1.3   Byte Order

`Byte_order` is a member of the message header only in GIOP 1.0. It indicates the byte ordering used in subsequent elements of the message (including `message_size`). A value of FALSE (0) indicates big-endian byte ordering and TRUE (1) indicates little-endian byte ordering.

4.11.1.4   Flags

The flags member of the header is available only in GIOP 1.1. The CORBA specification changed the member `byte_order` to `flags` in order to support fragmentation. The least two significant bits of the flag are currently used. The first such bit indicates the byte ordering used in subsequent elements of the message (including `message_size`). A value of FALSE (0) indicates big-endian byte ordering and TRUE (1) indicates little-endian byte ordering. The second least significant bit indicates whether more fragments follow the current message. A value of FALSE (0) indicates this message is the last fragment, and TRUE (1) indicates that more fragments follow. The other 6 bits (for example, the six most significant bits) of the `flags` member are reserved. The six reserved bits must have value of zero for GIOP version 1.1.

4.11.1.5   Message Type

The `message_type` member, as its name implies, indicates the type of the message (see Table 4.5). The actual value of the message type member is the corresponding enumeration value of type `MsgType_1_0` if GIOP 1.0 is used or `MsgType_1_1` if GIOP 1.1 is used. The member `message_type` is an enumeration, so its representation should be a `long`. The OMG, however, chose to encode it differently. One byte instead of 4 can be used to represent all message types, so the OMG chose to represent it in this way in order to improve call efficiency.

4.11.1.6　Message Size

The `message_size` member holds the number of octets in the message following the message header. The message size is the size of the message body, minus the 12-byte message header and including any alignment gaps. As mentioned previously, the message size is encoded using the byte order specified in the `byte order` bit. Currently, no Request, LocateRequest, Reply, or LocateReply messages should have a message size of zero, as it is reserved by the OMG for future use.

4.11.2　Object Service Context

Currently, object services such as the transaction and security services require service-specific context information to be passed implicitly with requests and replies. This information is piggybacked on a Request or Reply message outside the scope of a normal operation. Three requirements apply to the use of the object service context.

1. When an object service specification creates a new context, it must be specified as an OMG IDL data type.

2. The ORB needs to provide a set of APIs for use in the calling process. These APIs allow the setting and retrieving of context information. Service implementors then make handlers that call those APIs and set the service-context information as needed.

3. The ORB is responsible for determining when to send service-specific context information. It also decides what to do with service-specific context information that it receives from incoming messages.

The following is the IDL for the object server context:

```
module IOP { // IDL
    . . .
    typedef unsigned long ServiceId;

    struct ServiceContext {
            ServiceId context_id;
            sequence <octet> context_data;
    };

    typedef sequence <ServiceContext> ServiceContextList;
```

```
const ServiceId TransactionService = 0;
const ServiceId CodeSets = 1;
    . . .
};
```

The service context IDL specifies no service-specific information. Any information regarding a particular service will be found in its specification. The purpose of the service context IDL is in describing the structure of the information that will be passed. The service context is a very useful part of the message headers. It is a convenient way for CORBA developers to pass information back and forth between clients and servers without passing it at the IDL layer.

The service context is very useful for passing information for transactions, security and other services. For example, a developer implementing security can use the service context to pass information such as a call sequence number (to stop replay attacks by keeping track of invocations), the security session ID, user credentials, etc. The service context allows developers to pass information over CORBA invocations outside of the IDL interface. This frees architects to define IDL interfaces without worrying about how to pass service information.

The Request and Reply message headers contain a list of service contexts. This allows multiple services to add information to the message, each one placing a new `ServiceContext` structure into the list. There is no requirement for the ordering of the `ServiceContext` structure within the list. A service can place its service data anywhere into the list. It identifies the service data looking for its ID contained in the `context_id` field of the `ServiceContext` structure.

The environment specific inter-orb protocol (ESIOP) for DCE is also a consumer of this IDL. The OMG aimed to make the service context as generic as possible. It is the OMG's responsibility to allocate a unique service context ID (the member `context_id` of the type `ServiceID`), to each Object Service that requires the passing of an implicit service-specific context through GIOP. There are currently two `ServiceID`'s defined by the OMG (as of the publication of the CORBA V2.2 specification):

- `CosTSInteroperation::PropogationContext` defined by the transaction service.
- `CONV_FRAME::CodeSetContext` defined for code sets.

A service's IDL definition specifies its encoding of the context data for that service. This encoding is held in the `context_data` member. The `context_id` contains the serviceID value that identifies the service and data format. GIOP defines the context data as an octet sequence so as to allow the handling of unknown context data. This also allows the ORB to handle the data without unmarshalling it. It is the ORB's responsibility to insert and remove service-context data. During the marshalling phase of a Request or Reply message, the ORB collects all service-context data associated with it into a `ServiceContextList`, which it includes at the beginning of generated messages. Note that GIOP does not specify an ordering for this data within a `ServiceContextList`. Placing this data at the beginning of the message supports security policies that might apply to the majority of the data in a request, including the message headers. This is important, for example, when everything following the service context is encrypted and the service context contains an unencrypted flag informing the receiver of that fact. If there was no way to communicate to this, the receiver would be unable to decrypt and unmarshall the message.

4.12 GIOP Messages in Detail

The next sections examine each of the eight GIOP message types, focusing on the two most often used messages, Request and Reply.

4.12.1 Request Message

When a client invokes on a CORBA operation, that invocation is encoded as a Request message. For example, suppose we use the following IDL:

```
interface foo {
    long run (in short bar);
}
```

If a client invokes the `run` operation on an object reference to a `foo` instance, a Request message will be created and sent from the client to the `foo` instance. When the `foo` instance is done with the `run` operation it will reply to the client with a Reply message (the Reply message will be covered later). Other operations on objects that are invoked using the Request message in this manner include the attribute accessor operations, the CORBA::Object::get_interface and CORBA::Object::get_implementation operations. The attribute accessor operations are the get and set operations generated by the IDL complier for interface attributes (only get operations are created for read only attributes). These operations follow the same rules for messaging as IDL defined operations.

There are three components in a Request message, encoded in the following order: GIOP message header; Request header; and Request body.

Figure 4.12 shows the order of the components.

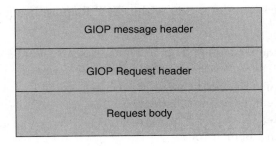

FIGURE 4.12   Order of a Request Message Stream

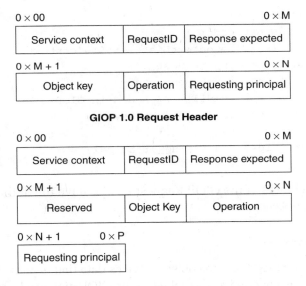

FIGURE 4.13   GIOP Request Headers

4.12.1.1   Request Header Structure

Figure 4.13 shows the layout of the Request header, in the two versions of GIOP.

The Request header contains information that specifies which operation is being invoked on which object. This information is held in the object key and operation fields. The response-expected field indicates if the sender expects a response from the recipient. The service-context field passes any special information, such as the sender's user name. This information may be added by developers, in an interceptor. The requestID is used to match up the corresponding Reply message. The requesting principal is used for security purposes to indicate the client issuing the request. Version 1.1 of GIOP added a reserved field for future use.

Here is the exact definition of the GIOP Request header.

```
// GIOP 1.0
struct RequestHeader_1_0 { // Renamed from RequestHeader
    IOP::ServiceContextList service_context;
    unsigned long request_id;
    boolean response_expected;
    sequence <octet> object_key;
    string operation;
    Principal requesting_principal;
};

// GIOP 1.1
struct RequestHeader_1_1 {
    IOP::ServiceContextList service_context;
    unsigned long request_id;
    boolean response_expected;
    octet reserved[3]; // Added in GIOP 1.1
    sequence <octet> object_key;
    string operation;
    Principal requesting_principal;
};
```

The members of the GIOP Request header have the definitions given in the following subsections.

Service Context

The service context contains object services data that is passed from the client to the server. It is encoded as described in the GIOP message header section, 4.11.1.

RequestID

When a client sends a Request or LocateRequest message, it usually expects a reply. Since a client might send multiple requests to a server and the server might reply to them in different orders (assuming a multithreaded client and server), a requestID is used to associate a particular request to a particular reply. This ID must be a value that prevents the possibility of a reply to a request being used for a wrong request. Because it is the client that uses requestIDs, it is responsible for generating them in a unique way. Specifically, the client must not reuse a requestID value during a connection if the previous request containing that ID is still pending or if the previous request containing that ID was canceled and no reply was received.

Response Expected

Most CORBA clients issuing a request on a server expect a reply and indicate this by setting the response-expected flag to TRUE (1). In some cases, however, a client sends a request and neither expects nor wants a reply from the server. If the client is invoking a one-way request or if the invocation was via the Dynamic Invocation Interface (DII), with the INV_NO_RESPONSE flag set, it might choose not to receive a response from the server. In both these cases the response-expected flag is set to FALSE (0). However, a oneway or DII call may also be done when the client expects a response. If the flag is set to TRUE (0), the client can receive replies that indicate both system exceptions and LOCATION_FORWARD responses. When a server is executing a one-way operation and the response-expected flag is set to TRUE (1) it may send a reply to the client as soon as it receives the request but before the operation completes. For example, a response may be an acknowledgement or LOCATION_FORWARD response.

Reserved

This member was added in GIOP 1.1. It is always set to 0 and is reserved for future expansion.

Object Key

In CORBA, a client does not invoke an operation on a server directly, but on an object contained in a server. Since servers may contain more than one object, the client's knowing the port number, hostname, and processID of the server is not enough; it also must know the target object, the object that is being invoked on. This object's key or ID information is stored in the object key member of the Request header. The object key is a server-only value and has no meaning to and may not be modified by the client.

Operation

A client invokes an operation on an object. Thus in addition to its identifying the target object in the request, it must indicate which operation on that target object it is trying to invoke. The mechanism for identifying the operation in the message header is to use IDL identifier naming, within the context of the interface, but not a fully qualified scoped name. If the operation being invoked is an attribute accessor, _get or _set are prepended to the attribute name for the get and set operations, respectively, to arrive at the value of the operation member, _get_<attribute> or _set_<attribute>. An example is an automobile interface with the attribute cost of type float. In this case, the IDL compiler generates two operations (using C++ binding), as shown in Table 4.6.

Table 4.6   IDL and C++ Binding

IDL Name	C++ Binding Name	CIOP Name
Cost-set	void cost (float c)	_set_cost
cost-get	float cost (void)	_get_cost

Table 4.7   Operation Name Mapping

CORBA::Object Name	Invocation Value
get_interface	_interface
get_implementation	_implementation
is_a	_is_a
non_existent	_not_existent

The operation names are case-sensitive, so they should match the case of the operation name specified in the IDL source. All objects have, in addition to the operation defined in the IDL, a set of invokable operations defined in CORBA::Object. The mapping of the operation names is shown in Table 4.7.

Requesting Principal

For security purposes, a server might want to know who the requester is. The requesting_principal member contains this information. This member was added to support the BOA::get_principal operation.

4.12.1.2   Request Body Structure

The Request body contains the in and inout parameters to the operation, encoded in an encapsulation. The encoding of these parameters is in the order in which they are specified in the operation's OMG IDL definition, from left to right. Following the parameters, an optional context pseudo-object may be encoded. This is included only if "the operation's OMG IDL definition includes a context expression, and only includes context members as defined in that expression." As in the headers, the parameters must be aligned based on their type's alignment rules.

4.12.1.3   Example

Here is a GIOP request stream generated by Visibroker 3.0. The following IDL was used to create a client-server pair. This pair can be used to follow a series of messages to examine the streaming protocol used by GIOP. Later we examine IIOP's role in establishing the connection between the client and server as shown in Figure 4.14. The streaming protocol, however, is based completely on GIOP and as such is independent of the transport protocol.

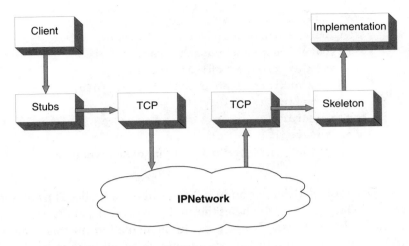

FIGURE 4.14 Flow of a Request through CORBA

```
enum VehicleType { car, truck, minivan, SUV };

typedef sequence <string> TripLocations;

exception CannotReturnData { string reason; };

union SpecialInfo switch (VehicleType) {
    case car:boolean hatchback;
    case truck:float bed_length;
    case minivan:unsigned short seats;
    case SUV:boolean four_wheel_drive;
    default:boolean unknown;
};

const long OccupantBound = 10;
typedef string occupants[OccupantBound];

struct VehicleInfo {
    short doors;
    string make;
    string model;
    float cost;
    VehicleType auto_type;
};

interface automobile
{
```

```
        attribute float speed;
        attribute TripLocations destinations;
        attribute occupants passengers;
        readonly attribute VehicleInfo auto_info;
        readonly attribute SpecialInfo spec_info;
        attribute any misc_info;
        boolean start();
        boolean stop();
        boolean get_info() raises (CannotReturnData);
    };
```

The example IDL defines an interface to an automobile. The automobile stubs are provided to a driver, which has the ability to control certain aspects of the vehicle. The skeleton is provided to a car implementation. In this example, the car implementation is a Ford Probe. An automobile, whether a car, truck, or whatever, has certain attributes and behavior. In this example, it can start and stop. Other behavior, such as a vehicle's speed, should be modeled as an attribute. The speed, occupants, and destination are defined as attributes of an automobile that may be changed by the driver. Some information about a vehicle is fixed, such as the vehicle type; for example, the driver cannot magically change a truck into a car. Using these methods and attributes, we can show the details of the GIOP protocol.

In this stream, there is no connection information. It has only the operation name and the in and inout parameters, if any, of the request. It does not contain the target object of the invocation, the host name of the server that contains the object, or the port number on which the server is listening. All of this information must be communicated via IIOP beforehand so that a connection can be established between the client and the server. Once this connection is established, the client may begin invoking requests on the server. More information on the connection establishment procedures is presented later in the IIOP section.

Once a connection is established, the client performs an invocation. It invokes the start operation on the car object. This results in a Request message being created and sent to the server that contains the car object that was the invocation's target. The automobile object on the client side which the client is actually invoking, is a proxy to the real car object; for example, it contains the implementation on the server side.

An operation often has one or more parameters. These parameters can be in, inout, out, or a return value. For a Request message, only in and inout parameters are of interest. These are turned into a data stream by converting them into CDR format in the order in which they were declared in the operation IDL definition. This data stream is called an encapsulation. This encapsulation must have certain information attached. To "start," a Request header is added to the front of the encapsulation and contains, as described previously, the operation name and other information necessary to allow the request to be handled by the server.

Next, a general header is needed to describe information that all requests and replies need in order for the recipient to understand what the stream is trying to do. This is the GIOP message header, which was described in section 4.11.1 Before the stream is sent to the server, it is tagged with the byte order of the current machine. This byte order tag is put into the message header so that the receiver can know immediately whether it will need to convert the data to a different order. For example, suppose the client machine is a Sparc. The byte ordering is big endian and this is indicated in the message header. The server is an Intel-based machine running Windows NT. It receives the request, reads the byte order flag from the message header, and converts the parameters to little endian.

The message header, the Request header, and the encapsulation containing the data are sent to the TCP layer by way of a socket call. The TCP layer fragments the message into however many datagrams are necessary and puts its header on the message, and sends each datagram to the IP layer, which puts its header on each. These IP datagrams are then sent to the hardware layer for transport to the server machine.

Figure 4.15 shows an example of a request stream. The first line of the stream is the message header stream in hexadecimal format. Subsequent lines

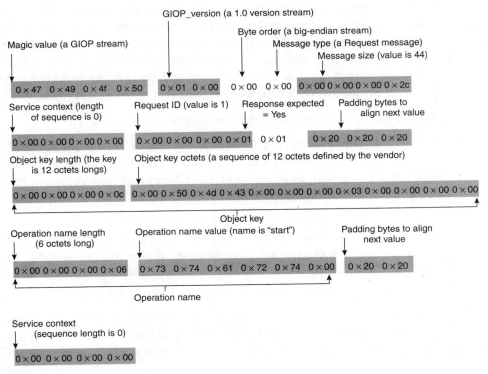

FIGURE 4.15   An Example Request Stream

contain the Request header stream followed by the Request body. The entire stream represents a GIOP Request message for the start operation on the car object. Its parts are discussed next, beginning with the message header.

- The first element of the message header is a 4-byte magic value that contains the protocol being used, including the value GIOP, since this is a GIOP-based message.

- Next is the version number of GIOP that is being used. This is a structure containing two octets, one for the major version number and one for the minor version number. It has two valid values: major 1, minor 0, and major 1, minor 1. In the example, it is 1.0.

- The byte order has two possible values: zero if it is a big-endian stream and 1 if it is a little-endian stream. This message, with a byte order value of zero, is a big-endian stream.

- The message type tells the type of message: Request, Reply, and so on. In the example, the value of zero indicates a Request message. The message types are an enumeration that is normally encoded as a long. In GIOP, however, the value is forced into an octet (for example, 1 byte instead of 4).

- The last value in the message header is the size of the message, which is the entire length of the message minus the message header size. The message header is 12 bytes long, so the size value will always be $l - 12$, where l is the length of the message. Message size is of type unsigned long; hence it is encoded as 4 bytes and must be byte-aligned. However, it starts at position 8 in the stream, so it is already aligned and no padding bytes are needed. This is always the case with a message header because of its structure.

Following the message header is the Request header.

- The first element is the service-context sequence. As a sequence, it begins with length. This stream has no service context, so the sequence length is zero. The length is an an unsigned long and four zeros are used to represent it in order to maintain byte alignment.

- The requestID, an unsigned long, has a value of 1.

- The next value is the response-expected flag and indicates whether the client expects a response to this message. A zero value indicates it does not and a 1 indicates that it does. This stream expects a response.

- Three padding bytes force byte alignment for the next value.

After starting the car, the driver will change its speed to 65.2 miles per hour. Speed is defined as a read/write attribute in the IDL, so two methods are generated for it by the IDL compiler. This example was programmed in C++, and the IDL binding for C++ results in the IDL compiler's creating the following overloaded methods:

```
float speed();
void speed(float);
```

The first method returns the speed as a floating-point value and the second method takes the speed value of type `float` as an input parameter. The client invokes the latter method to change the car's speed. Invoking this method with a value of 65.2 results in a request method's being generated. The stream is broken down as shown in Figure 4.16.

Recall that the encoding of attribute accessor operations involves prepending a _get and _set to the attribute name for the get and set operations, respectively. In this example, the speed attribute results in the operation names _get_speed and _set_speed. Within the encoding of the stream in the figure is the set accessor function of the attribute, _set_speed. The Request body contains the speed, a floating-point value. Recall from section 4.5.1.1 that a floating point is a 32-bit value, consisting of an exponent field, a mantissa, and a sign bit.

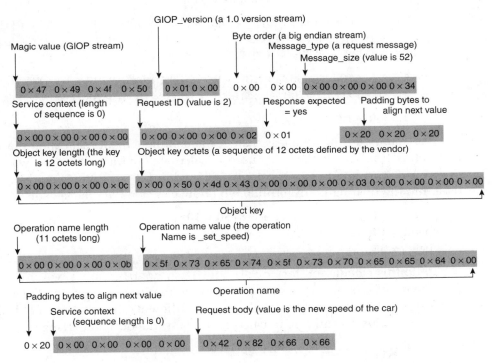

FIGURE 4.16 A Request Stream That Changes the Car's Speed

The binary representation of the exponent is a signed number using a bias of 127, that is, a decimal value that is the power to which two is raised. In other words, you calculate the exponent field value and plug it into the formula:

$$e = 2^{x-127}$$

In the example, the exponent field contains the value of 133, which gives the exponent:

$$e = 2^{133-127}$$
$$e = 64$$

To calculate the fractional part of the speed variable, first calculate the mantissa. Calculating the mantissa in decimal is more complicated than calculating the exponent. The mantissa has n bits, so the bits can be viewed as $x_1 x_2 \ldots x_n$. The calculation requires a polynomial of the form

$$m = \sum_{i=1}^{n-1} x_i 2^{-i}$$

In the example, the value of the mantissa is 00000100110011001100110. Using the previous formula to calculate it yields

$$m = (0)2^{-1} + (0)2^{-2} + (0)2^{-3} + (0)2^{-4} + (0)2^{-5} + (1)2^{-6} + (0)2^{-7} + (0)2^{-8} + (1)2^{-9} + (1)2^{-10}$$
$$+ (0)2^{-11} + (0)2^{-12} + (1)2^{-13} + (1)2^{-14} + (0)2^{-15} + (0)2^{-16} + (1)2^{-17} + (1)2^{-18} + (0)2^{-19}$$
$$+ (0)2^{-20} + (1)2^{-21} + (1)2^{-22} + (0)2^{-23}$$

$$m = 1.5625 \times 10^{-2} + 1.9532 \times 10^{-3} + 9.7656 \times 10^{-4} + 1.2207 \times 10^{-4} + 6.1035 \times 10^{-5} + 7.6293 \times 10^{-6} + 3.8146 \times 10^{-6} + 4.7683 \times 10^{-7} + 2.3841 \times 10^{-7}$$

$$m = 1.8750 \times 10^{-2}$$

The mantissa is a value less than 1; the complete mantissa, called the *significant,* is 1.m. This is the value used to calculate the fraction. m is always in the range $0 < m < 1$, so 1.m is calculated by adding 1 to m. Plugging the mantissa into the floating-point formula, you now can calculate the speed:

$$\text{speed} = -1^0 \times 2^{(133-127)} \times (1 + 1.8750 \times 10^{-2})$$
$$\text{speed} = 1 \times 64 \times 1.01875$$
$$\text{speed} = 65.2$$

To do this calculation for `double` and `long double` values, you increase the amount of bits in the mantissa; otherwise, the formula remains the same. The exponent must be calculated using a different bias, and its field size increases, but its overall role in calculating the value does not change.

4.12.2   Reply Message

Recall that a client that wants a reply to a Request message indicates this by setting the response-expected flag to `True`. The server, when finished with the request, replies with a Reply message. In this message, it acknowledges receipt of the message and returns any inout and out parameters and any return values, such as exception values. The Reply message may also return object location information.

A Reply message has three components, encoded in the following order:

- GIOP message header, which is always included
- Reply header
- Reply body, which includes all of the parameters and return values resulting from the execution of the operation specified in the Reply header

Figure 4.17 shows the order of the components.

4.12.2.1 Reply Header Structure

Figure 4.18 shows the layout of the Reply header.

The Reply header has three parts:

- Service context, used to return special information
- RequestID, used to matchup the corresponding Request message
- Reply status, used to return the status of Request, as well as LocateRequest, messages

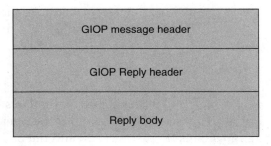

FIGURE 4.17   Reply Message Components

0 × 00   0 × 0M

Service context	RequestID	Reply status

FIGURE 4.18   GIOP Reply Header

Following is the exact definition of the GIOP Reply header.

```
enum ReplyStatusType {
     NO_EXCEPTION,
     USER_EXCEPTION,
     SYSTEM_EXCEPTION,
     LOCATION_FORWARD
};

struct ReplyHeader {
     IOP::ServiceContextList service_context;
     unsigned long request_id;
     ReplyStatusType reply_status;
};
```

The members are discussed in the following subsections.

Service Context

The `service_context` member contains the object services data that the server returns to the client, encoded as described in the GIOP message header Section, 4.11.1.

RequestID

When a server sends a reply to a Request or LocateRequest message, it obtains the requestID from the Request header and puts it in the Reply header's `request_id` member.

Reply Status

The server, in a reply, needs to indicate the completion status of the associated request, since not all requests are successful. If the operation was successful, the `reply_status` value is NO_EXCEPTION and the body contains any return values. If the operation was unsuccessful, thereby causing it or the ORB to throw an exception, the Reply body either contains the exception or directs the client to reissue the request to contain an object at some other location. If the Reply body is an exception `reply_status` will contain USER_EXCEPTION or SYSTEM_EXCEPTION.

4.12.2.2   Reply Body Structure

When a server replies to a client's Request message, the content of the Reply body depends on the status of the operation. The operation could have executed successfully, failed, or been deferred to another server. Each of these results requires a different `reply_status` value and Reply body. These are discussed in the following subsections.

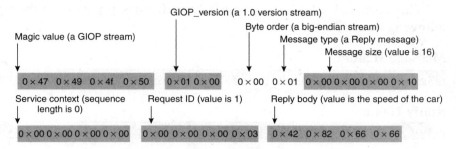

FIGURE 4.19   An Example Reply Message

Operation Succeeded

When the operation succeeds, reply_status contains the value NO_EXCEP-TION. The Reply body is encoded like a structure to hold the return data (if any). The return value is encoded first, followed by the inout and out parameters (if any) in the order they were specified in the operation's IDL definition.

Figure 4.19 shows an example of a GIOP Reply message send for a successful operation. This example continues the earlier Visibroker scenario.

The stream in the figure replies to a get request for the speed of the car. It contains the speed, 65.2 miles per hour, encoded as a float. Notice that the message type is 1, indicating a Reply message.

Following is another example of a Reply message. The message has a structure in the Reply body of the type VehicleInfo, whose IDL definition is as follows:

```
. . .
struct VehicleInfo {
    short doors;
    string make;
    string model;
    float cost;
    VehicleType auto_type;
};
. . .
```

An instance of VehicleInfo is then populated with the following data.

```
. . .
VehicleInfo vi;
vi.doors = 2;
vi.make = CORBA::strdup("Ford");
vi.model = CORBA::strdup("Probe");
vi.cost = 21000.00;
vi.auto_type = car;
. . .
```

This instance of `VehicleInfo` is returned in a Reply message that has the following headers.

Message Header

```
0x47 0x49 0x4f 0x50 0x01 0x00 0x00 0x01 0x00 0x00 0x00 0x30
```

Reply Header

```
0x00 0x00 0x00 0x00 0x00 0x00 0x00 0x05 0x00 0x00 0x00 0x00
```

Figure 4.20 shows that the data within the structure is byte-aligned. No special encoding tags are used to indicate that the data is within a structure. The data is simply encoded in the order that the corresponding members are declared in the IDL definition of the structure.

Operation Failed

If the operation failed, `reply_status` contains the value USER_EXCEPTION or SYSTEM_EXCEPTION. The Reply body will not contain the return value or inout and out parameters, but it will contain the exception raised by the operation. The exceptions that may be returned are limited to the CORBA-defined

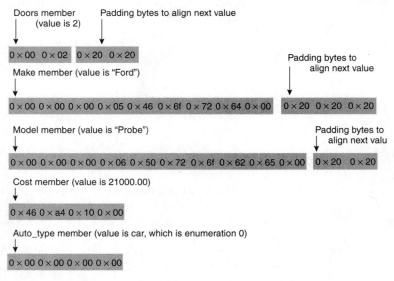

FIGURE 4.20   Another Example Reply Message

standard exception and the exceptions defined as raiseable by that operation in its IDL. For example, the body of the Reply message returning a system exception must contain the following structure.

```
struct SystemExceptionReplyBody {
    string exception_id;
    unsigned long minor_code_value;
    unsigned long completion_status;
};
```

The `minor_code_value` member is for ORB vendors that define their own system exceptions; standard system exceptions do not use it. The minor code value member, an `unsigned long`, is 32 bits long. The high-order 20 bits contain a 20-bit vendor minor codeset ID (VMCID). The remaining 12 bits contain a minor code. The OMG issues unique VMCIDs to vendors who wish to define specific sets of system exception minor codes. A VMCID of zero is special in that any vendor may use it without previous reservation. However, using a minor code assignment with a codeset of zero might cause conflicts with other vendor's assignments. The OMG has officially deprecated the use of the zero VMCID.

Next are two examples of returning exceptions in a Reply body. The first, shown in Figure 4.21, is a CORBA marshall exception, raised because the server's skeletons were unable to marshall a structure. The structure was to be returned within a CORBA any, but the skeleton could not understand the structure due to a programming error. When the skeleton tried to pull the structure out of the any so that it could convert it to CDR format, it was unable to

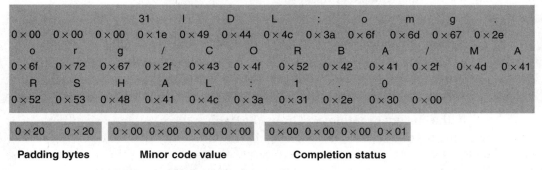

FIGURE 4.21   An Example CORBA System Exception Stream

detect the any's content. Thus it could not marshall it, and so it raised an exception. The headers are shown next.

System Exception Message Header

```
0x47 0x49 0x4f 0x50 0x1 0x00 0x00 0x1 0x00 0x00 0x00 0x38
```

System Exception Reply Header

```
0x00 0x00 0x00 0x00 0x00 0x00 0x00 0xe 0x00 0x00 0x00 0x2
```

As Figure 4.21 shows, the Reply body contains the three distinct members of a SystemExceptionReplyBody structure:

- exception_id
- minor_code_value
- completion status

exception_id contains the identifier of the exception, the exception's IDL definition. The OMG has defined the identifiers of system exceptions within the scope of the CORBA module version 1.0. This gives the exception omg.org::CORBA::MARSHALL:1.0.

The value of minor_code_value is zero. The stream in the example contains a standard OMG system exception, so the minor code is not used.

A completion status of 1 indicates that the operation executed successfully and that it was during the return that the exception was thrown. If the exception occurred before the operation could be successfully invoked, the completion status would be zero.

Here is the second example of returning an exception. This exception is user-defined. Recall from the automobile IDL in the earlier examples that an exception, CannotReturnData, was defined, as was an operation, get_info, that could raise the exception.

```
    . . .
    exception CannotReturnData { string reason; };
    . . .
    boolean get_info() raises (CannotReturnData);
    . . .
```

In the current example, we throw the CannotReturnData exception when we call the get_info operation on the automobile object. Following is the code for get_info. It creates a CannotReturnData exception and then adds the string "Test exception message" as the reason for the exception.

```
CORBA::Boolean
Car::get_info() {
    CannotReturnData crd;
    crd.reason = CORBA::strdup("Test exception message");
    throw (crd);
}
```

Once the exception is ready, it is thrown. This results in the Reply body shown in Figure 4.22. The message and Reply headers were removed to simplify the example.

This exception has two components, just as the encoding of the exception type requires:

- The repositoryID, defined from the exception's IDL definition. The repositoryID value is IDL:CannotReturnData:1.0, which is the `CannotReturnData` defined as throwable by the `get_info` operation.
- The exception member, which is a string that describes why the exception was thrown. In this example, a piece of sample data has returned the string "Test exception message".

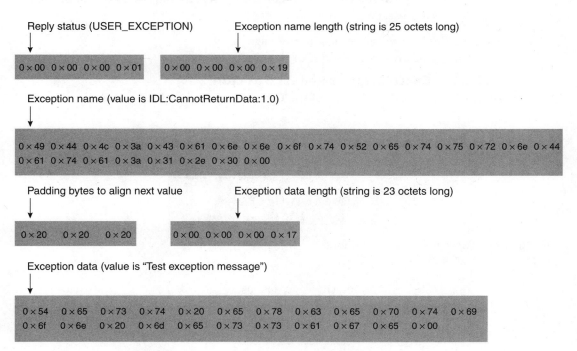

FIGURE 4.22   Reply Body of an Example User-Defined Exception

Operation Deferred to Another Object

If the server receiving a request of an object does not contain the object, but knows where it is and has a handle to it, it can return the handle (IOR) to the requestor. When the server replies in this fashion, it issues a Reply message with `reply_status` set to `LOCATION_FORWARD`. The Reply body contains the IOR of the object that can handle the desired request. Once the client receives this reply, it must resend the original request to the new object. This should be done at the stubs/ORB level so that it is transparent to the client program making the request. Note that the object key field in any specific GIOP profile is server-relative, not absolute. GIOP does not guarantee that the object key field embedded in the new object reference's GIOP profile will have the same value as the object key in the GIOP profile of the original object reference.

4.12.3   CancelRequest Message

A CancelRequest message has two components, encoded in the following order:

- GIOP mesageheader, which is always included
- CancelRequest header, which contains only the requestID of the original Request message

A CancelRequest message has no message body.

Figure 4.23 shows the order of the components.

4.12.3.1   CancelRequest Header Structure

Figure 4.24 shows the layout of the CancelRequest header.

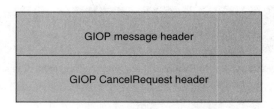

FIGURE 4.23   CancelRequest Components

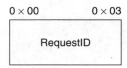

FIGURE 4.24   CancelRequest Header

The only information in the CancelRequest header is the requestID. Following is the IDL definition of the CancelRequest header.

```
struct CancelRequestHeader {
        unsigned long request_id;
};
```

A client that wants to cancel a Request or LocateRequest message must specify which message it wants to cancel. It does this by sending in the CancelRequest header, the same requestID value specified in the original Request or LocateRequest message. This CancelRequest is advisory only; the server is not required to acknowledge the request and may subsequently send the corresponding reply. The client should expect to receive a reply containing a result or an exception from the server once the CancelRequest is sent.

4.12.4   LocateRequest Message

A client has certain needs when dealing with a remote object. Often, for example, it obtains object references from a third party, such as a naming service. Sometimes problems can occur between the mapping of the object reference to the object itself. The object might not exist, have been moved to a different domain, or not be currently active. The client, to determine information about the object reference, can use a LocateRequest message. This message can be used to determine if an object is valid or whether the server containing the object is capable of receiving requests and if it is not to which address to send requests for the object.

A LocateRequest message has two components, encoded in the following order:

- GIOP message header, which is always included
- LocateRequest header, which contains the requestID of the original Request message and the object key of the object to be located

A LocateRequest message has no message body. Figure 4.25 shows the order of the components.

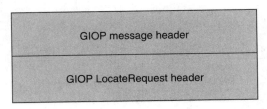

FIGURE 4.25   LocateRequest Components

4.12.4.1. LocateRequest Header Structure

Figure 4.26 shows the layout of the LocateRequest header.

The LocateRequest header has two fields:

- A requestID, used to match up the corresponding LocateReply message
- The object key field, which holds the object to be located.

Following is the exact definition of the GIOP Locate/Request header.

```
struct LocateRequestHeader {
    unsigned long request_id;
    sequence <octet> object_key;
};
```

The members are defined in the following subsections.

RequestID

In the same way that the requestID associates Reply messages to Request messages, it also associates LocateReply messages with LocateRequest ones. As always, the client is responsible for generating the ID values.

Object Key

The `object_key` member identifies the object being located in the request. The IIOP profile of the target object's IOR, in an IIOP context, contains the value of the object key. Specifically, the `object_key` field of the encapsulated `IIOP::ProfileBody` holds the value. If GIOP is using a transport mechanism other than TCP, then IIOP is not used. This means that GIOP mapping requires that the new IOR profiles must also contain an appropriate corresponding value for obtaining the object key. This key is a server-only value; it has no meaning to and may not be modified by the client.

4.12.5 LocateReply Message

A LocateReply message has three components, encoded in the following order:

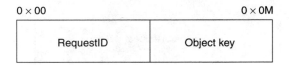

FIGURE 4.26 LocateRequest Header

- GIOP message header, which is always included
- LocateReply header, which contains the requestID of the corresponding LocateRequest message and the results of the location attempt
- LocateReply body, which contains the IOR of the located object

Figure 4.27 shows the order of the components.

4.12.5.1 **LocateReply Header Structure**

The LocateReply header has two fields, shown in Figure 4.28:

- A requestID, used to match up the corresponding LocateRequest message
- The LocateStatus field, which holds the results of the location attempt

Following is the exact IDL definition of the GIOP Locate/Reply header.

```
enum LocateStatusType {
UNKNOWN_OBJECT,
OBJECT_HERE,
OBJECT_FORWARD };
struct LocateReplyHeader {
unsigned long request_id;
LocateStatusType locate_status;
};
```

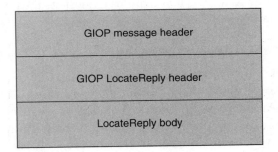

FIGURE 4.27   LocateReply Components

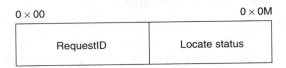

FIGURE 4.28   LocateReply Header

The members are discussed in the following subsections.

Request ID

When a server sends a LocateReply to a LocateRequest message, it obtains the requestID from the Request header and puts it in the LocateReply header's `request_id` member. As mentioned previously, GIOP uses the requestID to associate replies with requests.

Locate Status

The `locate_status` member returns the status of the attempt to locate the object specified in the corresponding LocateRequest message. It has three possible values with the following meanings.

- `UNKNOWN_OBJECT`. The server has no knowledge of the specified object. If this value is present, then there is no LocateReply body.
- `OBJECT_HERE`. The server has the specified object and can receive requests for it. If this value is present, then there is no LocateReply body.
- `OBJECT_FORWARD`. If this value is present, then there is a LocateReply body.

4.12.5.2   LocateReply Body

When the `locate_status` member contains `OBJECT_FORWARD`, the LocateReply body contains an IOR. This IOR handles requests to the object specified in the LocateRequest message.

4.12.6   CloseConnection Message

When a server intends to close a connection with a client, it issues a Close-Connection message. This tells the client that it is not expected to provide further responses. Any requests for which the client is awaiting replies will never be processed, so the client may safely reissue them on another connection. Only servers may issue a CloseConnection message. A CloseConnection message has one component, the GIOP message header, which identifies the message type.

4.12.7   MessageError Message

If a recipient of a GIOP message does not understand the message's type or version number, it will respond with a Message/Error message. This message is also sent in response to a message that has an improper header (for example, it has the wrong magic value). Error handling is context-specific. A Message/Error message has only one component, the GIOP message header, which identifies the message type.

4.12.8   Fragment Message

The GIOP 1.1 specification adds support for fragmented messages. Recall from Chapter 1 that a Request or Reply message can be broken into multiple fragments. The first fragment is a regular message with the more-fragments bit in the flags field set to `True`. The initial fragment can be followed by one or more Fragment messages. The last Fragment message has the more-fragments bit set to `False`. The client may send a CancelRequest message before the final Fragment message is sent, in which case the server should assume that no more fragments follow.

The message size field of the GIOP message header gives the total size of a message following the header. Sometimes, it is impractical or undesirable to ascertain the total size of the message when it is first being constructed, so the accurate size cannot be entered in the header. In this case, GIOP 1.1 provides an alternative way to indicate the size.

4.13 Final Thoughts on GIOP

In this chapter, we discussed the three primary elements of GIOP: CDR transfer syntax, transport assumptions, and messaging model. To build a messaging system that is interoperable with other CORBA-compliant systems, one must understand these elements. GIOP uses CDR to allow an exchange of data between disparate systems. Without this standard exchange syntax, defining a standard set of messages would be useless. Likewise, having a transfer syntax, but no common way to pass data, would not prove very useful.

We also discussed the relationships among the three GIOP components. It is important to remember the following:

1. A connection must be established between client and server that adheres to GIOP's transport assumptions.
2. All data must be marshalled to the correct byte order.
3. Marshalled data must be byte-aligned based on its type.
4. Aligned streams must have the appropriate message type header before they are sent.
5. Streams with the message type header must have a general message header.
6. Finally, a message may be sent.

Each of these steps must occur in order for a CORBA object invocation to take place. It also must be remembered that invocations usually take place as a request-reply message pair.

Now that we have addressed the fundamentals of GIOP, in the next chapter we look at its more popular cousin, IIOP.

5

Internet Inter-ORB Protocol

5.1 Introduction to IIOP

In this chapter, we provide the details of the IIOP messaging protocol. We cover the problem that IIOP solves and review related and derivative technologies by examining their context, the solutions they provide, and their strengths and weaknesses.

GIOP defines a protocol that is independent of any particular set of network protocols, such as IPX or TCP/IP. Given the explosive growth of the Internet, the most common networking protocols have become TCP/IP. Recall that IIOP, the Internet Inter-Orb Protocol, is the protocol adopted by the OMG that must be supported by CORBA-compliant networked ORBs, either as a native protocol or through half bridges. Essentially, IIOP is just a mapping of GIOP onto the Internet's TCP transport layer. Mappings onto other transport layers may be defined in the future.

An ORB may support optional ESIOPs (Environment-Specific IOPs) as its preferred ORB protocol. DCE-Common IOP (DCE-CIOP) is the first such protocol that has been publicly specified. It uses a subset of DCE-RPC facilities and reuses parts of GIOP.

IIOP compliance requires that agents that are capable of accepting object requests or providing locations for objects publish their TCP/IP addresses in IORs. Any client needing the published object's services initiates a connection with the object, using the address specified in its IOR. The agent may accept or reject connection requests, although the OMG suggests that they generally should accept them if possible. ORB vendors, however, may establish any connection acceptance policy they want. The OMG allows flexibility in this policy so that the vendors can enforce fairness or optimize resource usage.

5.2   **Connecting Client and Server**

GIOP itself is insufficient for enabling client-server interaction. IIOP is the glue that binds GIOP and TCP/IP. An examination of TCP/IP shows that it falls short (intentionally) in several areas. The first is in providing a consistent language that allows clients and servers to speak. The second is in defining a standard method to allow clients to discover services. By discovery is meant not dynamic discovery in the sense of finding objects through the naming service, but rather what information must be in a handle or reference in order for clients and servers to communicate. For a client to communicate with an object, it must have a reference to it. This object reference in IIOP is the IOR, which contains a host address and port number. A client wanting to invoke on the object can send a Request message to the host and port listed in the IOR. (It actually sends it to the server that contains the object.) The object that is the target of the invocation lives within a server process in the host machine. The server listens at the port for requests and, when they come in, dispatches them to the object. This scenario requires that the server is always running and actively listening on the port for requests. The IOR is defined in the following IDL.

```
module IOP { // IDL
   //
   // Standard Protocol Profile tag values
   //

   typedef unsigned long ProfileId;
   const ProfileId TAG_INTERNET_IOP = 0;
   const ProfileId TAG_MULTIPLE_COMPONENTS = 1;

   struct TaggedProfile {
           ProfileId tag;
           sequence <octet> profile_data;
   };
   //
   // an Interoperable Object Reference is a sequence of
   // object-specific protocol profiles, plus a type ID.
   //

struct IOR {
           string type_id;
           sequence <TaggedProfile> profiles;
   };
```

```
//
// Standard way of representing multicomponent profiles.
// This would be encapsulated in a TaggedProfile.
//

typedef unsigned long ComponentId;

struct TaggedComponent {
        ComponentId tag;
        sequence <octet> component_data;
};
typedef sequence <TaggedComponent> MultipleComponentProfile;
};
```

The CORBA specification requires that an object reference have at least one tagged **profile.** The profile holds information that allows the networking protocol to identify the object, in the case of IIOP, the host address, port number, and object key. This information is sufficient to drive a complete invocation. The structure of the IIOP profiles is defined in the IDL, as follows.

```
module IIOP { // IDL extended for version 1.1
    struct Version {
    octet major;
    octet minor;
};

struct ProfileBody_1_0 { // renamed from ProfileBody
    Version iiop_version;
    string host;
    unsigned short port;
    sequence <octet> object_key;
    };

    struct ProfileBody_1_1 {
    Version iiop_version;
    string host;
    unsigned short port;
    sequence <octet> object_key;
    // Added in 1.1
    sequence <IOP::TaggedComponent> components;
};
};
```

The profile structure marshalls into an encapsulation octet stream. This encapsulation is the `profile_data` member of the `IOP::TaggedProfile` structure that represents the IIOP profile in an IOR, and the tag has the value `TAG_INTERNET_IOP`. If version 1.1 of IIOP is used, then the `ProfileBody_1_1` structure is used. If version 1.0 is used, the only profile that likely will be supported is of type `ProfileBody_1_0`. The members of `IIOP::ProfileBody1_0` and `IIOP::ProfileBody1_1` are IIOP-version, host, port, object-key and component. Each is described in detail in the next sections.

5.2.1 The IIOP Version Member

The `IIOP version` member contains the version of IIOP that the agent at the host address specified in the IOR is prepared to receive. Note that the GIOP version number is neither equivalent nor related to the IIOP version number. Each is an independent value that describes only its particular protocol. For example, a GIOP 1.1 message header does not necessarily mean that the IOR is a version 1.1 IOR. However, the core CORBA 2.1 specification states that IIOP 1.0 is based on GIOP 1.0. The OMG allows IIOP 1.1 to be based on either GIOP 1.0 or GIOP 1.1. An agent must be able to support the current version it has specified as well as all previous versions of IIOP. For example, if a server publishes an IOR that indicates it is using IIOP 1.1, then it must support both GIOP 1.0 and 1.1 Request messages. It must also send Reply messages in the GIOP version that the client understands. This backward compatibility allows clients that have older object references to be supported. Object references, if stored on disk, could persist for an arbitrarily long period. Not allowing the use of previous versions of IORs would render such object references obsolete and severely hamper the ability of systems to upgrade smoothly and seamlessly.

For clients, supporting backward compatibility means that an IIOP 1.1 client must support GIOP 1.1 and optionally may support GIOP 1.0. If a client is of a previous minor version, it may attempt to invoke operations on objects that are of a higher minor version number. The client is required to send only the information defined in the lower minor version protocol and may ignore the extra information defined in later versions.

At the time of this writing, the highest major version number of IIOP specified by the OMG is 1; the highest minor version number is 1. As long as any new changes to the profile body are backward-compatible, the major version number may remain the same.

According to the OMG, compliant ORBs must generate version 1.1 profiles, and must accept any profile with a major version number of 1, regardless of the minor version number. As mentioned in section 5.2, there are two profile body structures:

- `ProfileBody_1_0`, used if the minor version number is zero
- `ProfileBody_1_1`, used if the minor version number is 1

If an IOR's minor version number is greater than 1, then the length of the encapsulated profile may exceed the total size of components defined for profiles with minor version number of 1. If an ORB supports only version 1.1 (and by default, the lower version 1.0), then the IIOP profiles ignore, but preserve, any data in the profile that occurs after the `components` member.

5.2.2   The Host Member

The `host` member identifies the Internet host on which the object lives. Later in the chapter, we discuss in more detail exactly where an object resides and the TCP/IP information in its IOR. For now, it is sufficient to say that the client expects that it will be communicating (using GIOP messages) with an object that is on the host encoded in the IOR. The OMG recommends using the host's fully qualified domain name, rather than an unqualified (or partially qualified) name, so as to alleviate scoping problems for the names. Within a subnetwork, specifying only the machine name rather than the full name, is usually sufficient. But there could be many common names that, without the fully qualified domain name, would conflict once they left the subnetwork. For example, it is easy to imagine that there is more than one machine named *mustang* on the Internet. If a subnetwork IOR for a machine named *mustang* is used outside of the subnetwork, the only information about the host name that the IOR contains is the name *mustang,* instead of, say, *mustang.ford.com.* The ORB either would not be able to route the request to any object or might route it to the wrong one.

Note, the `host` member may also be expressed using the standard dotted decimal form of the host name. For example, instead of the host name t2.concept5.com the IP address for it, 207.123.142.10, could be stored.

5.2.3   The Port Member

The `port` member contains the port number of the TCP/IP port on which a server listens for connection requests. This port number is the one that is used by agents to communicate with clients. Usually, a well-known port number is stored in the IOR. In this case, the only time a client sees the real port number is in the body of a reply to a LocateRequest or Request message. We cover in Chapter 6 the relationship between well-known port numbers and the port numbers actually used for invocations.

5.2.4   The Object Key Member

The `object_key` member identifies the object that is the target of the invocation. The `host` and `port` members of a profile together identify only the machine and socket of the server with which the client will communicate. Since it is likely that the server process will contain more than one object, the client needs to identify the invocation's object. The object key must be distinct enough to allow the server to route the request correctly.

5.2.5   The Components Member

The `components` member is a sequence of `TaggedComponents`. This sequence allows additional information to be attached so that it is available when invocations are made on the object described in the profile. The information put into a component must be standard.

If it is not, then there is no guarantee that any of the nonstandard components will remain in the IOR. The OMG has defined, as part of the IIOP 1.1 conformance standards, a set of optional, standard components for profiles. Since these components are standard, they cannot be dropped from an IIOP 1.1 IOR.

- TAG_ORB_TYPE
- TAG_CODE_SETS
- TAG_SEC_NAME
- TAG_ASSOCIATION_OPTIONS
- TAG_GENERIC_SEC_MECH

The OMG might add other components later, to support, for example, enhanced versions of IIOP, ORB services such as security, and other GIOPs, ESIOPs, and proprietary protocols.

According to the OMG specification, every IIOP version specifies a set of standard components for itself, as well as the components' conformance rules. These rules specify the requirements concerning the presence of the components in an IOR. A component is either mandatory or optional. Also, a component may be dropped. The conformance rules defined for the IIOP version are the only rules with which the implementation must conform.

New components cannot be added to an existing IIOP version's conformance rules. If one needs or desires new rules, then one must create a new version of IIOP. This new version of IIOP will then specify the rules and as a result new components.

5.3   Code Sets

As mentioned earlier in the wide string description in Chapter 4, 8-bit characters and wide character data are mapped to numeric codes. The set of these codes for all of the characters in a language is known as a code set, for example ASCII. CORBA has more than one notion of a code set. It uses the notions of a native code set, a transmission code set, and a conversion code set.

The native code set is the code set that is used by the application. It is also the one that the application communicates to the ORB with. The application may use different code sets for character and wide character data. For example, an application may use ASCII for character data and Unicode for wide characters.

The transmission code set is the character or wide character encoding that ORBs use to pass character data to each other. During a session there are two transmission code sets, one for byte character data and one for wide character data. The transmission code sets for the byte characters and wide characters can be the same code sets.

The conversion code set is the set of character codes to which the ORB can convert. For all of the codes in the conversion code set, the ORB will maintain appropriate conversion procedures and advertise that ability.

When a client and a server communicate, they must negotiate their code sets, both the 8-bit and wide character code sets. The negotiated code sets will be the ones used for the duration of the connections. The negotiation between client and server occurs by the client ORB determining the server's native and conversion code sets. This information is found in the target object's IOR, specifically in the code set component of the multiple profile structure. This component is tagged as `TAG_CODE_SETS`. The IDL below is used to hold the code set component of the IOR.

```
module CONV_FRAME {
    typedef unsigned long CodeSetId;
    struct CodeSetComponent {
        CodeSetId native_code_set;
        sequence<CodeSetId> conversion_code_sets;
    };
    struct CodeSetComponnentInfo {
        CodeSetComponent ForCharData;
        CodeSetComponent ForWcharData;
    };
}
```

It lists the native code set and the conversion code sets of the target object, for both character and wide character data. The conversion code sets are listed in the target object's order of preference.

The IDL below is used to identify the code sets used in a CORBA invocation. It is located within the service context of Request and Reply messages. It identifies both the 8-bit and wide character code sets used.

```
module CONV_FRAME {
   struct CodeSetContext {
      CodeSetId char_data;
      CodeSetId wchar_data;
   };
};
```

The client side ORB determines its side's native and conversion code sets from client side configuration data (OS variables, etc.). Based on the client's and server's code sets, the client side ORB determines the transmission code set for 8-bit and wide characters. If the client and server are using the same code sets then the transmission code set is the same as the native code set. When the server receives the character data, it will convert it to its native code set if it is not already in that format.

In figure 5.1, you can see the ORB will transmit character and wide character data using a transmission code set. It will use one code set for 8-bit character data and another for wide character data if necessary.

It is important for character code sets to be convertible so clients and server can understand one another. In distributed environments, clients and servers can be running in different countries and their users using different languages. Even if they are running in the same country, they may be on different machine architectures that don't understand each other (for example, both users speak American English but one using ASCII, the other EBCDIC). For them to have any chance to communicate, they must at least be able to translate messages into an understandable format, hence code set negotiation.

5.4 Example of an IOR

For an example of an IOR, we created an instance of the automobile interface defined in Chapter 4, a Probe. We start it on a machine named *apus*, which has the IP address 140.188.18.70. Following is a breakdown of the IOR, which was created using a VisiBroker 3.0 server.

The example, shown in Figure 5.1 is an IIOP version 1.0 object reference. The host's IP address is encoded in the IOR, as is the port number on which the Probe object will be listening. VisiBroker assigns the port number at runtime. (The reasons for this and its implications are discussed in Chapter 6). As a result, if we were to restart the server that created this IOR and create a new instance of the Probe object, the new IOR would probably contain a different port number.

The object key has VisiBroker-specific information, the IDL interface name, and the object's instance name. It is important to note that this IOR is not the same as the object reference that the client will use to talk to the implementa-

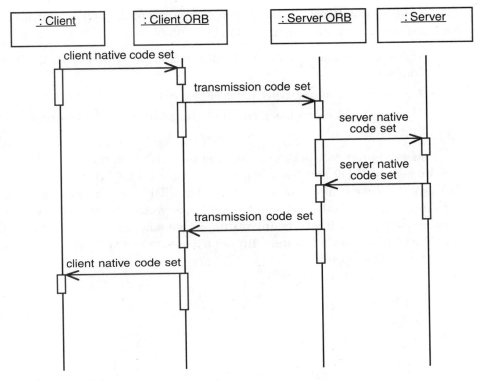

FIGURE 5.1   Example IOR

tion object. The object reference will use information contained in this IOR, but it needs to do marshalling to create a CDR stream and then send that stream in a Request message.

5.5   **Final Thoughts on IIOP**

The Internet has become a worldwide phenomenon, consequently increasing the presence of TCP/IP. TCP/IP has become the de facto standard networking protocol. IIOP was created to address the particulars of these protocols. Specifically IIOP provides the following:

- Host addresses, through IP addresses
- Machine process addresses, through port numbers

This chapter has provided all of the details on the specialization of GIOP into IIOP. It has shown how the IOR and message header are formed in IIOP.

The reader should have a complete understanding of the IIOP protocol definition and mechanics. Following are the key points covered.

- The IOR contains both the host address and port number for the TCP/IP connection
- A server is always actively listening for requests
- The object reference has a complete set of information to drive an IIOP invocation

Separating the networking addressing protocol from the messaging protocol, by keeping IIOP and GIOP separate, has given CORBA greater flexibility. IIOP was kept very thin, providing only what GIOP needs in order to establish a connection. The OMG has avoided adding any complexity to GIOP, such as new message types. It will be interesting to see what new changes to the protocols will occur in the future, with the expansion of IIOP's and GIOP's capabilities (such as multicast).

Vendors' Approaches to IIOP and Interoperability

6.1 The Reality of IIOP and Interoperability

Even though IIOP and GIOP specify a standard interoperability protocol, obstacles still exist to seamless interfacing between products from different vendors. While it is possible for clients and servers from different vendors to connect and interoperate, using correctly formed IORs, other unsolved problems remain. Foremost of these are server location independence and the initial bootstrapping of a connection. The first comes from having the host and port values embedded in the IOR. Solving that problem leads to the second problem, since each vendor has solved it in a slightly different way. Do not be discouraged, however, for even though the vendors have solved these problems in different ways, interoperability is still feasible. In this chapter, we cover three vendors' solutions: Inprise's VisiBroker, Iona's Orbix, and Object Oriented Concept's OmniBroker. At the end of the chapter, we give an example of interoperability between two of these products.

The act of establishing a connection between a client and a server creates an *object reference* on the client. An object reference that can work between different vendors' ORBs is an IOR. It is on this object reference that the client invokes all of the operations on the target object. The object reference then delegates the call to the real object, which is located somewhere on the other side of the connection. In this chapter, we focus on establishing the proxy object on the client.

6.2 Location Independence and IORs

Where's the object? Have you ever wondered how to migrate an object from one server to another in a live system? For example, suppose you want to do load balancing by moving a lot of objects from one server to another, but you do not want to shut down the server to do this. Recall from Chapter 5 that an object indicates its location to the machine (via the hostname) and the port number in its IOR. So if you migrate an object from a server located on machine A to a server on machine B, then when the client tries to invoke on it, it won't work. Right? The client using the original IOR pointing to machine A will try to open a connection and make a call to the object on machine A, but the object is now on machine B. How can this work? The answer is *location forwarding.* We take a look at that in more detail next.

In CORBA, the location of objects is of primary importance, in more ways than one. Issues quickly arise, such as security, what platform the object's implementation is written, and the load of a specific host (it is not a good idea to run everything on the same machine). Although this is not supposed to be the case (at least for the client), all of these issues nevertheless manifest themselves at the system level. When one begins to deal with the lower layers, where IIOP is located, they become more challenging to manage. This is because the exact network resources that are being used are hard-coded into IORs. Unless the ORB vendors have made the IOR/resource relationship flexible, you will have to give a great deal of thought regarding from where those IORs are going to come.

For example, if the specific host and port are hard-coded into an IOR and the object is moved to a different host or restarted on a different port, any client that has the IOR will be unable to contact the object. Thus services such as naming and trading are made largely useless in systems that are in a high state of flux, since the IORs that are registered with these services quickly become invalid. Every time a service starts, it could reregister itself with the naming and/or trading service by unbinding its old IOR and registering the new one. However, this helps only clients that have obtained the new IOR. This will not help the client that is using an IOR it had made persistent earlier (for example, by using the `object_to_string` call), since that persistent object will still have the old port and/or host.

One partial solution to help object location independence is to have a server reload its persistent IOR, the same IOR distributed to its clients. When the server reloads the IOR, it extracts the port number and listens on that port. This allows the port number in the IOR to remain valid no matter how many times the object starts and stops. It does not, however, solve the problem that results from moving the object from one host to another. ORB vendors have solved this problem through a variety of means.

To provide object location independence, some ORB vendors use IORs that are used only to obtain the object name; the host and port number are obtained through other means. Once the connection is established to the server, a new IOR is returned to the client. This IOR contains the actual host and port on which the object is listening. The client now should send its requests on that object to the new host and port. We call this solution a *locator solution.*

The locator solution depends on the port on which the server is really listening being returned. This adds the requirement that the server is always up and listening. However, leaving a server with low utilization constantly running is a waste of resources. A solution is to set the activation mode of the object so that the server is not constantly running. It could start up, if not already running, upon an invocation on it. It then would remain running for a fixed amount of time, unless it receives another invocation, in which case it would reset its countdown to shutdown. This mode is referred to as running *automatic server startup mode.* When running in this mode, the server is not actively listening at its IOR-advertised port number. Thus an error will occur if the client tries to invoke on the object. For this reason, many ORB vendors put a well-known port number in the IOR. Currently, the CORBA specification does not specify a standard "well-known" port number. However, the new Interoperable Naming Service Specification (INSS) introduces a well-known port at port 900. See the specification for more details. Instead, it recommends that "individual agents will need to assign previously unused ports as part of their installation procedures." Multiple such agents per host may be supported. The agent will then run on this port and listen for LocateRequest and Request messages. If such a message comes in, the receiver replies with a LocateReply or Reply message, respectively. The value of the `reply_status` member in the replying message is `LOCATION_FORWARD`. In the body of the message is the IOR for the desired object. This IOR contains the actual host and port on which the client will be communicating with the object. Once the client and server have connected, the client will have a proxy object upon which it can begin invoking operations (without passing an IIOP header every time). Remember, however, that a client should be prepared to be forwarded at any time, even after it has performed successful invocations. This allows runtime object migration and fault tolerance. In the first case, if the object is moved to a new host or port, a client's request may be forwarded there so that it can continue. In the latter case, if the server that the client was using becomes unavailable, for example, it crashes, then another server may handle the request. This allows for the seamless use of redundant servers for fault tolerance.

In addition to an agent that provides forwarding capability, CORBA also specifies three other methods that an agent may use regarding a request to an object. First, the agent may handle them directly. However, it might not have the object implementation. If it does, it processes the request as usual; if it does not, it passes on the request to another process to handle. Second, the agent may handle some requests and forward others. Using this method you could, for example, create an agent that has administrative capabilities. The agent would provide an object interface for administration, but would forward other calls to servers that hold the object implementation.

The third method that an agent may use regarding an object request is to process a request at one time and then forward it at another time. In other words, it may turn its forwarding capabilities on and off. This method might be useful for agents that want to take on some of the load from the servers to which they are forwarding requests. It also can be used to provide some level of redundancy. By bringing all of the objects normally forwarded online within the agent, you can shut down the server to which it forwards.

Whatever method the agent chooses, there is no requirement for location forwarding. In this case, the agent supports direct access to objects. However, if it cannot support direct access, it sends a LocateReply message with a status of UNKNOWN_OBJECT and the status returned is OBJECT_HERE.

If the client receives a Reply message with a LOCATION_FORWARD status, it should make no assumptions about the IOR it received for the target object. The client may use on subsequent invocations either the original IOR or the new one. On connection failure with the object (after forwarding), the client should use the original IOR to begin the reconnection process. This is because the forward location dropped the connection, so going to the beginning point might bring it to an agent who will forward you to the new location.

As of the GIOP 1.2 specification, the client may receive a Reply message with a status of LOCATION_FORWARD_PERM. This means that the client should use the new IOR in the future—that is, the forwarding is permanent. If an invocation returns a status of UNKNOWN_OBJECT, then the client should assume that the object does not exist at that location and that further attempts to connect to it there will be fruitless.

The OMG allows the implementation of location forwarding mechanisms to be at the discretion of ORB vendors. This allows them to use various strategies for optimization and to support dynamic object location and migration behaviors.

It is the agent's responsibility to activate or find a third party that can activate the server that contains the target object. Both VisiBroker and Orbix use the notion of a daemon process running on a well-known port. They use an operating system environment variable to indicate the well-known port that clients and servers use.

In the following several sections, we examine in more detail how several major vendors handle connecting clients and servers, beginning with Inprise's VisiBroker.

6.3   Inprise's VisiBroker

VisiBroker's osagent, or Smart Agent, is the program responsible for forwarding requests to the proper object. When an object is created within a server, the osagent must be informed of it through calls it makes to `BOA::impl_is_ready` and `BOA::obj_is_ready`. Only one call to `impl_is_ready` is needed no matter how many objects a server contains. The `obj_is_ready` call must be made for each CORBA object that is instantiated in the server; otherwise, clients cannot see the object.

To locate an osagent to register with, a server uses a broadcast message. The first osagent to respond is the one with which the server registers. Clients obtain the osagent in the same manner. Once the osagent has been located, clients look up requests and servers send registration requests using a point-to-point UDP connection. VisiBroker picked UDP over TCP for its broadcast capabilities. UDP allows an agent or process to dynamically discover agents that are located on the same LAN.

If you create an object that is to be activated on request, the osagent alone would be unable to direct a client's request to your object. VisiBroker has added an object activation daemon, or OAD, to handle situations like this. The object's implementation needs to be registered with the OAD. This allows the OAD to start up the object implementation. The OAD will register each object registered with it with the osagent. When the osagent receives a request, it forwards it to the OAD, which then will start the server and forward the request to it.

When VisiBroker's locator service, the osagent, runs in verbose mode, one can begin to see the steps necessary for the server and client to connect to each other. We use the car server and driver client from our previous example to show the use of IORs. Recall that in the example from Chapter 4, the driver client connected with a car object (Probe) and invoked operations. Using a bind interceptor, we show the driver trying to bind to the car. The first object reference shown is the one it received when it did the VisiBroker proprietary bind call. The second object reference is the IOR returned by the LocateReply message. This is shown in Figure 6.1.

```
>driver
Installing Sample Interceptors
  bind to car

Bind Int: bind
object reference is
IOR:002020200000001349444c3a6175746f6d6f62696c653a312e30002000000001564
9530000000035000100200000000100200000000000002500504d4300000000000001349
444c3a6175746f6d6f62696c653a312e3000200000000100

Bind Int: bind_succeeded
object reference is
IOR:002020200000001349444c3a6175746f6d6f62696c653a312e300020000000010000000000000046000
100200000000e3134302e3138382e31382e373000818f0000002a00504d4300000000000001349444c3a61
75746f6d6f62696c653a312e30002000000000670726f626500
```

FIGURE 6.1   Client Bind Interceptor Output

Using VisiBroker's IOR printing utility on the first IOR results in the following.

```
Interoperable Object Reference:
  Type ID: IDL:automobile:1.0
  Contains 1 profile.
  Profile 0-Unknown profile:
struct TaggedProfile{unsigned long tag=1447645952;sequence
<octet> profile_data={53 bytes: (0)(1)(0)[ ](0)(0)(0)(1)(0)[
](0)(0)(0)(0)(0)[%](0)[P][M][C](0)(0)(0)(0)(0)(0)(0)(19)[I][D]
[L][:][a][u][t][o][m][o][b][i][l][e][:][1][.][0](0)[ ](0)(0)(0)
(1)(0)};}
```

Printing the IOR returned in the LocateReply message produces the following.

```
Interoperable Object Reference:
  Type ID: IDL:automobile:1.0
  Contains 1 profile.
  Profile 0-IIOP Profile:
  version: 1.0
  host: 140.188.18.70
  port: 33177
  Object Key: PersistentId[repId=IDL:automobile:1.0,object
  Name=probe]
```

```
Bound to the following UDP port  :  14045
Bound to the following interfaces:
   Address: 140.188.18.70  Subnet: 255.255.255.0  Broadcast:
140.188.18.255

*********************************************************
Time: Thu Apr 16 16:57:53 1998

*--- Received a login message from client ----*
Host Name: apus
Client User name: pklinker
Process id: 1182
*********************************************************


*********************************************************
Time: Thu Apr 16 16:57:53 1998

*--- Received a getProvider message from client--*
Host Name: apus
Client User name: pklinker
Process id: 1182
Service Name: '140.188.18.70_IDL:visigenic.com/Activation/OAD:1.0'
Service Type: (4)
Argument type: NCObject
No such provider in my database.
Sending requests to other agents
   *-----------------------------------------------------------*
```

FIGURE 6.2   Osagent Output Screen #1

As this shows, the port number assigned at runtime to the automobile server is embedded in the new IOR.

Figures 6.2 through 6.5 show the output from the osagent as the client and server go through the connection process to return the new IOR to the client.

As can be seen in Figure 6.2, the well-known port of VisiBroker's locator service to 14045 is set, via an environment variable. The service now will listen only on that TCP port for connection requests. This allows multiple osagents or ORBS to run on different port numbers and not conflict. Setting discreet domains in this manner is useful in creating testing environments or running parallel networks on the same machine or an intersecting set of machines. Other ORB vendors, such as Iona, support this feature.

When the osagent runs in verbose mode, it binds to port 14045. At this point, the osagent binds to the following interfaces:

- The address 140.188.18.70, the machine on which it was started
- The address 255.255.255.0, the subnet mask
- The address 140.188.18.255.

```
****************************************************************
Time: Thu Apr 16 16:57:53 1998

*--- Received a registerSvc message from client ----*
Host Name: apus
Client User name: pklinker
Process id: 1182
Service Name: 'IDL:automobile:1.0'
Service Type: (4)
Argument type: NCObject
Internet address: 140.188.18.70
Port number: 33177
****************************************************************


****************************************************************
Time: Thu Apr 16 16:57:53 1998

*--- Received a registerSvc message from client--*
Host Name: apus
Client User name: pklinker
Process id: 1182
Service Name: '140.188.18.70_IDL:automobile:1.0'
Service Type: (4)
Argument type: NCObject
Internet address: 140.188.18.70
Port number: 33177
****************************************************************
```

FIGURE 6.3 Osagent Output Screen #2

Currently, host addresses are restricted, in IIOP version 1.1, to Classes A, B, and C Internet addresses. Class D Internet addresses are not allowed, as the OMG has reserved them for future versions of IIOP.

When a program starts up, it uses the broadcast address to send a broadcast message, looking for an osagent. If an osagent is listening at the broadcast address for messages from clients, it can begin a dialog with them. Broadcasting allows a subnet to have just one locator running for all hosts, rather than one per host. If two objects that are not in the same subnet must communicate, the osagent processes need to be configured to forward requests to osagents on other subnets.

Next, we start up the server, which creates and registers an instance of an automobile object, Ford Probe. See Figure 6.4. The ORB shows that the `Probe` object has registered itself, embedded in a server with the processID of 1182, running on the machine *apus,* and listening on the port number 33177. It is registered both with the IP address in the service name and without it. The osagent looks for an object activation daemon that can automatically start the `Probe` object upon an invocation; using an autostart mechanism prevents the

```
****************************************************
Time: Thu Apr 16 16:57:53 1998

*--- Received a registerSvc message from client ----*
Host Name: apus
Client User name: pklinker
Process id: 1182
Service Name: '140.188.18.70_IDL:automobile:1.0_probe'
Service Type: (4)
Argument type: NCObject
Internet address: 140.188.18.70
Port number: 33177
****************************************************


****************************************************
Time: Thu Apr 16 16:57:53 1998

*--- Received a registerSvc message from client--*
Host Name: apus
Client User name: pklinker
Process id: 1182
Service Name: 'IDL:automobile:1.0_probe'
Service Type: (4)
Argument type: NCObject
Internet address: 140.188.18.70
Port number: 33177
****************************************************
```

FIGURE 6.4   Osagent Output Screen #3

server from having to run continuously. It did not find an OAD, so it now registers the service. The service has the IDL interface automobile.

Finally, it registers the instance of the service, a `Probe` object. When the interface is registered, it is assigned a port number with which it will communicate with clients. It is this port number that is returned after the initial LocateRequest or Request message that was issued.

Now we start up the client, with the processID 23183, that will communicate with the server. The client does a Visibroker proprietary bind call, specifying the instance name and the interface of the object. The osagent replies to the client's get provider message with the IP address and port number of the automobile server. The client and server can now communicate on the port and address returned to the client. Once the communications are over, the client and then the server are shut down. The client is removed from the osagent process, since it will no longer be requesting services. The server is removed from the osagent process because it will no longer be offering services. The osagent reports to the client and server that each is requesting to be removed and then removes them.

```
*********************************************************
Time: Thu Apr 16 16:58:18 1998

*--- Received a login message from client ----*
Host Name: zeus
Client User name: pklinker
Process id: 23183
*********************************************************


*********************************************************
Time: Thu Apr 16 16:58:18 1998

*--- Received a getProvider message from client--*
Host Name: zeus
Client User name: pklinker
Process id: 23183
Service Name: 'IDL:automobile:1.0'
Service Type: (4)
Argument type: NCObject
Replying with the following provider.
Internet address: 140.188.18.70
Port number: 33177
*********************************************************
```

FIGURE 6.5   Osagent Output Screen #4

6.3.1   Diagram of Interactions during Connection

This section looks at a sequence diagram of the interactions between client, server, and osagent during the initial connection process.

Looking at the sequence diagrams in Figure 6.6, you can follow the flow of messages used to start and use a connection between a client and a server.

1. When the client and server start up, they first must check the environment to see if a broadcast port has been specified. The environment variable OSAGENT_PORT is used for this purpose. If it has not been set, the default port of 14000 is used.

2. The client and server also must obtain the address of the osagent. This is done using the UDP mechanism mentioned previously.

3. Once the address and port are determined, the server instantiates its object(s), registers them with the Basic Object Adapter (BOA), informs the osagent it is ready to receive requests, and finally listens for incoming connection requests. Note, the server must export its IOR to clients. For this example, assume that the client obtains the IOR from a naming service.

4. Once the client has the IOR and is ready to invoke an operation, it calls an operation on the proxy object and the proxy object issues a LocateRequest message.

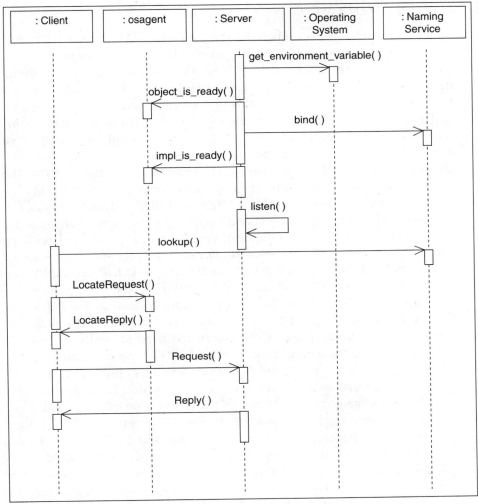

FIGURE 6.6 Sequence Diagram of a VisiBroker Connection

5. The osagent receives the message, finds the real IOR, and returns it to the client in a LocateReply message.

6. The client sends a Request message to the server pointed to by the returned IOR.

Note, this sequence will differ slightly if the client initially had the real IOR. In this case, the LocateRequest will go directly to the server instead of to the osagent.

6.4 Iona's Orbix

Iona's Orbix product uses much the same scheme as VisiBroker's in that it uses a daemon process that is running on a well-known port. Before a client invokes an operation on an object whose IOR has the same port as the port defined in the IT_DAEMON_PORT variable, it first sends a LocateRequest message. This message is received by the Orbix daemon, which then looks up the target object and replies with a LocateReply message. The LocateReply message has the reply_status set to LOCATION_FORWARD. Orbix does not use a UDP broadcast mechanism like VisiBroker. Instead, it uses a daemon process run on every machine that has a client or a server. However, this daemon also fills the role of VisiBroker's OAD, which is also required to run on every machine.

In this section, we look at the workings of IIOP in Orbix version 2.3. It is important to distinguish the version, as Iona made many changes to Orbix's IIOP implementation in moving from version 2.2 to 2.3. Orbix uses a proprietary protocol called POOP (Plain Old Orbix Protocol), and in versions 2.2 and earlier, the daemon process listened on one port for POOP connections and on a different port for IIOP connections. As with VisiBroker, these ports were well-known port numbers, defined by an environment variable. For POOP connections, the variable IT_DAEMON_PORT was used. This variable's value was typically set to the port address 1570, which has been officially assigned by the IETF (Internet Engineering Task Force). For IIOP connections, the variable IT_IIOP_PORT was used, generally having a value of port address 1571.

Iona simplified establishing a connection within the 2.3 version of Orbix by using the same port for IIOP and POOP connections. The standard variable and port number are IT_DAEMON_PORT and 1570, respectively. For the same port number to be used by different protocols, the daemon must have some way of determining what kind of connection is being established. It accomplishes this by looking at the message's Request header and forwarding the request to a decoder. Orbix's IORs use a proprietary object key, a regular Orbix object reference (for example, a POOP object reference).

Orbix requires that the port embedded within an IOR be valid throughout the lifetime of the system. This means that no matter how many times the server that holds the object is started and stopped, it must be able to be connected to, using the port in the IOR. There are two approaches for ensuring that the same port is used: An object can read its own IOR's port number and listen on that number, or the IOR can embed a well-known port number. Orbix uses the latter scheme, which lets the server use different port numbers whenever it starts up. Again, the port number is identified by the IT_DAEMON_PORT environment variable and is valid as long as the daemon process is running.

To connect to an object's server process using its IOR, Orbix 2.3 clients send a LocateRequest message to the object. Remember that the port number that the message is being sent to is not the port on which the server is listening. Rather, it is the port number on which the daemon process is listening. In previous versions of Orbix, a full Request message was sent; a Request message can be much larger than a LocateRequest message. The only benefit of sending a full Request message is that you might get a valid connection on the first try (for example, the port number in the IOR is the one on which the server is actually listening). Unless your system is exporting the IORs using the `object_to_string` call, your IORs will be embedded with the well-known port number. This means that it always takes two calls to get the real IOR. It is therefore desirable to make the first message as efficient as possible. Hence, Iona migrated from a full Request message to a LocateRequest message. Once that message is received by the daemon process, that process launches the server if necessary and responds with a LocateReply message. This message contains an IOR that indicates the port number on which the server is actually listening for requests.

Orbix has several features for manipulating IORs and port numbers. One is to make available a command line flag during object registration to ensure that the server is always assigned the same port by the daemon. Whenever the daemon launches the server, it instructs the server to listen on the port that was indicated during the registration process. Orbix also uses what is called a **persistent server,** a server that is launched by a mechanism other than a daemon process. When the object is registered with the daemon, a flag is used to tell the daemon not to generate a port number for the persistent server's objects. The persistent server handles embedding its own port number in its objects' generated IORs. When a client issues a LocateRequest message to the daemon process, the daemon routes the message directly to the server. The server responds using a LocateReply message that contains a status of OBJECT_HERE. This status indicates that the server can handle Request messages for the indicated object.

6.4.1   Diagram of Interactions during Connection

The Orbix connection sequence diagram, shown in Figure 6.7, is almost the same as VisiBroker's.

1. When the client and server start up, they first must check the environment to see if a broadcast port has been specified using the IT_DAEMON_PORT variable.

2. Once the port is determined, the server instantiates its object(s), registers them with the BOA, informs the daemon that it is ready to receive requests, and finally listens for incoming connection requests. Note, the server must export its IOR to clients. For this example, assume that the client obtains the IOR from a naming service.

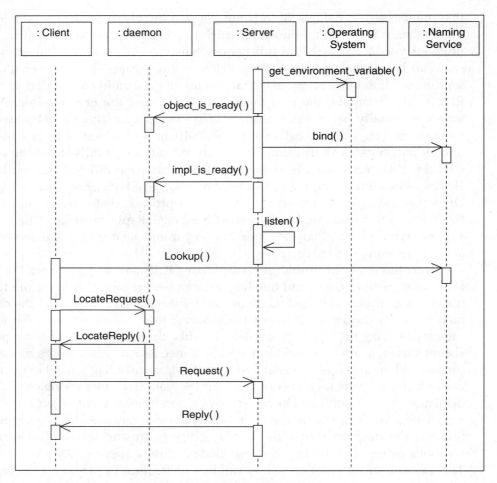

FIGURE 6.7 Sequence Diagram of an Orbix Connection

3. Once the client has attained the IOR and is ready to invoke an operation, it calls an operation on the proxy object and the proxy object issues a LocateRequest message.

4. The Orbix daemon receives this message, finds the real IOR, and returns it to the client in a LocateReply message.

5. The client sends a Request message to the server pointed to by the returned IOR.

6.5   Object Oriented Concept's OmniBroker

Object Oriented Concept's OmniBroker product does not use a well-known port number in its IORs. For the system to be bootstrapped, at some point a proxy object must be created to the real object on the server. Once this proxy object is created, other dynamic object references can be obtained at runtime (such as from a naming service). Creating a proxy object to the real object in the server requires first that an IOR with valid values be obtained. Once that is obtained, it is a simple matter to use the `string_to_object` call on the ORB to create an active object reference upon which operations may be invoked. Obtaining the initial IOR is generally done by reading it from a file.

All of this, of course, depends on the server's creating the IOR and then consistently running on the advertised host and port. The IOR can be stringified using the `object_to_string` call on the ORB, saved to a file, and then exported to clients for their subsequent use. To allow an object to consistently run on the host and port advertised in the IOR, OmniBroker provides a set of flags when the BOA is initialized. These flags allow the host name and port number to be set explicitly. When a server starts up, its IOR is read, the values extracted, and the BOA initialized to those values.

6.5.1   Diagram of Interactions during Connection

Figure 6.8 shows a sequence diagram of the interactions between client and server during the initial connection process. This sequence diagram differs somewhat from the previous two.

1. When the server starts up, it reads in persistent IOR and sends it to the naming service so that the client can retrieve and use it.

2. Once the client has done this and is ready to invoke an operation, it calls an operation on the object reference. It is important to remember that the act of a client's retrieving an IOR and taking it into its local process space (not as a stringified object reference) creates a proxy object.

3. The proxy object issues a LocateRequest message to the target object, which in turn sends back a LocateReply message, indicating the object is the correct one.

4. The client then sends a Request message to the target object to invoke the desired operation, and client and server interaction continues as normal.

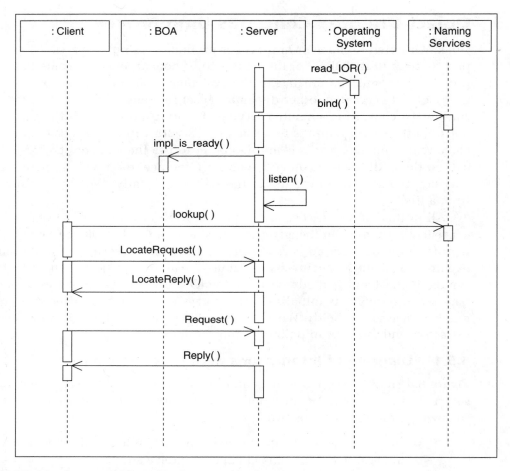

FIGURE 6.8   Sequence Diagram of an OmniBroker Connection

6.6   Interoperability between Different ORBs

Typically when you develop CORBA-based systems, you use a single ORB vendor's product. In some organizations, however, different departments might have independently picked different ORB vendors, and now you are tasked with making their components talk to yours. Or perhaps you are integrating a legacy system and the ORB you need to integrate it differs from the one you have been using. Whatever the motivation, you are tasked with making two ORBs interoperate.

If the ORB vendors' products are IIOP-compliant, as all major ones now are, interoperability is easy. By interoperability, we mean either of the following situations:

1. A CORBA client that was written using one ORB vendor's product (vendor A). The client uses stubs generated by vendor A's IDL compiler, as well as its IDL compiler. It also uses vendor A's CORBA libraries so CORBA messages sent by the client are generated by that vendor's GIOP implementation.

2. A CORBA object implementation that was written using another ORB vendor's product (vendor B). The object uses skeletons generated by vendor B's IDL compiler, as well as the vendor's CORBA libraries for reading and writing GIOP messages.

Now, given a client implemented with vendor A's ORB and a server containing objects implemented with vendor B's ORB, the client needs to use the object's resources. First, the client needs to obtain an IOR to the object so that it can connect to it. Once it has the IOR, it can invoke on the object as if it had been written using the same ORB product as the client. The primary problem with interoperating between IIOP-compliant ORBs is obtaining IORs to the desired objects. This is typically solved by flattening the IOR into a string and exporting it, by using a naming service or other directory service, or by retrieving it from a trading service.

Since all of the vendors have different ways of initially connecting clients to their desired objects, we felt the best way to test interoperability was to use standard OMG mechanisms. The first one that came to mind, and in our opinion the most straightforward, is a stringified IOR. Using Omnibroker's "Hello World!" example,[1] we rebuilt the client using VisiBroker 3.2 for C++ on Solaris.

Following is the IDL for the "Hello World!" example.

```
interface Hello
{
   void hello();
};
```

This is a single interface with one operation that takes no parameters and returns no data. For our purposes, this example will suffice. The main point of this interoperability example is to show that IORs can be used to connect clients and servers from different vendors, not to show that the vendors' GIOP streams are compliant. The best way to guarantee interoperability of the GIOP streams is to examine the message buffer in an interceptor, which should contain the GIOP message stream, for errors in compliance.

Next is the server code of the "Hello World!" example. The first set of code shows the implementation of the Hello object. The first operation is the

---

[1] All of the example code (excluding some extensions and comments by the authors) comes from Object Oriented Concept's OmniBroker demo code, Object-Oriented Concepts, Inc., 1977 (Billerica, Mass.).

interface's implementation class constructor. The second is the implementation of the `hello` operation. It simply prints out the message "Hello World!" to standard output.

```
// Hello object constructor
Hello_impl::Hello_impl()
{
}

// The hello operation, prints out a message.
void
Hello_impl::hello()
{
    cout < "Hello World!" < endl;
}
```

The next set of code is the main routing of the server code. It creates the `Hello` object and exports that object's IOR to the file system for clients to obtain. It exports its IOR to the file system by making an `object_to_string` call and then saving the string to a file named `Hello.ref`. Once the IOR has been exported, the server calls `impl_is_ready` to tell the BOA that the server can now accept requests from clients on the IOR it has just published.

```
int main(int argc, char* argv[], char*[])
{
    try
    {
      //
      // Create ORB and BOA
      //
      CORBA_ORB_var orb = CORBA_ORB_init(argc, argv);
      CORBA_BOA_var boa = orb -> BOA_init(argc, argv);

      //
      // Create implementation object
      //
      Hello_var p = new Hello_impl;

      //
      // Save reference to the file system. The reference is
      // stored in a file named "Hello.ref"
      //
      CORBA_String_var s = orb -> object_to_string(p);
```

```
const char* refFile = "Hello.ref";
ofstream out(refFile);

// Error handling code.
if(out.fail())
{
    extern int errno;
    cerr < argv[0] < ": can't open `" < refFile < "`: "
        < strerror(errno) < endl;
    return 1;
}

// Write the IOR to standard out.
out < s < endl;
out.close();

//
// Run implementation
//
boa -> impl_is_ready(CORBA_ImplementationDef::_nil());
}
// Catch any system exceptions that may be raised.
catch(CORBA_SystemException& ex)
{
  OBPrintException(ex);
  return 1;
}

return 0;
}
```

Finally, the client code invokes the `hello` operation on the `Hello` object. The client imports the `Hello` object by loading the contents of the `Hello.ref` file into a string. It then does a `string_to_object` call to create a proxy object that it can use for invocations. Next, it invokes the `hello` operation on the object and displays its contents to standard output.

```
int main(int argc, char* argv[], char*[])
{
    try
    {
      //
      // Create ORB
```

```
    //
    CORBA_ORB_var orb = CORBA::ORB_init(argc, argv);

    //
    // Get the "hello" object by reading it in from the
// "Hello.ref" file that the server created.
    //
    const char* refFile = "Hello.ref";
    ifstream in;
    in.open(refFile);

    // Error handling code.
    if(in.fail())
    {
        extern int errno;
        cerr < argv[0] < ": can't open `" < refFile < "': "
            < strerror(errno) < endl;
         return 1;
     }

    char s[1000];
    in > s;

    CORBA::Object_var obj = orb -> string_to_object(s);
    assert(!CORBA::is_nil(obj));

    Hello_var hello = Hello::_narrow(obj);
    assert(!CORBA::is_nil(hello));

    //
    // Main loop
    //
    cout < "Enter 'h' for hello or 'x' for exit:\n";
    char c;
    do
    {
        cout < "> ";
        cin > c;
        if(c == 'h')
            hello -> hello();
    }
    while(c != 'x');
}
```

```
    catch(CORBA::SystemException& ex)
    {
      return 1;
    }

      return 0;
}
```

By now, you should be familiar with how the client and server operate. To show an example of interoperability, we kept the OmniBroker server, using OmniBroker's ORB libraries and initialization code. We then recompiled the client using the VisiBroker 3.0 ORB libraries. Next, we ran the server and client and produced the expected, correct, results.

Figure 6.9 shows the steps that take place in the example. The following output shows the results of those steps. First, we look at the IOR that was written to the operating system and used to establish the connection. The stringified representation of it can be viewed in the Hello.ref file:

```
IOR:000000000000000e49444c3a48656c6c6f3a312e300000000000000001000000
000000003a000100000000000f3134302e3138382e31382e323139002013890000
0000001a4f422f49442b4e554d0049444c3a48656c6c6f3a312e30003000
```

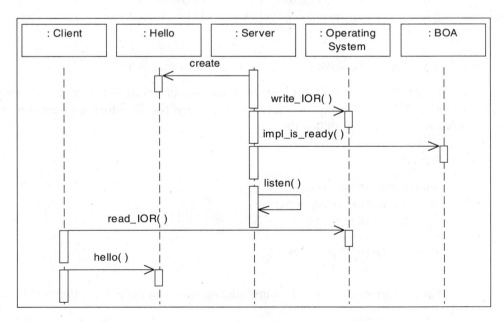

FIGURE 6.9   Sequence of Events in the Example

Using VisiBroker's IOR printing utility, we can examine the contents of the IOR:

```
>printIOR Hello.ref
Interoperable Object Reference:
Type ID: IDL:Hello:1.0
Contains 1 profile.
Profile 0-IIOP Profile:
   version: 1.0
   host: 140.188.18.219
   port: 5001
   Object Key: ForeignId[object_key={26 bytes:
[O][B][/][I][D][+][N][U][M](0)[I][D][L][:][H][e][l][l][o][:][1][.]
[0](0)[0](0)}]
```

Embedded in the IOR is the version number, host address, and port number. Note that the object key is a foreign key created by OmniBroker (by the prefix OB); it contains the IDL definition of the object.

Following are the results of the client and server processes executing. The client is running on the machine *apus,* and the server is running on the machine *zeus.*

Client

```
apus:/home/zeus/pklinker/test_stuff/example3: client
Enter 'h' for hello or 'x' for exit:
> h
> x
apus:/home/zeus/pklinker/test_stuff/example3:
```

Typing "h" on the client results in the server printing the message "Hello World!" Before running the server, we look up the IP address of *zeus* to see what it is and if it matches the IOR.

Server

```
zeus:> nslookup zeus
Server: buster.epd.prc.com
Address: 140.188.18.232

Name: zeus.epd.prc.com
Address: 140.188.18.219
```

The IP address of *zeus* is the same address that is in the IOR printed previously.

```
zeus:> server
```

```
Warning: ORB::BOA_init: gethostbyname() returned domainless name
using dotted decimal notation instead of hostname
Hello World!
zeus:>
```

This example shows that bootstrapping disparate systems is fairly easy, as long as:

- the client can get the IOR and
- the server uses the advertised IOR elements.

Both of these criteria were met in this example, so the client and server were able to connect and communicate successfully. The VisiBroker client had a valid IOR and used the information in it to connect directly to the Omnibroker server. It went straight to the server with the LocateRequest message, and Omnibroker replied that the IOR was valid. Because we had a valid IOR, we were able to bypass the osagent service and connect immediately. This is the case internally with VisiBroker as well. The osagent service and other vendors' proprietary location services are provided as a convenience mechanism. They are not able to find another ORB's objects. This is the reason for IIOP and IORs.

6.7   Interoperability from IIOP

As was shown in Section 6.6, although the various ORB vendors have slightly different strategies for handling bootstrapping and location independence of IORs, basic interoperability between them is quite easy. The real issue becomes enhancing interoperability between clients and servers that have no prior knowledge of each other. Perhaps extending IORs to include a field for XML (eXtended Markup Language) links could greatly increase interoperability. An IOR is simply metadata about an object that describes its location and name. A client could use an XML link as metadata about the object's semantics to download an XML document that defines a mapping or translation from the object's interface semantics to the client's. Extending the IOR to provide more metadata about an object is the key to CORBA's continuing success.

This chapter has given the reader detailed insight into how IIOP has been implemented by three different vendors. The key points of this chapter were:

- There is more than one way to implement IIOP
- IIOP works as advertised and ensures interoperability between ORBs
- Location transparency is directly related to how host and port information is handled in the IOR
- These example implementations are not the only methods of implementing IIOP

Emerging CORBA
Specifications and IIOP

7.1   Requirements of the Next Generation

The OMG has a number of pending changes to base CORBA technologies. These include asynchronous messaging, passing objects by value, and firewall security. When implemented in future ORBs, these will greatly increase CORBA's usefulness in the enterprise.

In this chapter, we introduce you to some of the emerging technologies that will have a profound effect on how GIOP and IIOP will work in the future.

7.2   CORBA Messaging

CORBA traditionally offers two modes of operation invocation: synchronous and deferred synchronous. During a synchronous operation, the caller is blocked until the operation is finished and a reply is returned. This type is the only invocation method available to statically compiled stubs. During a deferred synchronous operation the caller continues execution after the call is made, but continues polling for the operation's results. Deferred synchronous operations are available only by using the Dynamic Invocation Interface (DII). The DII, however, is difficult to use (we have yet to meet anyone who uses it in a real system). There is a need for truly asynchronous communications. Asynchronous capability would give developers much more flexibility and power when developing applications.

Specifically it will touch on the new types of asynchronous messages. These new types of messages are described in the *CORBA Messaging Specification*. The new types are polling, time independent invocations, and extensions to the existing oneway invocation type. In covering these, they will be compared to the existing callback model that may be used with the current CORBA specification.

There is a need for truly asynchronous communications. For an invocation to be asynchronous, the requesting client must not be in a blocked state while the server processes the invocation. With the current invocation-response model, however, the client *is* blocked while the invocation is processed. This is not always desirable; examples of when this is problematic are easy to find. For example, suppose you have a set of clients and a server that serves up automobile images. Clients retrieve images from the server that they display to users. The clients can specify the image format that they require, and the server will convert the image to that format. For application programmers, designing clients and server-side objects with the current ORB implementations usually requires the use of one of two techniques. The first is to simply have the client block on the retrieve image call. The second is to have the client create a callback object and pass a callback object reference to the server.

The second method uses standard CORBA. It requires that the client recreate a callback object and pass it to the server. The server then immediately returns control to the client and begins processing the request. When the server is done loading and converting the image, it passes it to the client via the callback object. The key to the second technique is the use of threads. The server, when it receives the request for the image, schedules a thread to handle the request and then returns. This technique has several drawbacks. First, programming this multithreaded model can be complicated. Second, this technique requires that the thread be available. Last, and most important, by passing an object reference to a server the client itself becomes a server and thereby incurs all of the added complexity and expense that being a server implies. Now that we have seen two standard ways CORBA may be used to retrieve information, we can look at new models of communication. These new models extend the asynchronous capabilities of CORBA, providing store and forward capabilities. They are the callback model, the polling model and time-independent invocation model.

7.2.1   Asynchronous Invocation Models

Asynchronous invocations are so common, and so necessary, that the OMG put out an RFP for an asynchronous messaging specification. In response, a coalition of CORBA vendors submitted the *CORBA Messaging Specification.* This specification defines two asynchronous invocation models:

- Callback
- Polling

According to the callback model, clients pass a reference to a callback object as part of operation. The polling model calls for the invocation to return an object that may be queried at any time to obtain the status of the pending request. In the first case, the client creates the object, and in the second, the server creates the object.

7.2.1.1 Callback Model

The callback model uses the notion of a callback object that the client passes to the server. This callback object is used by the server to return information to the client. Using a callback prevents the server from having to block while it waits for the server to finish processing its request. However, how does a client know when the server has invoked upon the callback? Threads can solve the problem of callbacks.

The use of threads allow the client's main thread of execution to continue while another thread waits for the callback to receive an invocation. However, they make programming an application more complex and can introduce more errors. It often requires synchronization, uses extra resources, and can introduce memory management problems. For example, if an object exists in a separate thread, when may it be deleted? If it is a callback object, maybe it can be deleted after it receives an invocation, but maybe not. It might be a callback that requires a series of invocations before it is deleted. Generally, deletion policy must be dictated by the system, and maintaining the memory in a separate thread makes it all the more difficult to obtain the reference to delete it. To solve these thread issues, at least in regard to asynchronous invocation, the *CORBA Messaging Specification* has callback and polling mechanisms.

The *CORBA Messaging Specification* callback mechanism behaves in the same way as the application-level multithreaded callback model. The client object passes a callback object to the server as part of an invocation. When the server is ready to reply, the callback object gets invoked upon and the data is passed to the client.

The polling model differs from the callback model in that the invocation object returns an object that might be queried at any time to obtain the status of the outstanding request. Instead of using application-level threads, the specification's callback model uses a callback object that is handled automatically by the ORB. For this model to work, there can be no requirement for application-level multithreading on the client-side developer's part. This model is the "fire and forget" callback style. The "fire and forget" style means once the client has passed the callback object to the server, it may continue processing without blocking or checking on the server's progress. When the server is done, it will use the callback to inform the client so that the client does not have to poll for the results. The model allows for deferred synchronous behavior, if desired. It uses the concept of a ReplyHandler. This ReplyHandler is a CORBA object that is implemented by the client application. It gets passed via an asynchronous method invocation. When the server is ready to return the results, it invokes on the ReplyHandler, passing it the results. If you are making a time-independent invocation (discussed shortly), then the ReplyHandler must be a persistent object reference, as opposed to a transient object reference.

7.2.1.2 Polling Model

Another messaging model is the polling model. This model has a CORBA value, called a **poller,** that is implemented by the messaging-aware ORB. When an asynchronous method is invoked, using the polling model, a poller is returned from that invocation. The client then uses the poller to either poll or block while in deferred synchronous mode until a response is available. Use of the polling model during a time-independent invocation results in a persistent poller's being returned. A time-independent invocation is an invocation in which the reply may outlive the client process that sent the request. We cover this concept in more detail next. (In both the callback and the polling models, if you use a time-independent invocation, you must use a persistent object.) A reference to this poller can be passed from one client to another so that any client can query its state to determine the status of the invocation.

7.2.2 Time-Independent Invocations

We need to cover time-independent invocations because they might demand the definition of an interoperable store-and-forward capability that IIOP currently does not support. This capability provides a better level of delivery reliability. As you will see, a client may receive a reply far removed in time from the corresponding request. Rather than the client's application having to be running continuously, it may be shut down and reactivated later, when the reply arrives. If the client is unavailable or unable to be reactivated, the ability to store and forward the reply later enhances the chance of its delivery. Time-independent invocations require that a routing protocol be defined, along with several other extensions to GIOP, including additions to the protocol, such as additional service context definitions, and a newly defined IOR tag component. These extensions, along with the Request and Reply routing agents, provide enough functionality to satisfy the requirements of time-independent invocations. Currently, no known vendors have implemented these extensions to GIOP, and the *CORBA Messaging Specification* has not been formally adopted, as of this writing. We cover it, however, because we assume that ORB manufacturers will support it at some point. We do not show the extensions in the main IIOP and GIOP chapters, since no current implementations exist.

Essentially, a **time-independent invocation** is a request for results for which the client does not want to wait. Such a request may be, for example, an overnight batch job, and the client application should not be left running all night just to wait for the results. The motivation for a time-independent invocation is to decouple the request-reply cycle from the life span of the client process. In other words, the client may issue a request and then, rather than wait for a reply from the object, shut down. When the reply is sent, the client is reactivated and receives it. For a time-independent invocation, the client creates an object that will receive the results of the invocation. Suppose that in the batch job example, you are going to do a series of operations that do calculations and then store the results of those calculations in a file for later viewing. You do not need to see the results of the operations right away and instead want the batch job to handle creating all of the necessary results files. As each calculation is finished, the results are written to a file; you have no idea how long each operation takes you to complete. By necessity, these operations are time-independent. As you can see by this example, if you wish to inquire at any point in time about the status of the batch job, you need to be able to obtain a persistent object reference. Once this is obtained, you can query it for the status. The object need not always be running; it may be started by an activation daemon upon an invocation. When the ORB detects an invocation on an object that is not running, it hands off the information to the activation daemon. That daemon will start the object, which must reinternalize its state, so that it may handle the request.

7.2.3 One-Way Invocations

In keeping with the need to manage time resources during an invocation, the *CORBA Messaging Specification* allows one-way operations to be synchronized to control when the ORB returns control to a client. One-way invocations are not truly asynchronous, but rather deferred synchronous. There are four types of synchronization, identified by the type `SyncScope`:

1. *SYNC_NONE*. The ORB returns control to the client before the Request message is passed to the transport layer.

2. *SYNC_WITH_TRANSPORT*. The ORB returns control to the client after the Request message has been passed to the transport layer and is accepted.

3. *SYNC_WITH_SERVER*. The operation is passed to the server, but before the operation is executed, a Reply message is sent to the client.

4. *SYNC_WITH_TARGET*. The operation is passed to the server, the operation is executed, and then a Reply message is sent to the client. This is the same as a standard synchronous request.

We have shown the different possible techniques for asynchronous communications in CORBA, assuming the adoption of the *CORBA Messaging Specification*. The addition of these new methods will allow greater flexibility in the decoupling of communications. They are of particular interest to those who need messaging systems such as pagers, notification services, and event services. They allow CORBA invocations to be held and sent at a later more opportune time, such as when a pager is turned on. These new extensions, however, will require some updates to the CORBA communication protocol.

7.2.4   IIOP and GIOP Messaging Changes

In this section, we cover the primary focus of this book—the changes to GIOP and IIOP required by the *CORBA Messaging Specification*.

The *CORBA Messaging Specification* is designed to support communications where the client and target are disconnected for long periods of time. To support this the target should be able to specify a temporary destination for messages. This temporary destination is a router and is specified in the target's IOR. The router is used to forward messages to other routers and to synchronously deliver a message to its target. The router will need to modify the Request header of a message in order to store it or forward it to another router.

The specification addresses four issues that arise when an attempt is made to use routing agents to redirect individual Request and Reply messages along the path to and from caller to target.

1. *Inability to remarshall the header without remarshalling the entire message.* The marshalled arguments are in the same CDR stream that starts at the beginning of the message. This means that the lengths of the service contexts and object key affect the way in which the message payload is marshalled. This is due to the alignment restrictions mentioned in Chapter 4.

2. *Use of* `RequestHeader::response_expected`. This field must be defined specifically so that the synchrony of the call can be determined.

3. *Fragmentation.* The fragments cannot be interleaved because only the lead fragment has the requestID.

4. *Version requirements.* A new version of GIOP is required.

These four issues are solved with a new Request header and new messaging rules, described next. Following is the new GIOP 1.2 Request header IDL definition. None of the other headers, including the message header, change for GIOP 1.2.

```
module GIOP { // IDL extended for version 1.2
  // GIOP 1.2
  typedef MessageHeader_1_1 MessageHeader_1_2;

  struct RequestHeader_1_2 {
    IOP::ServiceContextList service_context;
    unsigned long request_id;
    octet response_flags;
    octet reserved[3];
    sequence<octet> object_key;
    string operation;
    Principal requesting_principal;
  };
};
```

GIOP 1.2 changes the Request header in only one way: The `response_expected boolean` member becomes the member `response_flags` of type `octet`. `Response_flags` can be one of three values:

1. 00000000 (binary) for a `SyncScope` of `SYNC_NONE` or a `SyncScope` of `SYNC_WITH_TRANSPORT`
2. 00000001 (binary) for a `SyncScope` of `SYNC_WITH_SERVER`
3. 00000011 (binary) for a `SyncScope` of `SYNC_WITH_TARGET`

In GIOP 1.0 and 1.1, the Request body was placed in the CDR stream directly after the Request header. In GIOP 1.2, the Request body is aligned on an eight-octet boundary. Recall from Chapter 4 that the maximum alignment of a primitive type is eight octets. Placing the Request body after the order-aligned Request header guarantees it will not require remarshalling if the message header or the Request header is modified. This is because no more padding will be needed at the start of the body, no matter how much or how little data is added to the header.

The Reply message is similar to the Request message in that it must be able to support routing-induced adjustments to its header. Thus, the increased potential of change to the Reply header means that the Reply body should start on an eight-octet boundary. Similar to Request headers, if the Reply header changes, the Reply body will not have to be remarshalled.

The Fragment message should support being multiplexed. To support this capability, the requestID is added to each message fragment, not just to the initial fragment. As with a nonfragmented Reply message, the requestID in every fragment of a Reply identifies the corresponding LocalRequest or Request for which the Reply is being returned.

With the addition of the *CORBA Messaging Specification* IIOP will have a new version number. It now supports version 1.2. Note also that `Principal` has been deprecated and should be removed from the protocol.

7.3   Pass by Value

7.3.1   Introduction

If you have ever tried to use CORBA to pass large amounts of especially complex data, you've probably wished you could create an object locally, fill it with data, and then hand it off to some other component. This was not possible, however—until the addition to the CORBA specification of the ability to pass objects by value. Until then, all objects passed as parameters were passed by reference. Passing by reference is usually a good thing, because the client's language and platform might be separate from the object, yet the client might still use the object. A client might be, for example, a Java client running on an NT workstation, while the server is written in C++ and running on a Solaris server. Often, however, it's useful to create an object to hold data and then pass it to a distributed server. The server then has its own local copy of the object, thereby leaving the client free to delete it. Passing an object in this way is passing it *by value* rather than by reference.

7.3.2   Why Pass by Value?

What is the rationale behind passing objects by value instead of by reference? As mentioned in the previous section, often you want to pass data encapsulated within an object. Encapsulation data in an object allows you to protect it to some degree, provide additional processing capability on the data, and express complex data easily.

Using the example from Chapter 4, we change the `VehicleInfo` structure to a value type and an interface (Table 7.1). We then can pass around vehicle

Table 7.1   Changing the `VehicleInfo` Structure

CORBA Interface	CORBA Value Type
```interface VehicleInfo {```	```valuetype VehicleInfo {```
``` attribute short doors;```	``` public short doors;```
``` attribute string make;```	``` public string make;```
``` attribute string model;```	``` public string model;```
``` attribute float cost;```	``` public float cost;```
``` attribute VehicleType auto_type```	``` public VehicleType auto_type;```
```}```	```}```

information by passing the object either by reference or by value. These different methods have very different design models.

In the case of passing by reference, suppose that the object was created remotely. As shown in the reference row of Figure 7.1, the object implementation will live on the server side. Suppose also that a client wants to pass a `VehicleInfo` object to an automobile dealer object on the server. It remotely calls a factory to create a `VehicleInfo` object. The factory then returns a reference to the newly created object (for simplicity, assume the factory and the automobile dealer object are in the same server process). Next, the client makes a remote call back to the server to set each of the attributes of the `VehicleInfo` object. When the client is done setting the object data, it passes the object reference to the automobile dealer object. This method of data passing requires a large number of network calls in order to populate the `VehicleInfo` object.

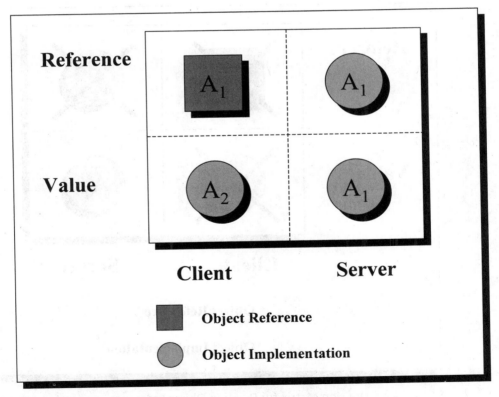

FIGURE 7.1   Decision Matrix for Object Reference and Implementation

When the object is passed by value instead of by reference, the client creates the `VehicleInfo` object locally and subsequently sets the attributes locally. When done, it passes the object to the automobile dealer object. At this point, the receiver will have its own local copy of the project. As shown in the Value row of Figure 7.1, there are two copies of the object implementation, one on the server and one on the client. If the client is finished with the object, it may delete its own local copy without affecting the automobile dealer's copy. This is shown in Figure 7.2, where the value A_2 is deleted from the client side, but A_1 still exists on the server side. When the automobile dealer is finished with the object, it too may delete its local copy, without affecting the client's copy.

The management of an object passed by reference is more complex. If the client deletes the object (using the lifecycle service, it could delete the actual implementation object) before the server is finished with it, an error will occur. This also is shown in Figure 7.2, where object A_1 is deleted from the server by

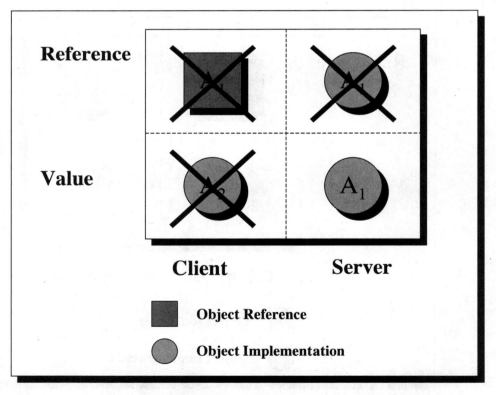

FIGURE 7.2.   Decision Matrix for Deleting Object Reference and Implementation

the client, thereby rendering all references no longer valid. An object activation scheme could be employed to reactivate it, but this is inefficient; the object should not be deleted if it is still being used. Reference count would not help either, since the factory that created the `VehicleInfo` object returned a reference to it only once (to the client), even though two entities have reference to it. To protect if from accidental or premature deletion, you need to use locks. Alternatively, you could programmatically let both parties know that the automobile dealer object now controls the lifecycle of the `VehicleInfo` object, even though the client created it. As you can see, managing an object is easier and more efficient by creating it locally and passing it by value, rather than creating it remotely and passing it by reference.

To sum up, passing by value allows a client to create an object, populate it with data, pass it to a server, and be done with it. To create the object on the server side and begin setting the parameters puts you back to passing data across the wire. Either the parameter data is passed in chunks via a mechanism like a Name-Value list, or every attribute must be set via a set option(s). What is the purpose of using an object if the object's state must be set by passing it across the wire and then a reference to the object passed to an awaiting recipient, who most likely itself must extract the data across the wire. In this case, designers usually use structures. Something between a structure and a standard CORBA interface would be useful—an object type that allows us to create the object locally, set the parameters locally, and pass the object to the receiver, where the data can then be extracted locally. CORBA value types may be used to pass complex data around, whereas interfaces are primarily used for services (coarse-grained objects as opposed to fine-grained objects). The values support the description of complex state, so any relationships that an object has with other objects, for example, a cyclical graph, also can be supported with the value type.

By now, you might be asking, why not create a nonvalue CORBA object on the client side, set the data there, and pass the object reference to the server side? If the client creates an object locally to hold data and passes a reference to it to a server, this adds several constraints on the client.

1. It becomes a server capable of handling requests on the object that it created.

2. The client cannot delete the object until it is sure that the server it passed it to has finished using it. This makes programming the client much more complex and error-prone. It also makes the client a heavier-weight client. In the age of thin clients, written with small applets, HTTP, and JavaScript, many organizations do not want to add a lot of capabilities to their clients, such as the ability to receive requests. In these cases, pass by value might be a natural fit.

7.3.3   How It Works

The OMG, recognizing that sometimes objects should be passed by value rather than by reference, added to the CORBA specification the capability to pass CORBA objects by value. The addition of value objects extends CORBA to support the passing of objects that encapsulate data or for copying objects. It is not designed for replication or caching. Pass by value in CORBA is similar to pass by value in standard programming languages. In those languages, when a parameter is passed by value the receiver of the parameter gets a new instance of that parameter that has a completely separate identity from the original parameter. Therefore, once the parameter passing is complete, no relationship exists between the original and the new parameters. So it is with pass by value in CORBA.

When an object is passed by value, the receiving side must create an instance of that object. Thus it must know something about the object's state. CORBA extended the OMG IDL to support the addition of the `value` type. The OMG decided to allow flexibility when an object is received so that the object may be received as a standard CORBA object reference or as a value. To support this, it defined an abstract interface type that allows an operation to explicitly support receiving either the value or the interface type at runtime. Like a structure, a value object is always local to the context in which it is used because it is copied when it is passed as a parameter.

A value, like classes in C++ and Java, supports both public and private data members. Because of this, values may be used to specify the state of an object's implementation. This means that they may support data members from an ordinary interface. Values, however, are not CORBA objects—they do not inherit from CORBA::Object. A value object, however, like any other object can support a CORBA interface. A value type that is declared as supporting an interface may be passed by reference, as long as it has been registered with the ORB, like a standard CORBA interface implementation. The essential property of the value type is that its implementation will always be local. Thus any operation on a value type will always be a local call and never a remote call.

Value types come in two flavors: concrete and abstract. Concrete value types may be stateful, whereas abstract cannot. Abstract value types are essentially a collection of operations that may be invoked upon locally. Concrete value types are more advanced; they allow for inheritance from both multiple interfaces and a single value type. Abstract types, on the other hand, may inherit from multiple value types. Concrete value types allow for arbitrary recursive value type definitions so data structures may be defined. Concrete types also support the notion of null objects.

When a concrete data type is passed as a parameter, the sending context needs to marshall the object's state data and pass it to the receiving context. The receiving context will then instantiate a new (local) instance of the value.

All of the information passed must be sufficient to recreate the object and must be passed in a GIOP message. An object transmits its type information and state data as a repositoryID. The specification assumes that both the sender and receiver have available implementations of the value object. All that happens on the receiving end is that an instance of the value time is created and set with the state data. It also might be downloadable, for example, by using Java. This downloadable code can be pointed to using a URL. Using a URL is a standard and well-known way to advertise resources. URLs enable the on-the-wire format to support an optional callback object called a **codebase,** which allows the receiving context to download the implementation. The loading of the code is outside of the scope of the GIOP specification.

Value objects also introduce the notion of truncation. To truncate an object is to cut off part of its type information so that it becomes one of its base types. A value object may be truncated if it is specified in the IDL as `truncatable`. This indicates that it is safe to truncate the object to its immediate nonabstract parent value. When an object is passed, it may be sent as normal but received as a truncated type. For this to occur, GIOP must provide information about to what types the object may be truncated.

Having discussed the basis of pass by value, we examine how it affects IIOP and GIOP.

7.3.4   GIOP/IIOP Extensions and Mapping

The ability to pass objects by value has led to new messaging requirements in the GIOP 1.2 specification. The extensions to the GIOP message protocol support the passing of complex object state by value, specifically, the transmission of an object's state and type information (encoded as repositoryIDs). The new specification states that the loading (and possible transmission) of code is outside of the scope of the IIOP definition but that enough information must be carried to support recreation of the object at the destination. This means that when one CORBA application, A, is passing an object by value to another CORBA application, B, it must pass enough information so that a new object can be created in B, and then the object's state is reinternalized. The GIOP format also allows for custom marshalling so that a value object may be encoded using application-defined code. Custom types cannot be truncated. Custom marshalling was included in the value extensions for CORBA to help integrate "existing 'class libraries' and other legacy systems." The OMG recommends that as a standard practice, you do not write your own custom marshalling.

The encoding compactly supports all of the features of value types. It also supports the splitting of value types into fragments or chunks. Value objects may have references to or contain other value objects. When a value object is passed by value, all of the value objects it contains or references must be passed as well.

The encoding of the object values occurs in a depth-first manner and is recursive, similar to that used for TypeCodes. If a value occurs more than once in an encoding, an indirection is used to point to it, rather than its being encoded again. The data members are written beginning with the highest possible base type to the most derived type in the order that they were declared in the IDL.

A value encoding starts with a value header and is followed by a list of value chunks. The header contains the following (in this order):

1. A value tag
2. A codebase URL, if appropriate
3. The repositoryID
4. An octet flag of bits

The value tag indicates the presence of type information and codebase URL information in the encoding. This information is not necessary for all encodings—only when features such as truncation are used. The value tag is a `long` with a range of `0x7fffff00` and `0x7fffffff`, inclusive. The last octet indicates if additional information is present. If the least significant bit (<value_tag> & `0x00000001`) equals 1, then a codebase URL follows the value tag in the encoding. If the least significant bit is 0, then no codebase URL is present. The second and third least significant bits (<value-tag> & `0x00000006`) are used to indicate type information. If the value is 0, then no type information is present in the encoding, thereby indicating that the actual parameter is the same type as the formal argument. A value of 2 indicates that only a single repositoryID is present in the encoding. Therefore, the actual value's most derived type is the same as the static type of the position being marshalled. Finally, if the value is 6, then the partial type reformation host of repositoryIDs is present in the encoding as a long, thereby indicating the number of repositoryIDs followed by the repositoryIDs themselves. These repositoryIDs indicate all of the base types to which it is safe to truncate the value.

The same repositoryID and codebase URL may be repeated many times in a single request when a complex graph is being sent. However, adding the repositoryID and URL every time that they occur wastes space. Instead, they are encoded as a regular string the first time that they appear and then as an indirection for later occurrences. The octet flag, which currently has a value of zero and is reserved by the OMG for later use, contains information that simplifies operating on value types.

7.3.4.1 Partial Type Information and Versioning

The GIOP format provides support for partial type information and versioning issues in the receiving context. The type information is specified by providing a list of repositoryIDs, preceded by a `long` specifying the number of repositoryIDs.

The first repositoryID identifies the real type of the value; it must always be present. The value's real type may be a derived type, in which case the base types must be sent as well. The sender is responsible for listing the repositoryIDs for all of the base types from which the real type is derived. These base types go up the derivation hierarchy and include, if appropriate, the formal type. If the typing information received by the receiving context is insufficient, the receiving context may go back to the sending context to look up more typing information based on the repositoryID. CORBA repositoryIDs also contain standard version identification (major and minor version numbers). The ORB is responsible for determining whether the version of the value being transmitted is compatible with the version expected and to apply any appropriate truncation/conversion rules (with the help of a local interface repository or the `SendingContext::RunTime` service). The RMI model of communication/conversion across versions can be supported here.

7.3.4.2   Scope of the Indirections

To direct the decoder to go somewhere else in the marshalling buffer to find what it is looking for, we must use a special value. A value of `0xffffffff` introduces an indirection, which may be either a URL that has already been encoded or another value object that is shared in a graph. The tag `0xffffffff` is always followed by a `long` indicating where to go in the buffer. As mentioned in Section 7.3.4, the encoding used for value object indirection is almost the same as that used for recursive TypeCodes. The two differ only in that object value indirections are assumed to work across more than one parameter so that the same value object can be shared across multiple parameters of an IDL call. This keeps a value from being sent more than once.

7.3.4.3   Fragmentation

An object, with all of its state data, can get rather large—and when the object is a graph, it can get extremely large. Sending one of these large objects over a network can potentially cause problems. For example, the program that is sending or receiving the object might need to dedicate most, if not all, of its processor and I/O resources to moving the object. If the object is being transmitted over a low-bandwidth connection, such as a modem-based connection, the problem is significantly exacerbated. A server serving up a large number of objects by value to multiple clients could have a serious problem meeting load requirements. However, if the server could time-slice and send the object a chunk at a time rather than all at once, it could increase the number of clients that it can handle simultaneously.

The drafters of the pass by value extension, recognizing this problem, added support for splitting serialized objects into an arbitrary number of chunks. No restrictions apply to what types may be fragmented; any given

CDR type representation may be split. Fragmentation of the CDR stream should be invisible to the upper layers of the ORB. Specifically, the CDR stream is responsible for reassembling the chunked data for the marshalling code's use.

When chunking is used, the stream indicates to the ORB that chunking is occurring by adding a tag at the beginning of the value. At the beginning of each chunk is its length, encoded as a positive `long`. An end tag indicates when a value is terminated. The end tag is a nonpositive `long`, which differentiates it from the start of another chunk.

Chunking is usually a relatively straightforward task. It can get complicated, however, if values that contain other values are chunked (e.g., linked lists). In these situations, the "recursive" value is started without an end tag. When the end tag finally appears, it indicates how many values are being terminated.

The ORB uses this tag to determine how many levels of recursion exist so that the relationship may be correctly reconstructed. Following are the rules concerning chunking.

- End tags and value size tags are encoded using non-overlapping ranges. This is done so that when the ORB is unmarshalling the stream, it can determine after reading each chunk whether
  - another chunk follows (positive tag), and
  - one or multiple value types are ending at a given point in the stream (negative or null tag).
- As mentioned previously, the end tag is a nonpositive `long` indicating the number of value types ending at a specified point in the CDR stream. The number of value types indicates the recursion level. A recursion depth of zero means that more than 2^{31} recursion levels are ending and that at least one more end tag follows that represents the number of recursion levels to be added to the previous end tag. All value types using a chunked encoding are terminated, at a minimum, with an end tag of −1. A value of −2 terminates a nested value. It is important to remember that data members are encoded in their declaration order. Declaring a data member that contains value type last will yield the smallest encoding of the CDR stream. This is because encoding maximizes the number of values ending at the same place, thus reducing the number of end tags. The canonical example of this is the encoding of a linked list.

Truncating a value type in the receiving context might require keeping track of unused buffer chunks (only during unmarshalling) in case further indirection tags point back to values that appear in the unused chunks. These unused chunks then must be unmarshalled. Custom-marshalled value types are encoded as chunks so that the ORB runtime knows exactly where they end in the stream without having to rely on user-defined code.

7.3.5   Notation

The ability to pass by value adds several new IDL definitions to the CORBA core. One is the IDL type `valuetype`, which obviously is an object that can be passed by value, as opposed to an `interface`. The IDL extensions also include `public` and `private` descriptors of value state members, which act like their counterparts in object-oriented programming languages. Other added definitions are beyond the scope of this book. The primary importance of the new types is their effect on GIOP in the form of new TypeCodes, as listed in Table 7.2.

The addition of passing by value adds several new minor exception codes, listed in Table 7.3.

Table 7.2   Two New TypeCodes

TCKind	Enum Value	Type	Parameters
tk_value	29	Complex	string (repositoryID), string (name), ulong (count){string (member name), TypeCode (member type)}
tk_value_box	30	Complex	string (repositoryID), string (name), TypeCode

Table 7.3   New Minor Exception Codes

System Exception	Minor Code	Explanation
OBJECT_NOT_EXIST	1	Attempt was made to pass an inactivated value as an object reference.
NO_IMPLEMENT	1	Local value implementation is missing.
NO_IMPLEMENT	2	Indicates incompatible value implementation version.
MARSHAL	1	Unable to locate value factory.
BAD_PARAM	1	Unable to register value factory.

7.4 Firewall Security

The Internet has had a profound impact on CORBA. Because of it, we have IORs, IIOP, and an IDL/Java binding. Its effects can be felt in many of the services, but perhaps none more so than the security service. Enforcing security for objects in a closed network is relatively straightforward. Once those objects are exposed to the outside world, however, security enforcement becomes much more complicated. It is no longer sufficient to protect just the object or application—the machine itself must be protected. This is usually done by placing the resources to be protected behind a firewall.

A **firewall** is a piece of hardware or software usually placed between an intranet and the Internet that restricts communication based on certain criteria. An attacker can do the worst damage if it is able to infiltrate a system as a trusted user. Usually a firewall is configured to protect against unauthenticated interactive logins from the Internet, locking all outside logins. Firewalls can be used to create an internal site that is accessible only to computers within a LAN. To make a server available to the rest of the world, it is placed outside the firewall. Then a break-in of the server will not breach the security of the inner network. This is depicted in Figure 7.3.

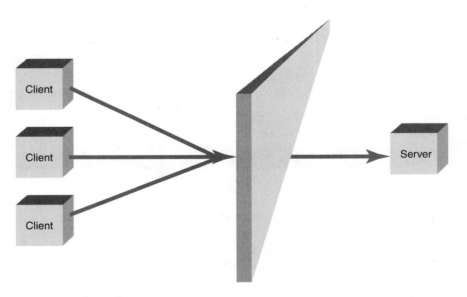

FIGURE 7.3 Server Firewall

There are two ways to access servers that are behind a firewall.

1. Using a screened host type of firewall, you selectively allow the firewall to pass requests for port 80 that are bound to or returning from the Web server machine. This allows clients on the Internet to send and receive requests to and from the Web server machine.

2. Using a dual-homed gateway type of firewall, you place a **proxy** on the firewall machine. A proxy is a small program that can see both sides of the firewall. The proxy intercepts requests for information from the Web server and forwards those requests to the server machine. It then forwards the response back to the requestor. This prevents a direct connection between outside clients and the servers behind the firewall.

In the next section, we look at the *CORBA Firewall Security Specification* in some detail.

7.4.1   The CORBA Firewall Security Specification

The goal of the *CORBA Firewall Security Specification* is twofold.

1. To show how firewall processing of IIOP can be done to permit access to some CORBA-based application services by clients outside the firewall, while providing internal access to those services that should be protected from external access.

2. To show how firewalls can process IIOP as an ordinary application protocol.

To support firewalls that handle the IIOP protocol, the specification adds new data elements to CORBA. Firewalls have effective but limited IIOP processing capabilities. The specification uses the term *enclave* to mean a collection of CORBA objects behind a firewall. A firewall is used to restrict access to a subset of objects within the enclave. This means that some objects may be invoked upon by clients on the other side of the firewall, while other objects may not be.

When a client and a server communicate, often two firewalls are involved. The first is between the client's domain and the Internet. The other is between the server's domain and the Internet. This means that both the client and the server are behind firewalls. For the client to be able to invoke on something outside of its firewall, the firewall must initiate the connection. This means that the firewall configuration must be set up to include the TCP ports that the client is going to use for the outgoing IIOP connection. Also, the server's firewall must be set up so that it can receive incoming connections from the clients outside the firewall. Usually, when the firewall is set up, the administrator restricts access to ports and hosts. This is a problem for IIOP, since object references usually have a dynamically assigned host and port. When an object is created and registered with an object adapter, it can listen on any port. (Recall that this problem was solved by VisiBroker and Orbix by using a daemon process to map well-known ports to the real port on which the object is listening.) Direct communication between a client and a server that must talk across the Internet cannot be done using standard firewall means, since the client might not have a direct connection to the server unless the firewall knows the host and port ahead of time. This is to be expected, since it is the job of the firewall to prevent this direct connection. But there must be some way around the inability to support a direct connection. This is done using a proxy.

If the clients use only well-known TCP ports for IIOP transport, then the standard TCP mechanisms can be used for outgoing traffic. If the ports are not known in advance, then the firewall uses the proxy technique. The proxy is a **SOCKS** proxy. SOCKS is a protocol specifically designed for firewall access. It allows a connection to be established to the SOCKS proxy and from there out to the Internet. On the server side, the server must listen on a fixed port for incoming IIOP requests. But the firewall must know the host and port for it to be able to tunnel requests through the firewall. The new *Firewall Security Specification* handles this by adding information to the IOR that tells the client how to contact the firewall. This allows the firewall to use one host and one port address that clients can use directly to contact the firewall so that the object behind it will be protected.

7.4.2 GIOP Proxy

The *Firewall Security Specification* defines a new network communication component, a *GIOP proxy,* that is used to support inter-enclave CORBA communication. The GIOP proxy supports inter-enclave communication in three ways:

- Firewall traversal
- SSL support
- Callback support

The GIOP proxy may be part of the firewall or may be deployed as a proxy server behind the firewall. It does simple TCP-level processing of IIOP traffic. The specification defines only a GIOP proxy for TCP; therefore it understands only IIOP messages. If other transport mappings of GIOP are to be used, a new GIOP proxy that supports that transport protocol must be created.

The GIOP proxy is an application-level firewall that understands GIOP messages and the specific transport-level IIOP. Its job is to relay messages between the client and the object. It is able to perform basic access control,

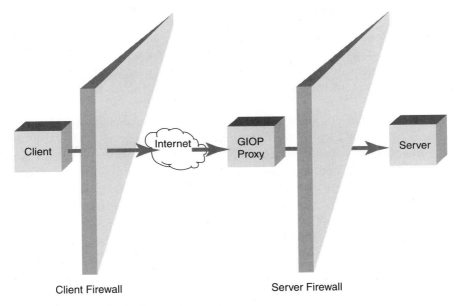

FIGURE 7.4.   GIOP Proxy in Action

based on information in the GIOP message. For example, it may restrict invocations based on the object key or the operation being invoked.

Essentially, a GIOP proxy acts as a middleman between the client and the server. Figure 7.4 shows this interaction in progress. The client sends a request to the server over the Internet. The request is then sent to the GIOP proxy listed in the IOR, which then forwards the message to the server behind the firewall. This connection between client and server, once established, is the connection that bidirectional GIOP will use, if permitted. A bidirectional connection is one that both clients and servers may use to issue requests and replies. For example, both a client and a server may issue *Request* message. A Server may restrict the bidirectionality of messages. This restriction may be due to a lack of support for bidirectionality or a configuration decision.

7.4.3   Bidirectional GIOP

Recall from Chapter 4 that GIOP connections are not symmetrical. Clients and servers do not send the same messages. The *CORBA Firewall Security Specification* changes all of this by introducing *bidirectional GIOP*. This is needed because when operating across firewalls, it is not practical to require potential client firewalls to have a GIOP proxy so that incoming connections may be established. Incoming connections to a client can occur if the client supports callbacks to itself. It also is not practical for any client that wishes to receive a callback to have its firewall proxy configured ahead of time. Remember that CORBA clients may be created on the fly, for example, by downloading an applet. The user might not even know that he is using a CORBA client, so how could he configure his firewall to handle something he doesn't even know he is going to use?

To solve this, the *Firewall Security Specification* reuses the client-initiated connection. Specifically, bidirectional GIOP still requires that a client initiate a connection to a server. However, any request from the server to an object that the client owns is sent back on the same connection. It is important to note that since messages can now flow in both directions, the role of the requestID changes. It no longer is used just to associate corresponding Request and Reply messages per connection. It now must associate corresponding Requests and Replies per connection *and* per direction.

Several steps are involved in creating a bidirectional connection.

1. The client creates an object to send to the server, for example, the callback object. The IOR of the object is sent as a parameter in a GIOP Request message to the server. It is up to the ORB to allow or disallow bidirectional connections. The Request message will indicate the bidirectionality of the connection in the `ServiceContext` field of the GIOP message header.

2. Once the server receives the request, it checks the service context to see if bidirectionality was indicated; only the client can force a connection to be bidirectional. If it is and the server supports it, the server may then send Request messages to the received object, over the same connection. However, the server might not support bidirectionality, either because it cannot or it is restricted from doing so. If such restrictions are relaxed for bidirectionality, then both the client and the server may issue all message types. Table 7.4 shows the messages available with unrestricted bidirectional GIOP. It shows who may issue a message, client or server. Notice how either side is now capable of issuing any message, under certain circumstances as mentioned above. Compare this table to Table 4.5 where much greater restrictions were placed on which side was allowed to issue messages. This table also shows what the message value is, as it is found in the `message_type` field of the Request header.

For the client and server to be able to issue the messages listed in the table, restrictions on which side of a connection may issue what must be relaxed. These bidirectional capabilities are policies defined by the ORB, and the poli-

Table 7.4 CORBA Message Types

Message Type	Issuer	Enum Value	GIOP Versions
Request	Both	0	1.2
Reply	Both	1	1.2
CancelRequest	Both	2	1.2
LocateRequest	Both	3	1.2
LocateReply	Both	4	1.2
CloseConnection	Both	5	1.2
MessageError	Both	6	1.2
Fragment	Both	7	1.2

cies need to be defined in a standard way. This definition has been coded in the IDL as follows.

```
module BiDirPolicy {
   typedef unsigned short BidirectionalPolicyValue;
   const BidirectionalPolicyValue NORMAL = 0;
   const BidirectionalPolicyValue BOTH = 1;

   const CORBA::PolicyType BIDIRECTIONAL_POLICY_TYPE = xx;
   // xx indicates value to be assigned by the OMG
   interface BidirectionalPolicy:CORBA::Policy {
      readonly attribute BidirectionalPolicyValue value;
   };
};
```

Currently, there two standard bidirectional policy values, NORMAL and BOTH. If BidirectionalPolicyValue is NORMAL, the default, then the standard GIOP message rules are applied. This means that bidirectional connections are not allowed. If BidirectionalPolicyValue is BOTH, then bidirectional connections are supported. For both the client and server to use bidirectional communication, both of their ORBS must have a bidirectional policy value of BOTH.

7.4.4 Bidirectional IIOP

Each mapping that GIOP has to a transport protocol should have a corresponding transport-specific bidirectional service context. It should also have an `IOP::ServiceID` defined for it by the OMG. The mapping for TCP, of course, is IIOP, and the bidirectional mapping is BiDirIIOP. The IDL definition of BiDirIIOP is defined next.

```
module IIOP {
    const IOP::ServiceID BI_DIR_IIOP=xx; // to be assigned by the OMG

    struct ListenPoint {
      string host;
      unsigned short port;
    };

    typedef sequence<ListenPoint> ListenPointList;
    struct BiDirIIOPServiceContext {
      ListenPointList listen_points;
      };
    };
```

For the client to contact the firewall, the IOR is given the host and port on which the firewall is listening.

The `BiDirIIOPServiceContext` structure is used in the service context of GIOP messages to support bidirectional IIOP. The `listen_points` member in the service context is used by the ORB to search through its listening point list of active client-initiated connections. If a host-port pair in the listening point list is found to match a host-port pair of an intended new connection, the server can reuse the existing connection to communicate with the client. The host and port values in the `BI_DIR_IIOP` structure are used only for bidirectional connections and not for new connections from server to client (for callbacks).

7.5 Adapting to Continuous Change

In this chapter, we presented an overview of three new specifications that will soon be adopted by the OMG. It is a testament to the flexibility and robustness of CORBA that such vast changes as asynchronous messaging, passing objects by value, and support for bidirectional communication do not fundamentally change the workings of GIOP or IIOP. We can expect many more changes in the future, but IIOP and GIOP should be able to meet these new challenges as well as they met challenges in the past.

Advanced Middleware Interoperability

IIOP and Security

8.1   Introduction to SECIOP

Security is a growing concern for those who manage distributed computing systems. Information resources are critical enterprise assets. Attacks against these resources can have expensive, even catastrophic, results. The challenges involved in distributed system security include the following:

- Protecting against unauthorized disclosure of transmitted sensitive information
- Protecting against unauthorized modification of transmitted sensitive information
- Establishing accountability of directed system execution and utilization
- Preventing malicious interruption of system availability

Object technology assists the development of complex distributed systems. Object-oriented software engineering methodology includes such techniques as abstraction, layering, encapsulation, and decomposition. Abstraction reduces complexity by allowing a system to be decomposed into multiple viewpoints. It removes extraneous detail and exposes only the relevant features within a certain viewpoint. Layering reduces complexity by restricting the interactions and responsibilities of components that are participating in providing a functionality. Encapsulation reduces complexity by removing implementation detail from the service interface of an object component. Decomposition breaks functionality into cohesive units that perform a single well-defined task, thereby reducing complexity.

Trust is a fundamental concept in system security. It involves the belief or confidence in the integrity or reliability of another person or thing. A trust model describes the relationships between principals and information technology resources and underlies all the security-related decisions in a system. The use of object technology obscures trust whenever implementation detail is abstracted or encapsulated or when functionality is divided into layers of fine-grained distributed components. It complicates the trust model within a system by obscuring detail and increasing the number of principals in the system to be trusted.

Recall that an ORB is software that translates abstract interface invocations from a client application into middleware Request messages. It then routes the messages to an object server, which dispatches them to specific object methods. ORB middleware enables object interface messaging regardless of the object server's location, host operating system, or programming language.

ORBs facilitate collaboration over information resources within enterprise networks. These new, distributed communication capabilities introduce new system security vulnerabilities. These in turn compound the many technical challenges of distributed messaging. The issue of secure distributed object messaging was first comprehensively addressed by the OMG in the January 1996 publication of the *CORBA Security Service Specification.*

This comprehensive specification is the most complex of the OMG specifications. It took several years for the OMG Security task force to reach agreement on the standard in 1996. It has since undergone several revisions. The specification deals with all aspects of distributed security. In fact, it is the only all-encompassing standard for security.

CORBA Security provides the following functionality to meet the distributed object security challenge:

- Authentication, to prove that principals are who they claim to be
- Access controls, to control which principals can access the system
- Secure communications, to protect information in transit between participants
- Security auditing, to record, for subsequent analysis, the directed utilization of the system
- Security administration, to manage security information, including security policies

SECIOP is only one small part of CORBA Security Services. SECIOP is involved with secure communications and authentication to provide secure network interoperability. However, it is not the only choice for secure interoperability in the CORBA environment. The other two choices are SSL and DCE-CIOP. Only two of the three options are in practical use today—SECIOP and SSL. We will focus on SECIOP in this chapter with some discussion on SSL. While implementations may vary, it is important to note that the concepts and designs discussed are applicable to any of these solutions.

In this chapter, we describe the Secure Interoperability Protocol (SECIOP) messaging protocol. SECIOP is an extension of GIOP and is the outcome of three years of effort by the OMG to define a security mechanism for interoperable distributed object systems. We begin by providing a primer on related security technology and then discuss the impact of security on GIOP and interoperable object references. We end with an example implementation that provides some insights regarding how an actual implementation of the specification might work.

8.2 Distributed Security Considerations and Requirements

Ensuring secure communication among entities in a distributed computer system is a challenging task. Network communications can be vulnerable to attack in several ways.

- *Denial of service.* In a denial of service attack, something dominates a system resource, slowing down or stopping the system's or network's performance. This can be as simple as flooding the network with messages. It can be hard to combat, particularly if the attacker is a trusted user.

- *Replay.* A replay attack occurs when an attacker records a legitimate message and then sends it again later. This kind of attack can be used, for example, to send a funds transfer a number of times to increase the value of the attacker's account.

- *Repudiation.* Repudiation occurs when a message is sent and the sender denies it was sent and/or the receiver denies it was received. Nonrepudiation services are used to prove that the sender of a message actually sent the message or that the receiver of a message actually received the message. Authentication services also help solve this problem.

- *Tapping.* Tapping is the act of intercepting communications. This can be done either actively or passively. In an active tap, the attacker taps into the communication line and modifies the information, thereby threatening the authenticity of the information being communicated. In a passive tap, the attacker simply eavesdrops on the communication.

- *Masquerade.* Masquerading is the act of an impostor pretending to be an authorized user. For obvious reasons, this type of attack, if successful, can be very dangerous.

There are four primary issues in network communications that security solutions need to address to provide a complete security solution.

1. *Confidentiality.* Networks must be protected against unauthorized access to transmitted information. Attackers should not be able to tap

into a communication line and understand messages. This can be prevented by using an encryption scheme that is strong enough to prevent the message from being easily decrypted and understood. A number of different types of encryption schemes can be used, but all can be classified as either *asymmetric* or *symmetric key algorithms.* These are discussed in Sections 8.3.2. and 8.3.4. For now, it is sufficient to say that for Internet applications, the typical method to secure information is to use an asymmetric key algorithm to exchange keys and then use that key to encrypt messages with a symmetric key algorithm.

2. *Availability of information.* Networks must be able to ensure access to information in a timely manner. It must have some resistance to denial of service attacks so that information is available when needed. A network that does not have some level of guaranteed delivery is useless.

3. *Verification of sender and receiver authenticity.* Networks must be able to verify the identify of who or what is using the system. It is often necessary (and always desirable) to know that the party with whom one is communicating is who they say they are.

4. *Data integrity.* Networks must protect data from unauthorized alteration or destruction. Not only must information be delivered reliably and be unreadable by outside parties, but it also should not be altered so that it is no longer the same as when it was sent.

Some of the most popular and well-known solutions in encryption and authentication that address these issues are discussed in greater detail in the following sections.

8.3   Encryption and Authentication Technology

When one machine communicates with another machine, the communication preferably should be unreadable by outside parties. However, it is difficult, if not impossible, to send data across a public network without someone being able to record it. The most efficient way to make the data unreadable is to scramble it in such a way that an attacker cannot understand it. To accomplish this, encryption can be used.

Encryption is the reversible process of transforming standard text, called **plaintext,** into **ciphertext** that is readable (one hopes) only by the intended recipient. Ciphertext is encrypted plaintext. The reverse of this process is called **decryption.** The process of converting the plaintext into ciphertext usually requires one or more keys and an algorithm. The strength of a particular encryption is based on the secrecy of the key(s) and the complexity of the algorithm. We discuss keys and algorithms in the following several subsections.

Authentication is the act of verifying that a principal is who it says it is. In the case of client-server, where two-way (mutual) authentication is used to establish a connection, the server typically authenticates itself to the client, proving it is who it claims to be. Once the client is convinced it is connected to the correct server, it authenticates itself to the server. If the server is convinced of the client the connection is established and communication may proceed. We will describe several popular authentications that all have encryption and influenced CORBA Security and SECIOP.

8.3.1   Types of Encryption

Encryption can be placed in several locations in the OSI stack. Where it takes place can affect not only performance but also security options. There are two alternatives in encryption:

- Link
- End-to-end

Link encryption takes place at OSI layer 1 or 2, while end-to-end is done at 6 or 7.

In link encryption, an encryption device is placed on each end of a vulnerable communications link. This makes all traffic secure. However, it also is expensive as each message is decrypted at each packet switch so that the switch can read the packet header to route the packet. This makes messages vulnerable at the switches. If the message is sent over a public packet-switching network, the sender has no control over the security of the nodes.

In end-to-end encryption, encryption is done at the sender and decryption is done at the receiver. Encrypted data is passed from sender to receiver. Since only the receiver may decrypt the communications, the entire packet cannot be encrypted. If it was, the switch could not read the header and route the packet. So only the user's data is encrypted. By contrast, in link encryption, packet headers are encrypted. This reduces the chances of traffic analysis. An attacker could still assess the amount of traffic on a network and the amount of traffic entering and leaving a node; however, it cannot analyze the source or destination of a particular packet. This threat can be reduced with traffic padding. **Traffic padding** is a random data stream of ciphertext output continuously in the absence of input plaintext (which is encrypted before being sent). This makes it impossible for an attacker to determine the amount of traffic being sent to a node, since a node is always receiving encrypted traffic. This defense is not possible in an end-to-end encryption scheme, although more limited solutions are possible.

For greater security, both link and end-to-end encryption can be used. In this scheme, the sender encrypts the data with one key, while the entire packet is encrypted using the link encryption key. This prevents the data from being read at the switch and prevents traffic analysis.

8.3.2 Private Key Technology

Private key technology, also known as **symmetric key technology,** uses a single key. This single key is used both to encrypt and to decrypt information. The sender and receiver of a message must share a common key, and this key must be kept secret, since anyone who possesses the key (and knows the algorithm) can decrypt the message.

Private key technology has three major advantages over public key technology.

1. Encryption and decryption using a private key is faster than using a public key because private keys are much shorter. (Public key technology is discussed later in this section.)

2. The use of private keys provides *authentication,* assuming the key has not been compromised.

3. The same key is used by both sender and receiver to both encrypt and decrypt the communication, thereby simplifying the process.

Using private key technology also has disadvantages.

1. If an attacker discovers the key, all communications that were encrypted with that key can be decrypted. Therefore keys must be changed often to minimize damage in the event of a key's being compromised. This further can cause a key management problem.

2. How to distribute keys can be a problem. Keys cannot be transmitted in the clear since anyone who steals the key would be able to decrypt the information. They can be transmitted physically such as on a disk by a courier or in pieces on separate channels. And once the keys are received, they must be stored securely.

3. The number of keys increases with the square of the number of people exchanging information. This problem can be solved by using a central clearinghouse or forwarding office that accepts an encrypted message from a sender, decrypts it with the sender's key, and then encrypts it again with the receiver's secret key. Another technique is for sender and receiver to exchange a secret key by encrypting it using a public key technology.

8.3.3 Data Encryption Standard

The **data encryption standard** (DES) is a private key system that encrypts data in 64-bit blocks using a 56-bit key. It was adopted in 1977 by U.S. government agencies as the official method of encrypting data. It is in wide use in hardware and software and is an accepted cryptographic standard both in the United States and abroad.

DES is based on several concepts from Shannon's theory of information secrecy. These concepts are confusion when a piece of information is changed, and diffusion when one tries to spread the effect of one plaintext bit to other bits in the ciphertext. The idea is to use two different ciphers applied alternately. Shannon noted that two weak but complementary ciphers can be made more secure by using them together. The two types of ciphers used are **substitution** and **permutation** ciphers. The substitution cipher systematically substitutes some bit patterns for others. The permutation cipher, also known as a transposition cipher, reorders the bits, thereby providing diffusion. This is accomplished by processing the plaintext into ciphertext in three phases:

1. An initial processing rearranges the bits into the permuted input.
2. The next process iterates 16 times. This iteration contains both substitution and permutation functions. The final iteration generates a 64-bit output. The preoutput is then created by swapping the left and right halves of the 64-bit output.
3. The preoutput is passed through the inverse of the initial permutation function, producing the 64-bit ciphertext.

The permutation function consists of a set of tables that generate an output bit from an input bit. The substitution function consists of a set of eight **S-boxes.** S-boxes are the classified internal structure of DES. An S-box accepts 6 bits as input and produces a 4-bit output. There is a known set of outputs for each of the eight S-boxes based on the inputs (breaking them into row and column).

The adequacy of DES has been questioned recently. One concern is if 16 iterations is sufficient to diffuse the information of the plaintext into the ciphertext. With only one cycle, a single ciphertext bit is affected by only a few bits of plaintext. Studies have shown that 8 iterations are sufficient to eliminate observed dependence. Another concern is key length. If an attempt is made to search all of the keys, the result is 256 56-bit keys, requiring a search time of 2,280 years. With a parallel processor attack, in which the processor works at the rate of one key per microsecond, the time to decrypt a message is 106 days. If, however, 106 processes were to work in parallel they could check all of the keys in one day. It has been estimated that the cost of such a machine is around $50 million, with a cost of about $20,000 per solution. This is easily affordable by governments and large corporations. Therefore, the key length is too short for practical protection.

8.3.4   Public Key Technology

Public key technology, also known as **asymmetric key technology,** uses two keys, a private key and a public key. Only the private key needs to be kept secret; the public key can be publicly distributed. The two keys are mathematically related, so messages that are encrypted with one can be decrypted by the other and vice versa.

Its primary advantage is that the private key does not need to be sent over the network; this reduces key management problems. Its primary disadvantage is its longer key lengths, making public key technology a lot slower than private.

8.3.5   Diffie-Hellman Public Key Algorithm

In 1976, Whitfield Diffie and Martin Hellman created the first published public key algorithm. This algorithm is used to allow for the secure key exchange between two users. Once the key has been exchanged, the algorithm can be used for the encryption of messages between the two users. The effectiveness of the Diffie-Hellman algorithm relies on the difficulty of computing discrete logarithms. A discrete logarithm is defined as follows. r is a primitive root of a prime p, where

> r mod p, $r2$ mod p, . . . , $rp - 1$ mod p are distinct and consist of the integers 1 through $p - 1$ in some permutation. For any integer a, a unique exponent i exists such that $a = ri$ mod p, where $0 <= i <= (p - 1)$.

The exponent i of r is the discrete logarithm.

With Diffie-Hellman, it is assumed there is a known prime number p and an r primitive root of p. Suppose two users, Bob (b) and Alice (a), wish to exchange keys. Bob selects a random integer bi that is less than p and computes $Yb = rXb$ mod p. Alice does the same thing, computing $Ya = rXa$ mod p. Both Alice and Bob exchange Y values, while keeping the X values private. Bob then computes the key as $k = (Yb)Xa$ mod p, while Alice does likewise with $k = (Ya)Xb$ mod p. These two formulas result in identical k values.

8.3.6   RSA

The **RSA algorithm** is a patented public key algorithm. Developed by Ron Rivest, Adi Shamir, and Leonard Adleman at MIT in 1977, it is the most popular public key system. It is the only publicly accepted public key technology in the United States and is used for authentication as well as encryption.

RSA is a block cipher in which the plaintext and ciphertext are integers between 0 and $n - 1$ for some n. Encryption and decryption in RSA involve raising an integer to an integer power of modulus n. The algorithm is as follows. Find the product of two large prime numbers p and q such that modulus

$n = pq$. A number e (the public exponent) is found that is less than n and relatively prime to $(p − 1)(q − 1)$ so that e and $(p − 1)(q − 1)$ have no common factors other than 1. Once e is found, d (the private exponent) must be found so that $(ed − 1)$ is divisible by $(p − 1)(q − 1)$. The public key is the pair (n, e), and the private key is the pair (n, d) with p and q no longer necessary.

To crack the private key from the public key (n, e), you factor n into p and q and then obtain d. However, RSA's security is based on the fact that this factoring is difficult. But, as the speed of computers increases, decrypting data encrypted with a fixed key size becomes easier and easier. Increasing the key length greatly increases security, but each doubling in the modulus length increases the public key operations (encryption) by a factor of 4 and private key operations (decryption) by a factor of 8. RSA recommends using 768-bit keys for personal use, 1,024-bit keys for corporate use, and 2,048-bit keys for extremely valuable keys.

8.3.7   Digital Certificates

A **digital certificate** is a message signed by a certificate authority attesting to a user's public key. Digital certificates are becoming the standard means of authentication on the Internet. To create a certificate, a user, say, Bob, sends his name and public key to the certificate authority. The certificate authority forms a message from the name and public key using its private key, and the message is used to create a signature. The message and signature are combined to form a certificate, and this certificate is returned to Bob. As part of this process a certificate receives a time stamp. A time stamp indicates date and time of creation. Now suppose Bob wants another user, Alice, to trust his public key, so he sends the certificate to Alice. Alice then verifies the signature contained in the certificate using the certificate authority's public key. If the signature is valid, Alice can accept Bob's public key.

Certificates would be placed on a certificate revocation list whenever an individual no longer has the rights given with the certificate. For example, if an employee leaves a company, it would be part of the termination process for the employee's certificate to be placed on the revocation list. A certificate would expire if it has been given a date or time length that is no longer valid.

The most widely used format for digital certificates is defined by the ITU-T X.509 standard. Several organizations have become certificate authorities, thus allowing systems to use them to verify a certificate's authenticity. These organizations are companies formed as profit-making ventures, public institutions such as the U.S. Post Office, and governmental bodies. Certificate authorities also hold certificate revocation lists so that systems may check to see if a certificate has been revoked.

A certificate can become invalid in several ways. For example, it can be placed on a certificate revocation list, which a system can check. Or it can expire, since certificates are time-stamped.

8.3.8 Kerberos

Kerberos is an authentication system developed by Project Athena at the Massachusetts Institute of Technology. Named after the three-headed dog in Greek mythology that guarded the gates of Hades, Kerberos is used to authenticate network users. Kerberos uses an authenticated token called a **ticket.** A ticket is an encrypted, unforgeable, nonreplayable data structure that contains the name of the user and the service that the user is allowed to use. It has a limited lifetime to help prevent brute force attacks; an attacker usually doesn't have time to complete an attack before the ticket becomes invalid. Tickets are provided to requesting applications by a Kerberos server. Working with Kerberos involves the following steps.

1. The user establishes a session with the Kerberos server by sending his identity at login to the Kerberos server.

2. The Kerberos server verifies that the user is an authorized user. If the user is authorized, the server sends the user a session key for communicating with the Ticket Granting Server and a ticket for accessing the Ticket Granting Server. Kerberos provides crytographic protection against spoofing by mediating each access request with the Ticket Granting Server. The session key is encrypted with the user's password. Note that passwords are stored at the Kerberos server rather than being sent across the network.

3. The user's application then sends a copy of the session key and ticket to the Ticket Granting Server. This information is encrypted by using a key that the Ticket Granting Server and the Kerberos server share.

4. Using the key, the user requests a ticket from the Ticket Granting Server to assess a particular service or talk with another user.

5. The Ticket Granting Server verifies the user's access permission, and if the user is authorized, it returns a ticket and session key to the user. The ticket is encrypted by using a key shared by the application, server, and user (user's workstation). The user then can use the ticket to use the service or communicate with another user.

Kerberos has several weaknesses, including its vulnerability to password guessing. However, the greatest weakness of the Kerberos system is its inability to scale. In this case, the Kerberos assumes that only one Kerberos server and only one Ticket Granting Server exist. In practice, multiple Ticket Granting Servers are allowed. Further, each user or server that uses Kerberos must have a unique key. If a new Ticket Granting Server is added to a Kerberos-based system, a duplicate set of keys is needed for all users or servers. Having duplicate keys laying about increases the risk of exposure, as well as the problem of key management. The Kerberos system is based upon a private-key concept. Having to generate private keys for every user and server on the system requires serious dedicated manpower for any sizeable organization. Furthermore, because of its focus on central authority it does not scale at all to Internet style communications resulting in sizeable management burden of the private keys.

One interesting note: a potential implementation option for SECIOP is to implement it on top of Kerberos. The messages would all be defined using SECIOP, but the encryption and authentication would all be provided through the Kerberos implementation. This will be discussed in detail in later sections.

8.3.9   Secure Sockets Layer

The Secure Sockets Layer (SSL) protocol, developed by Netscape Communications Corporation, provides privacy and reliability between two communicating applications. The goals of the SSL protocol are the following:

- Provide cryptographic security by establishing a secure connection between two parties.
- Allow cryptographic interoperability between SSL-enabled applications.
- Allow applications to be security-extendible by allowing new public key and bulk encryption methods to be incorporated as needed.
- Be relatively efficient.

Sessions in SSL are stateful, with the SSL handshake protocol responsible for coordinating the states of the connections. Certain handshake information about the state of the connection is cached to enhance performance. The SSL handshake protocol (abridged) is as follows:

1. The client sends a ClientHello message to the server, consisting of the following:
   - The SSL protocol version being used by the client
   - A random number
   - A sessionID so that the client can identify the session
   - A set of the ciphers that the client can use
   - A set of compression methods that the client can use

2. The server returns a ServerHello message, its certificate (if it is server-side authentication first), and a certificate request, if it wishes to authenticate the client. The ServerHello consists of the following:

   • The SSL protocol version being used by the server

   • A random number

   • A sessionID so that the server can identify the session. If the client's sessionID is nonempty, the server will look in its cache for a matching session cache. If it finds one, it resumes the session and the client and server proceed directly to the finished methods.

   • A cipher selected from the set of the ciphers that the client sent over

   • A compression method selected from the set of compression methods that the client sent over

3. The client responds with its certificate and a finished message.

4. The server sends its finished message.

The client and server may now communicate using secure sockets. The data will be encrypted using the negotiated cipher and keys. There are two keys: a client write key (the server uses this to read) and the client read key (the server uses this to write). When the connection is broken, if the client and server wish to communicate they must go through the handshake again.

SSL generally uses public key cryptography to exchange the keys. Once they are exchanged, secret key algorithms are used for increased performance.

All data sent in SSL is encapsulated in a **record.** A record contains (a) a header (which contains a record length, padding, and an IS-ESCAPE field) and (b) some nonzero amount of data. The header, which is transmitted before the data, has a 2- or 3-byte length code. If the most significant bit of this code is set in the first byte, then padding is used and therefore the length is 2 bytes. The receiver of the padded record decrypts the entire record to get the plaintext and then subtracts the padding from the record length.

The data consists of message authentication code (MAC) data, the actual data, and the padding data. The MAC data is a hash function of the secret key (depending on which way the message is going), the actual data, the padding data, and a sequence number. The receiver of a message then computes the MAC and compares it to the received MAC. If they match, the message is authentic.

SSL is based upon a public-key system. The choice of a public-key system should be obvious since the technology was developed for use on the Internet and private-key systems do not easily scale due to a key management problem. Due to the popularity of the Internet, SSL is one of the most popular technologies.

One alternative to SECIOP is to use SSL under IIOP. Many of the concepts and designs that will be discussed about SECIOP are applicable to this solution as well.

8.4 CORBA Security and SECIOP

SECIOP is only a portion of the CORBA Security Services. The SECIOP standard defines the structure declarations that a SECIOP message is built from. These SECIOP messages can then be transmitted between clients and servers to achieve secure interoperability. Strictly speaking, though interfaces are not part of the SECIOP specification, they are part of other CORBA Security Service modules. However, it is impossible to have a discussion about SECIOP without covering the interfaces and their use. CORBA Security Service interfaces do not change regardless of which optional interoperable secure messaging technologies the system is using—SECIOP, SSL, or DCE-CIOP. The discussion and examples in the following sections are applicable to the design and use of any of these choices.

Existing security standards and technology heavily influenced SECIOP design. For example, the Generic Security Service Application Programming Interface (GSS-API) from The Open Group played a role in the design of the structure declarations. Mappings of SECIOP were made to Kerberos, the Secure European System for Applications in a Multi-vendor Environment (SESAME) and the Simple Public Key GSS-API Mechanism (SPKM). Kerberos was discussed previously; SPKM and SESAME are similar technologies that are not yet as well known as Kerberos. SPKM is similar to Kerberos, but is based upon a public-key infrastructure. SESAME was developed as a research project partially funded by the European Commission. Kerberos, SPKM and SESAME have all used the GSS-API in their designs.

In order to understand SECIOP you must understand its relationship to GIOP and IIOP, and how it makes use of object references and message types. In the example that follows you will be able to understand how SECIOP works within the context of an ORB and the CORBA Security Services. Furthermore, as we have indicated, there are many alternatives to implementation of a "secure IIOP" such as SECIOP, SSL, DCE-CIOP, or the use of Kerberos, SPKM, or SESAME in SECIOP. In evaluating any solution it is important to know what decisions were made by the designers since each of these choices has different strengths and weaknesses that will impact system design.

8.4.1 SECIOP Design Origins

The basis for the SECIOP design is rooted in the Generic Security Service-Application Programming Interface (GSS-API). The GSS-API, specified by The Open Group, is a standard interface for security in distributed, heterogeneous systems. It enables software entities in a distributed application to authenticate one another and to protect communication between themselves. The DEC Security Service utilizes the GSS-API to provide access to its security services.

SECIOP consists of structure declarations that are used to create messages that provide interoperability with security services for use in distributed applications. SECIOP may be implemented using many different security mechanisms, such as Kerberos or public keys. Like GSS, SECIOP principals first must establish a **security context** by exchanging a set of tokens that contain authentication and security mechanism information. A security context represents the successful, mutual establishment of identity and confidentiality options. After the establishment of a security context, SECIOP provides for the per-message protection of messages between client and server.

8.4.2   SECIOP within GIOP and IIOP

CORBA security leverages the advantages of the GSS-API standard. Application of the GSS approach introduced several new message types to GIOP messaging. Throughout the security service adoption process, members of the OMG Security and ORB Task Force collaborated to coordinate SECIOP messaging within the GIOP/IIOP framework. Figure 8.1 depicts the SECIOP protocol relationship with GIOP messaging.

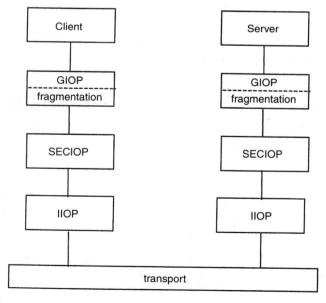

FIGURE 8.1   The Relationship of SECIOP to GIOP

SECIOP message types extend the GIOP message types while retaining GIOP's message header. The SECIOP message types extend the GIOP messages for the purpose of providing secure transmission of data. Clients and servers intending to participate in the SECIOP protocol must be able to process GIOP as well as SECIOP message types. Providing the GIOP-compatible message header for SECIOP messages is advantageous because processing a message buffer requires extracting a number of bytes equivalent to the size of the message header. The message header is defined as:

```
GIOP::MessageHeader header;
int length = sizeof(header);
header = read(message_buffer,length);
```

The GIOP message header has the following structure.

```
struct MessageHeader {
        char                    magic [4];
        //Version                GIOP_version; (deprecated)
        Version                 protocol_version;
        boolean                 byte_order;
        octet                   message_type;
        unsigned long           message_size;
};
```

SECIOP uses the same structure but uses different field values than GIOP in some cases, as follows.

- *Magic.* Identifies the protocol being used in the message. Typically, the field value is GIOP. SECIOP messages have been allocated the value SECP by the OMG.
- *Protocol version.* Identifies the versions being used for the protocol identified in the magic field. The previous variable was named GIOP_version; this has been deprecated for the new name, protocol_version. The initial protocol version value for SECIOP is 1 with a minor code of 0.
- *Message type.* Identifies the message type being used. Recall that in GIOP, the types are Request, Reply, CancelRequest, LocateRequest, LocateReply, CloseConnection, MessageError, and Fragment. In SECIOP, they are MTEstablishContext, MTCompleteEstablishContext, MTContinueEstablishContext, MTDiscardContext, MTMessageError, and MTMessageInContext.

8.4.3   SECIOP Components of Object References

The CORBA specification defines an IOR as a sequence of object-specific protocol profiles, plus a typeID. Recall from Chapter 4 that a profile is an interoperability mechanism that provides clients with information sufficient to successfully communicate with a server. Object references have at least one tagged profile per protocol supported. GIOP/IIOP profiles use the TAG_INTERNET_IOP tag and contain basic Internet IP host name and port address information.

ORBs that support only the IIOP profile use the TAG_INTERNET_IOP tag, not TAG_MULTIPLE_COMPONENTS, and set the length of the IOR::profiles sequence to 1. IOR::type_id is set to the object's type as defined on the object IDL interface in the interface repository.

IORs that use profiles in addition to the interoperability profiles require additional internal component tags and structures. These component tags are identified within the IOR using the TAG_MULTIPLE_COMPONENTS profile tag. The IOP::TaggedComponent and IOP::MultiComponentProfile structures are defined in the IOP module to provide support for profiles that consist of a number of tagged components. The SECIOP module uses ComponentId instead of higher-level ProfileIds to identify components within a profile. The SECIOP module is defined as:

```
module SECIOP {
        IOP::ComponentId  TAG_GENERIC_SEC_MECH = 12;
        IOP::ComponentId  TAG_ASSOCIATION_OPTIONS = 13;
        IOP::ComponentId  TAG_SEC_NAME = 14;

        struct GenericMechanismInfo{
                sequence<octet> security_mechanism_type;
                sequence<octet>  mech_specific_data;
                sequence <IOP::TaggedComponent> component;
        }
    ...
    }
```

The *Common Secure Interoperability Specification* (CSI) defines several mechanism-specific tags allocated by the OMG. TAG_GENERIC_SEC_MECH is a general tag available for security mechanisms that are not registered with the OMG and is placed in IOP::TaggedComponent::tag. GenericMechanismInfo is a structure that represents the octet data in IOP::TaggedComponent::component_data, which matches TAG_GENERIC_SEC_MECH. The security_mechanism_type data field in the GenericMechanismInfo structure is used to identify the security mechanism supported by the target. The mechanism type is an ASN.1 object identifier as described in IETF RFC 1508. The mechanism-specific data are octets that specify mechanism-specific information. The SECIOP::GenericMechanismInfo::components field is provided to hold additional components.

- TAG_ASSOCIATION_OPTIONS, which defines the supported and required options available at a target. Secure association includes the following options for a client: NoProtection, Integrity, Confidentiality, DetectReplay, DetectMisordering, EstablishTrustInTarget, and EstablishTrustInClient.
- TAG_SEC_NAME, which provides the security name of the target. The security name is useful in authenticating the target.

8.4.4   SECIOP Messaging

The following message types are defined for secure messaging.

```
module SECIOP {
...
        enum MsgType {
                MTEstablishContext,
                MTCompleteEstablishContext,
                MTContinueEstablishContext,
                MTDiscardContext,
                MTMessageError,
                MTMessageInContext
        };
...
    };
```

Prior to the exchange of SECIOP messages, the client and server should be authenticated within their respective domains, and have established credentials. Within the SECIOP protocol, the following activities are performed:

- Security-context establishment
- Protection-level option negotiation
- Per-message protection mechanism
- Security-context termination

8.4.5   An Example Implementation Using SECIOP

Figure 8.2 presents one possible example implementation of CORBA SECIOP to illustrate the physical interaction of SECIOP components. Allocated processes on client, server, or security machines are depicted by clouds. Stacked clouds represent the possibility of an indeterminate number of processes or threads allocated for an unknown number of client or server threads.

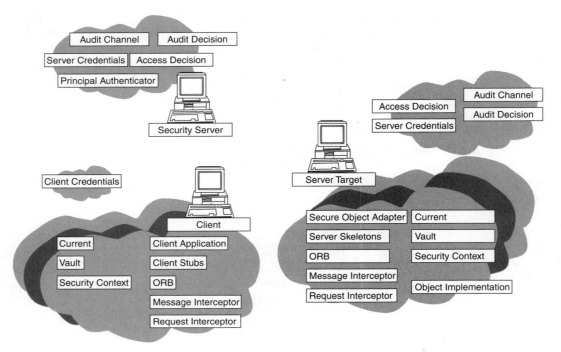

FIGURE 8.2   Example SECIOP Physical Architecture

On the client, a Credential object provides access to the login authentication information to any client application. The security runtime objects are initialized by the main thread of a client application. On the target, a secure object adapter listens for incoming connections. Access to thread-dependent security-context information, such as client credentials, can be obtained through the Current object. A separate process may be utilized to run the target security server proxy objects. These proxy objects cache security server object information. The security server proxy objects include AccessDecision, AuditDecision, and AuditChannel. The AccessDecision and AuditDecision objects download and cache invocation control and audit information. The AuditChannel object uploads audit log data to the security server.

At the security server, centralized control and maintenance of security-sensitive information is provided. Security objects can be run from single or multiple server/process configurations.

Figure 8.3 presents a representation of the nominal message interactions for secure communication within the security runtime. Security runtime

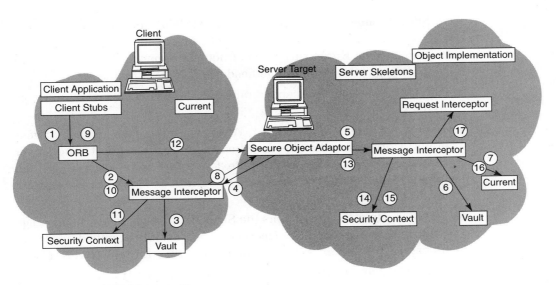

FIGURE 8.3   SECIOP Message Flow

objects on client server or security machines are depicted by shaded boxes. Operation invocations are depicted by numbered, annotated arrows. A description of each step is provided following the diagram.

1. Client stubs receive the invocation of an operation against an object with no security context and place a `prepare_request` to the client ORB.

2. The client ORB recognizes that security components exist in the target IOR and augment the GIOP processing of the invocation by calling `MessageInterceptor::prepare_request`. The MessageInterceptor obtains the security name and `security_mechanism_type` from the IOR. The client MessageInterceptor checks its dictionary cache to determine whether a SecurityContext for the security name and `security_mechanism_type` already exists.

3. If no security context is available, the MessageInterceptor creates one by calling `Vault::init_security_context`, passing in the target's security name, association options, mechanism type, and mechanism data. Internal to the `init_security_context()`, the Vault creates tokens appropriate for an EstablishContext message that is appropriate for the `security_mechanism_type` desired by the target. The tokens are returned to the MessageInterceptor. The MessageInterceptor creates

a SECIOP message by placing the SECIOP message header into `CORBA_MarshalOutBuffer`. It then places the `init_context_token` into the EstablishContext struct and appends the EstablishContext message after the message header in `CORBA_MarshalOutBuffer`.

4. The client MessageInterceptor transmits the EstablishContext message to the server.

5. The server listens to the socket. Whenever a message appears, it generates a process to handle the client connection request. The server determines that an EstablishContext message is being sent. It then transfers the message to `MessageInterceptor::prepare_request` for processing.

6. The MessageInterceptor opens the SECIOP message, reads the message type, and, since the message type is an EstablishContext message, processes `init_context_token` out of `CORBA_MarshalOutBuffer`.

7. The MessageInterceptor calls `Vault::accept_security_context()`, passing `init_context_token`. The Vault validates the client's credentials, reviews the association options, and, if everything is acceptable, creates a SecurityContext, client credentials, and the `final_context_token`. The Vault returns the `final_context_` token and the AssociationStatus to the MessageInterceptor. The MessageInterceptor reviews the AssociationStatus and, if the association was successful, continues to set the credentials for the client to the server's current as `received_credentials`.

8. The MessageInterceptor calls the `Current::received_credentials (SECInvocationCredentials)` operation to set the user's credentials for the thread. It then creates a SECIOP message and a CompleteEstablishContext header struct and places `final_context_token` into the struct and the struct into the SECIOP message. The SECIOP message is returned to the server ORB runtime.

9. The server ORB transmits the CompleteEstablishMessage over the socket. The client MessageInterceptor awaits the return of the message. The MessageInterceptor removes `final_context_token` from the SECIOP message. It retrieves the SecurityContext relevant to the security name, the `mechanism_type`, and the AssociationStatus. It then calls `SecurityContext::continue_security_context (final_context_token): AssociationStatus`, passing `final_context_token`.

10. The stubs stream the request arguments into the MarshalOutBuffer and invoke the ORB to `send_request()`.

11. The ORB streams the request arguments into the MarshalOutBuffer and invokes `MessageInterceptor::send_request()`. The MessageIn-

terceptor determines that a MessageInContext message is desired and creates a MessageInContext header struct, filling in the relevant struct fields. It then processes the struct into the SECIOP message.

12. The body of the GIOP message is encrypted by calling `SecurityContext::protect_message()`. Control is returned to the client ORB, which transmits the message.

13. The client ORB transmits the MessageInContext message to the server.

14. The server determines that a MessageInContext message is being sent. The server transfers the message to `MessageInterceptor::receive_request` for processing.

15. The MessageInterceptor retrieves the SECIOP header struct from the SECIOP message and removes the ContextId field value. It uses the ContextId to locate the SecurityContext and checks the validity of the SecurityContext by calling `SecurityContext::is_valid():boolean`.

16. Assuming the SecurityContext is still valid, the MessageInterceptor decrypts the message by calling `SecurityContext::reclaim_message()`. It then returns control to the server ORB runtime.

17. The server ORB runtime obtains the client's credential from Current by calling `Current::received_credentials()`.

18. The server ORB runtime performs the authorization by invoking `RequestInterceptor::target_invoke(CredentialsList, IOP::IOR):boolean`.

This example provides some insight into the operation of SECIOP. As discussed earlier in the chapter, SECIOP is only one of many choices for achieving a secure interoperable environment. In general, however, each mechanism works in a similar manner. The implementations may vary but the underlying concepts and designs remain the same.

8.5 Security as a Critical Requirement for Business Critical Systems

Computer network security is a broad and complicated topic. In this chapter, we touched on some of the more popular technologies currently in use. As computer networks become more widespread in use, especially in areas such as on-line transactions and accessing health records over the Internet, privacy and data integrity will become increasingly important. Much of the technology discussed in this chapter can help solve the security problems of networks. It is up to vendors to implement, install, and use these technologies correctly.

Java, HTTP, and IIOP

9.1 The Relationship of IIOP to Java and HTTP

Two of the most significant technologies to emerge recently are the Java programming language and the hypertext transport protocol (HTTP) for communicating between Web browsers and servers. Java is a programming language for creating distributed objects. HTTP is being redesigned to support distributed objects. Both of these technologies will be critical in the future for object-based systems, so it is important to consider them in the context of object interoperability. What are they, where are they going, and how does IIOP fit in their future?

In this chapter we will look at these two technologies and their relationship to IIOP. What makes the relationship of RMI and HTTP-NG to IIOP interesting are their competitive as well as complementary natures. The first part of the chapter deals with the RMI relationship while the second half deals with HTTP-NG.

9.2 Communication between Objects in Java

Java is an object-oriented programming language, developed by Sun Microsystems, that has achieved significant popularity in a relatively short period of time. The reasons for its success are its portability across heterogeneous platforms through the use of byte codes and a virtual machine (VM), as well as its ease of use in comparison to other popular programming languages.

The original Java concept was to allow **applets** to be sent across a network and executed on a local machine. An applet is a small, self-contained set of code that performs a specific function. Sun's original goal was to embed the Java VM in various devices and appliances, eventually leading to the "smart" home or office. However, it discarded this concept to focus instead on integrating Java into Web browsers to support Internet application development. The original

FIGURE 9.1   Socket-based Java

concept was discarded because the opportunity of the Internet far outweighed the market potential of smart appliances. However, Sun Microsystems continues to look for opportunity to apply Java towards meeting this initial goal. Over its short life, Java has been expanded to allow objects not only to be downloaded, but also to allow objects to communicate across a network.

However, with all of this emphasis on distributed objects there is no single method for communicating between objects using Java. Sockets, RPC, RMI, and IIOP are all supported communication mechanisms.

Basic communications using sockets and RPCs were the earliest forms of object invocation. While these mechanisms are the best-performing approaches, they require significant effort on the part of the programmer to implement applications. Specifically, sockets require the encoding and decoding of messages and parameters to be handled within the application, as shown in Figure 9.1. This process requires detailed specifications of interfaces between objects, is difficult to reuse, and means that errors are discovered at runtime rather than at compile time.

RPCs provide improved mechanisms for communicating that include the handling of parameters; however, they were not built for object-oriented application communication. The use of RPCs requires the application code to map Java communications to a procedure call structure, as shown in Figure 9.2.

Due to the programming deficiencies of sockets and RPCs for Java communications, two alternative approaches have emerged for higher-level, object-oriented communications. These are depicted in Figures 9.3 and 9.4.

- RMI, distributed object communications optimized for Java-to-Java object interactions
- IIOP, distributed object communications between Java objects, as well as between other object and non-object-based systems.

Sun Microsystems remains committed to supporting both of these mechanisms, leaving the selection of which to use to the user. Furthermore, Sun has integrated together the two technologies giving users the choice of a hybrid approach. It is important to understand their similarities and differences in order to make an educated selection of when to use one or both in developing an application. We discuss this in the following subsections.

FIGURE 9.2   RPC-based Java

FIGURE 9.3   RMI-based Java

FIGURE 9.4   CORBA-based Java

9.2.1   RMI and Java

RMI was developed to have a Java-only perspective. It assumed that business applications would be completely written in Java. This is both its biggest strength and its weakness. It is RMI's biggest strength because RMI was optimized for Java applications. It is its biggest weakness because many applications consist of a variety of non-Java applications, databases, and packaged applications that are integrated together with new Java code to comprise a system.

The original goals of RMI were as follows:

- Expand invocation support from a local VM to distributed VMs, including callbacks from the server.
- Align a distributed object model with Java language semantics, while making differences between the local and distributed object models transparent.
- Provide for simplicity of use.
- Preserve type safety provided in the runtime environment.

From the perspective of having achieved these goals, RMI is a success.

9.2.1.1 RMI Architecture

RMI is the mechanism for invoking a remote interface on a remote object using the same syntax as a local invocation. To accomplish this, RMI was architected as a series of three layers, as shown in Figure 9.5.

- *Stub/skeleton layer.* This is the layer that is visible to the application objects. A stub is visible to a client object, and a skeleton is visible to a remote object. A client object that wants to invoke a method on a remote object does so through the stub, which implements the interfaces from the remote object. The stub is responsible for initiating the request, marshalling and unmarshalling arguments and returning values, and closing the request on completion. The skeleton unmarshalls and marshalls the arguments and returns values and makes the call to the remote object. Other than the client object and remote object knowing how to communicate with a stub and skeleton, they are not aware that a remote invocation has occurred.

- *Remote reference layer.* This layer is responsible for interfacing between the stub/skeleton layer and the transport protocol. It was defined to allow different invocation strategies to be implemented as a protocol. Examples of strategies that might be implemented are point-to-point, replication, and persistent reference. In addition, these strategies can be tailored on both the client and server sides. This can allow the client side to handle

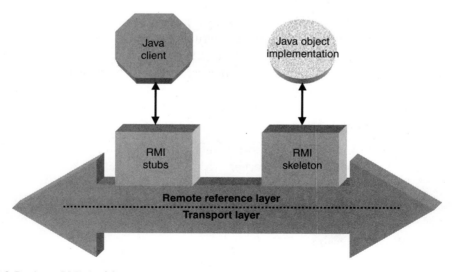

FIGURE 9.5   Java RMI Architecture

the replication of a request or a server side to communicate as necessary with replicated servers prior to passing the invocation to the skeleton.

- *Transport layer.* This layer is responsible for the management of a connection, including listening for, setting up, monitoring, and transmitting an invocation. It consists of four abstractions:

    - Endpoint, which is the address space of the Java VM machine.
    - Channel, which is the conduit between two address spaces. It manages the connection between local and remote endpoints.
    - Connection, which performs the input and output.
    - Transport, which manages the channels, setting up the channel between two endpoints. It does this by monitoring incoming calls, setting up a connection, and notifying the remote reference layer. Multiple transport protocols can be managed in a single RMI implementation of the transport layer.

The Java RMI architecture is supported by two protocols to format the on-the-wire transmissions:

- Java object serialization protocol for formatting the call and return data of an invocation as well as support for method reference and movement so that an object can be distributed
- HTTP POST to allow invocations through a firewall

9.2.1.2   The Native RMI Approach

RMI was designed and implemented around the Java language. Thus it removes a great deal of the complexity of the sockets approach without requiring an IDL. It supports garbage collection, the VM's common type system, and the dynamic distribution of applications. The initial implementation of this architecture also included a proprietary transport protocol, the Java remote method protocol (JRMP). As with the architecture and object serialization protocol, JRMP was optimized for an all-Java environment.

Recognizing the deficiencies of the all-Java approach, Sun has enhanced RMI by adding additional services for integration with legacy systems, remote activation of objects, and other mission-critical functions. However, the native RMI approach does not adequately provide for these other requirements:

- Improved support for interoperability with other languages, such as C, C++, and Cobol
- Platform independence and vendor neutrality
- CORBA support

9.2.1.3 Enhancing the Java and RMI Implementation with IIOP

Because of the strengths and weaknesses of the native RMI approach, IIOP was provided as an additional capability. IIOP complements the native RMI approach by addressing all of the shortcomings related to native RMI. IIOP can be used in three different architectural configurations:

- In conjunction with RMI and JRMP through a bridge
- RMI over IIOP
- As a replacement for RMI through Java IDL

By providing an IIOP half bridge to the native RMI approach, the developer can have RMI requests transmitted into a CORBA environment. This approach, shown in Figure 9.6, provides an excellent Java-to-Java integration, with access to external objects through CORBA. However, the access is very inefficient and might not be satisfactory for some applications. This half-bridge architecture is similar to using IIOP to communicate between two ORBs, each of which uses different internal object communications mechanisms, with IIOP half bridges to communicate between them.

RMI's layered architecture approach is meant to allow different technologies to be used at each layer; IIOP can be applied at the RMI transport layer. This approach, shown in Figure 9.7, uses IIOP as a native protocol and fixes the inef-

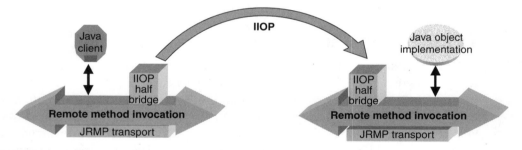

FIGURE 9.6   RMI-IIOP Half-bridge Architecture

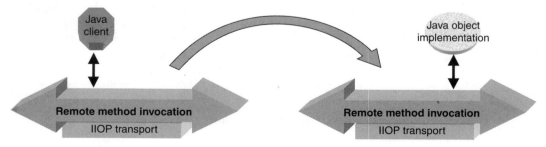

FIGURE 9.7   RMI with IIOP at Transport Layer

ficiencies of the half-bridge approach. It allows the developer to migrate from a Java-only environment to allow Java objects and objects in other languages to communicate. In addition, the RMI over IIOP solution solves all of the weaknesses described in Section 9.2.1.2. However, in both of these architectures the CORBA services are either not available to the developer or difficult to use.

Obtaining the full use of the CORBA services requires the use of a Java IDL option in which CORBA IDL interfaces are specified. This approach, shown in Figure 9.8, obviates the use of RMI. There are two different methods that can be used to apply JAVA IDL. In the first case, the developer writes an IDL for interface specification. IDL modules, interfaces, and operations are similar to Java packages, interfaces, and methods. Then a Java IDL compiler is used to generate the Java code for the developer. The IDL generates CORBA stubs and skeletons rather than RMI stubs and skeletons. These stubs are ORB-independent and perform functions similar to RMI stubs, such as data marshalling. An IIOP-based ORB is used to transmit the request. This ORB allows Java applications to run as either standalone applications or as applets in Java-enabled browsers. All of the CORBA services are available to the programmer, the most important being the naming service. This approach is the most heterogeneous, but it requires the developer to work with the CORBA IDL.

In the second case, the developer writes Java code and interfaces. Then applying Java IDL the Java interfaces are used to generate CORBA IDL interfaces. Other applications and programs can access the Java applications through an IIOP-based ORB using the generated CORBA IDL. This method of applying Java IDL has the benefit of not requiring the Java programmer to have

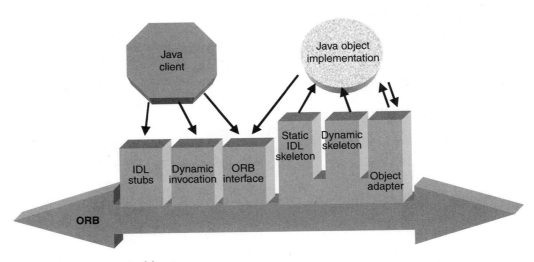

FIGURE 9.8 Java IDL Architecture

any CORBA IDL knowledge. Selection of the method will depend on the experience of the programmer with CORBA IDL. The first method will develop more efficient interfaces but the second is very easy and provides heterogeneous access that is lacking in the native RMI solution.

The OMG is committed to supporting Java. With the development of the objects by value specification, as described in Chapter 7, CORBA will support all methods of distributed invocation processing in Java. With the availability of products, the Java IDL and objects by value capabilities will give the programmer the equivalent of the RMI native solution as well as solving all of RMI's shortfalls that were described at the end of Section 9.2.1.2.

In November 1998, Sun Microsystems made the public commitment to promote the seamless integration of the Java 2 platform and CORBA. In conjunction with this commitment the OMG agreed to recommend to Sun selected APIs from CORBA for inclusion in the JDK core. In addition, when Sun includes these specifications they will only use those specifications that have been recommended by the OMG. This commitment moves CORBA and JAVA's relationship to a serious new level.

9.2.1.4 Important Considerations in Selecting a Java Distributed Invocation Strategy

In selecting a Java distributed invocation strategy, the developer has three choices:

- Java RMI
- Java IDL
- RMI over IIOP

Java RMI has two strong points in its favor. The first is its optimization for an all-Java environment. The second is the strong support from Sun Microsystems. Developers faced with a self-contained Java programming problem might opt for this solution. However, it will be the most limited solution.

Java IDL is a better solution for systems development when integration with existing systems and new development based on other languages is required. It has three benefits. First is vendor neutrality with wide industry and platform support. The second is interoperability between multilanguage objects. And finally is the support for CORBA services. Developers that need to develop interoperable systems in heterogeneous environments will prefer this option. However, it requires knowledge of IDL by the developer.

Finally, a developer can always choose to apply both technologies to application development using RMI over IIOP. This solution appears to provide the developer with the best of both worlds. This solution has been optimized by Sun Microsystems for JAVA. It has significant support from Sun and doesn't require knowledge of IDL. Its only shortfall is the limited support for the CORBA services.

9.3 Using HTTP for Web Communications

HTTP was designed as a protocol to support hypertext applications. This technology was ultimately applied to the Web, where it has gained wide and enthusiastic support. Using this protocol, developers can build applications to allow links to be established between documents, to transmit requests for document searching, and to provide some level of forms-processing capabilities. Due to the success of the Web, HTTP has been extended in a variety of directions to improve on its basic capability. However, the nature of the original protocol coupled with these extensions has led to a protocol that is complex to use and doesn't scale to large, mission-critical, Internet-based applications. Two of the most significant issues are the number of ever-increasing transport connections that are created to service requests and the need to extend the Internet to support distributed object-based applications based on CORBA, DCOM, and Java RMI.

The goal of the W3C regarding HTTP is to provide a protocol that has the following features:

- Has a robust architecture and framework definition
- Is extensible to new types of interactions and applications
- Is scalable to large-scale Internet applications

To satisfy these, the W3C has explored a next generation of HTTP, aptly entitled hypertext transport protocol—Next Generation (HTTP-NG). This effort to design, implement, and test a new architecture for HTTP was begun in July 1997 and completed in September 1998. The goal was to design a new Web protocol whereby the Web is expressed as a set of interfaces on top of a distributed object system designed with Internet constraints in mind. It is important to know that all information related to HTTP-NG is work in progress and therefore has not been formally endorsed by W3C membership at the time this book was written and is subject to change.

The types of issues addressed include these:

- Characterizing the usage on the Web that might be expected in the future
- Classifying layers that would support a protocol that is flexible and extensible
- Ensuring adequate transport support
- Providing scalability and efficiency through a variety of mechanisms, including replication and mirroring

One of the two groups established to develop the architecture, the requirements group, focused on characterizing the Web as the basis for the requirements. HTTP-NG would have to not only support static content and browser access, but also address dynamic content and first-class Web objects. This would significantly alter the utilization of the Web. As a result, scalability and performance would become increasingly more difficult.

To design HTTP-NG, the protocol design group used this information, as well as lessons learned from prior protocol efforts such as X.11, XNS, ONC, DCE, IIOP, RMI, DCOM, and TCP/IP. HTTP-NG is designed to be a layered architecture based on a distributed object-oriented model. The layering is expected to result in an architecture that is modular and extensible. This would make it easy to understand. It further would allow different technologies or approaches to implementation to be applied at each layer without the entire protocol having to be redesigned. In addition, the architecture emphasizes the need for scalability and efficiency in operation because of the nature of the Internet. The Internet is the world's largest network. What might work in a corporate environment may not scale for usage on the Internet. HTTP-NG was architected for the Internet. Three layers are currently envisioned for the architecture, as shown in Figure 9.9:

- Application
- Messaging
- Transport

Each is isolated by a well-defined set of APIs.

The Web application exists at the application layer. The protocol ensures that applications cannot interfere with each other. The Web application can be any of a variety of types, such as "the classic Web application" (TCWA), an HTML-based Web page with links operating across HTTP, or a set of object-based applications. The interface between the application and message layers is described through the definitions of operations and data types.

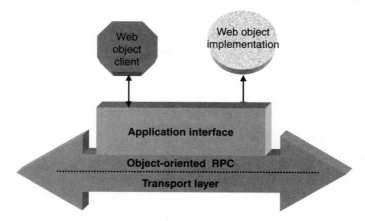

FIGURE 9.9   HTTP-NG Architecture

The type system is very robust and functionally compatible with CORBA, DCOM, and Java RMI. It supports the following types:

- Fixed
- Floating
- Boolean
- Sequence
- Array
- Enumeration
- Simplified union
- Abstract strings
- Reference pointers
- Pickles
- Local objects
- Remote objects

The type system has many interesting features. As an example, `char` is not supported. `Chars` are expected to be implemented using strings. The `pickle` type is used instead of the CORBA `any` type and supports both dynamic typing and externalization.

The messaging layer provides two important mechanisms. The first is the significant caching of methods, resource identification, and results. The second is session-context management that allows persistent connections, pipelining, and batch processing of requests. Both of these have obvious performance advantages over other approaches.

The messaging to transport layer interface is accomplished using a very basic concept: blocks of data are transmitted between these layers. The transport layer is further substrated as a set of abstract sublayers. This allows specific transformations to occur that can be added or removed at runtime. Examples of these sublayers might be security, compression, and multiplexing.

The transport layer has a special sublayer called the Webmux. The Webmux is a construct of four specific sublayers:

- Chunking, for splitting messages into arbitrary sizes
- Record marking, for identifying the last chunk
- Bidirectionality, for managing server callbacks over the same connection
- Multiplexing, for allowing multiple "virtual" connections to be mapped on a single transport connection

Combining these sublayers improves the overall efficiency of the protocol. Other types of sublayers that can be expected in the transport layer include synchronous and asynchronous messaging, notification and events, real-time and multicast, and advanced security features.

A solution to the scalability and efficiency questions for HTTP-NG are replication and mirroring. Distributed replication, multicast replication, and cooperative caches were all explored as possible designs. It is expected that replication and mirroring would be managed separately from the protocol but that the protocol would provide explicit guidance for implementation.

HTTP-NG was expected to capture a growing fraction of Web traffic, initially it would coexist with HTTP, eventually replacing it for all new Web applications. It was not expected to be backward compatible with HTTP but would continue to support the request-response nature of HTTP. However, the resource, basically the Web page pointed at by a link, would be expanded to be an object that can not only be a Web page but an application as well. TCP/IP will be supported as the default transport protocol.

In December of 1998 the initial work on HTTP-NG was presented at the IETF. At that time it was felt that HTTP-NG was too different to be accepted in one step. The work is being taken forward in smaller pieces in a variety of working groups, but it is unclear at this time what, if any, impact it will have. This activity bears watching for two reasons:

1. Lessons learned can be applied to future generations of IIOP

2. HTTP-NG may be adopted in some form by the IETF or WC3

9.3.1   HTTP-NG and IIOP

HTTP-NG was intended to allow general purpose distributed applications to directly participate on the Web rather than be layered on top of HTTP. This would have converted the Web to a distributed object system. A generic distributed object model has been considered by HTTP-NG to allow CORBA, DCOM, and Java RMI to coexist on top of this protocol. W3C states, as a part of the HTTP-NG draft goals from March 27, 1998, that it was not the intention of HTTP-NG to unify these object models; rather, to support an analogous system that would have CORBA, DCOM, or Java RMI components layered on top, with little effort or modification on the part of software vendors.

If this approach had been carried to its logical conclusion, developers would be faced with three architectures for interoperability:

- IIOP, optimized for interoperability
- Java RMI, optimized for Java applications
- HTTP-NG, optimized for Web applications

Given that most organizations are moving towards Java-based Web applications built by integrating existing systems, organizations would be forced to choose one of these technologies.

9.4   The Future of Object Interoperability

The OMG continues to be committed to object interoperability. Recognizing the failings in the original specifications, it added IIOP to ensure interoperability. Working with Sun Microsystems, it has provided Java programmers with a choice that is quickly becoming the preferred method of development, since few applications live within a vacuum. Applications based on heterogeneous technology must connect and communicate.

The work done on HTTP-NG by W3C has been followed by the OMG. The OMG is a member of W3C. In addition, there is significant overlap of members between both organizations. This means the membership of both have interest in ensuring consistency and interoperability in the technical solutions from each organization.

In the last year we have seen IIOP become the only viable candidate for building distributed object systems. Interoperability and heterogeneous environments are critical issues that only IIOP has addressed. Potential competitors are either integrating IIOP or are disappearing. At this time, IIOP has become the only logical choice.

Satisfying the next generation of distributed object systems will require the OMG to focus on several fundamental issues:

- Continuing to provide object interoperability, which will require greater emphasis on services interoperability
- Providing a fully functional, high-performance Java IDL system
- Increasing scalability and efficiency of IIOP for Web-based applications based on the results of work such as HTTP-NG

If the OMG manages to provide good standards and vendors provide solid products, then IIOP will continue to be the best choice for distributed object systems.

In this chapter we learned about several related technologies and their complicated relationship with IIOP. The key points of this chapter were:

- IIOP can complement RMI and provide improved interoperability outside of the Java environment
- The results of the HTTP-NG activities should be considered in the next generation of IIOP
- IIOP is the solution for today's applications

CORBA's Distributed Object Interoperability Architecture

10.1 IIOP and Object Interoperability

This chapter will place in context the role IIOP plays with regard to achieving distribution transparency and interoperability. IIOP is only one of the tools that must be applied to obtain interoperability. CORBA's interoperability architecture as well as scenarios for achieving interoperability will be addressed.

IIOP was created for the sole purpose of providing interoperability. The intent was to enable CORBA objects that were created and managed by two different ORBs to communicate without the need to understand each other's implementation. To accomplish this, any inter-ORB communication must provide the following:

- ORB-to-ORB communication
- Availability of all ORB functionality
- Content and semantic preservation

IIOP was intended to work within an interoperability architecture that provides a variety of configurations from which an implementor of CORBA software can choose, either as a native messaging protocol or through a bridging mechanism to the native protocol. This architecture is shown in Figure 10.1.

However, the enterprise will need to understand and manage interoperability in order to successfully apply distributed object technology. They cannot assume that these issues will be completely solved through the application of products that contain IIOP. In many cases, they will attempt to solve this problem by selecting a single ORB product in order to assure themselves of interoperability. However, the ability to select a single ORB product will not be feasible for the long term, for the following reasons.

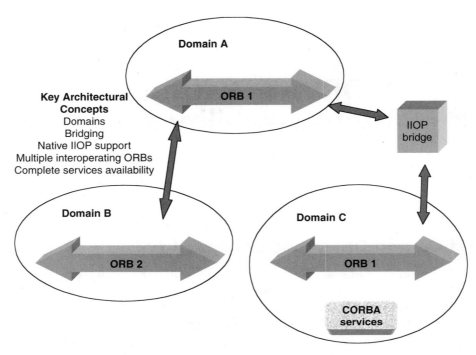

FIGURE 10.1   CORBA Interoperability Architecture

- *Implementation diversity.* As CORBA becomes widely accepted as the standard for distributed object technology, it is creating a marketplace in which ORBs are developed and used by a wide range of vendors, including those that sell ORBs directly and those that embed them in their products. In addition, in certain circumstances users will choose to develop ORBs to meet their own special needs.

- *Domain diversity.* Within any reasonably complex system, multiple domains will be created that model the manner in which the business operates. As an example, different security needs will exist for core systems, desktop applications, and Internet applications. Each security domain will have separate ORB's that are configured to the needs of the domain.

- *One size does not fit all.* ORBs will be optimized for a variety of scenarios. Some will be better suited to large-scale networks such as the Internet, while others will be optimized for real-time processing requirements. For example, new application development in Java would have an optimized Java ORB, with a separate ORB responsible for the integration of existing core systems, such as mainframe or relational database systems that have been given IDL interfaces. Furthermore, specialized packaged applications might have their own embedded ORBs.

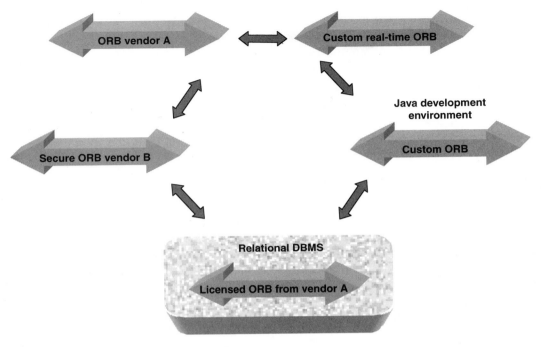

FIGURE 10.2   Examples of ORB Diversity

These configuration examples are shown in Figure 10.2.

10.2 The Need to Understand Interoperability in the Architecture

Combinations of the configurations given in Section 10.1 are most likely in any organization. Organizations will expect the ORBs to seamlessly interoperate. While IIOP will provide this interoperability, it will not *ensure* interoperability. Organizations will not be able to build systems to their requirements without carefully selecting and applying the technology. As an example, the use of IIOP in an RMI environment will not provide the higher levels of interoperability required for many distributed object systems. Interoperability of services and across language is also necessary.

Application designers, developers, system architects, and administrators will find that IIOP is not as transparent as touted. Since the implementation of interoperability is left to the developer of a CORBA product, each implementation will have different operational characteristics. For example, the system architect will need to ensure that a product provides interoperability in a manner conducive to meeting performance, reliability, scalability, and other system concerns. In this case, the specific implementation will significantly influence the system's ability to meet its required operating requirements. Thus, product selection and implementation will be important to the system architect. The application designer will need to pay careful attention to the support provided for services interoperability. While a robust IIOP implementation might exist, the ability to use the naming service across ORBs is equally important to object interoperability. The application designer will want to ensure that interoperability is supported at the services level. This will be important to building Java applications. The selection of RMI over IIOP versus Java IDL will extend beyond IIOP implementation to include the need to support services outside the Java application domain. This issue will continue into the development stage, in which the quality of interoperability with regard to services will require significant workarounds in a design. Further, in the absence of a unified interoperability architecture, test and quality assurance efforts will increase because an application's behavior might change when the application is accessed from other ORBs.

10.3 Key Considerations in Distributed Object Architectures

Following are the key considerations when managing a distributed object system:

- Creating and managing domains
- Identifying system services
- Understanding interoperability implementations

10.3.1 Creating and Managing Domains

Remember from our previous discussions that a domain is a collection of components unified because they share specific characteristics. Typically, these characteristics are related to some aspect of system operations, such as networking, security, or transactions. They might also be oriented around programming considerations such as languages, references, or representations. However, the definition of a domain has no bounds. They can be oriented around applications, functionality, organization, products, or any logical inclusion that is required by a system. An example of domains in an organization is shown in Figure 10.3.

In addition, domains can be related. A domain can be defined around the grouping of domains either by containing a domain within a new domain or federating or by grouping domains. Domains can also be temporal or geographical in nature. The important issue for the system architect is ensuring the interoperability across domains, setting up operating rules between

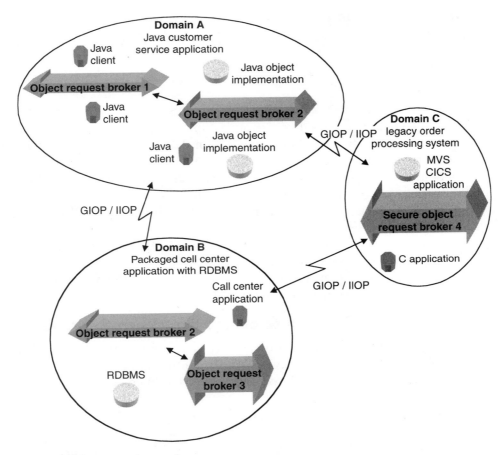

FIGURE 10.3   Examples of Domains

domains, and ensuring that the architecture supports the interoperability needs. As an example, if transactions do not cross domains, this will limit the need to provide interoperable transaction services, a very complex issue.

There are two important considerations to managing domains in an organization:

- Domains will evolve over time and cannot be completely specified for any organization.
- Domains should not be constantly in flux.

The creation, management, and deletion of domains are not well understood in system architecture. Understanding this, however, will be important in order to effectively build distributed object systems in organizations.

10.3.2 Identifying System Services

System services can be subdivided into two categories:

- Fundamental object services
- Advanced system services

Fundamental object services are those that are required in order to build distributed object systems. Every organization must have these, independent of function, organization, or domain definition. Fundamental services that need to be interoperable include those related to the handling of a request (such as representation, marshalling and unmarshalling, and message encoding) and those concerning reference management (such as location transparency, and reference resolution). Naming, persistence, and lifecycle are all examples of fundamental services.

Advanced system service selection is organization-dependent. For example, security, transaction, and conversion services are all system-unique.

In either case, the organization will need to ensure interoperability of services that satisfies its operational requirements.

10.3.3 Understanding Interoperability Implementations

Finally, a key to effective interoperability is understanding the implementation choices that CORBA software implementors have made in supporting interoperability. These are shown in Figure 10.4. In general, the approach in

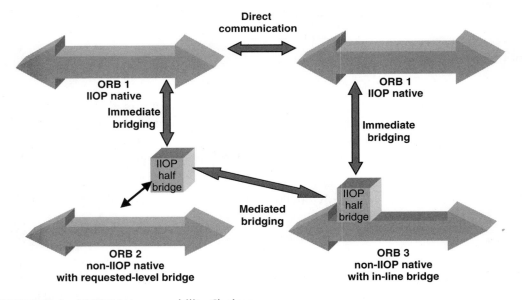

FIGURE 10.4   CORBA Interoperability Choices

which both ORBs natively implement IIOP is the most desirable solution. This is because the request will be handled in the same way, whether it is in the domain or external to the domain. However, this will not always be an optimal solution and should not be taken as the de facto choice. As an example, a real-time ORB will never support IIOP as its internal communications mechanism. The best performance for the system will be obtained through an immediate or mediated bridging approach. Mediated bridging can be much more flexible than immediate because the interaction can be optimized between specific domains as required. For example, ORBs can be optimized to handle the needs of a specific domain, such as a transaction-oriented system or Java development. The interactions with another ORB would be contained to the area of specialization and therefore the translation optimized by the mediated bridge to the needs of the interaction. Obviously, this requires significantly more work than an out-of-the-box solution can provide.

Every organization will need to trade off these considerations against time, money, organization, and criticality of the application. The most important thing to remember is that the flexibility provided by CORBA, IIOP, and their interoperability architecture places the decisions with the organization. But these decisions must be managed.

10.4 A Scenario for Interoperable Distributed Object Systems

Every organization will follow a different path to get to an interoperable object architecture. The availability of products will constrain or enable the final solutions that are reached. In this scenario, we try to give insight into how others are approaching distributed object technology and its impact on interoperability.

This scenario is broken into three stages. These stages describe how this technology enters into an organization and grows into use across the organization. These stages are:

- Project entry
- System expansion
- Core enterprise technology

10.4.1 Stage 1: Project Entry

In stage 1, the technology is brought into the organization for a specific activity usually by early adopters. In many organizations, the use of distributed object technology will begin with three likely entry points, shown in Figure 10.5.

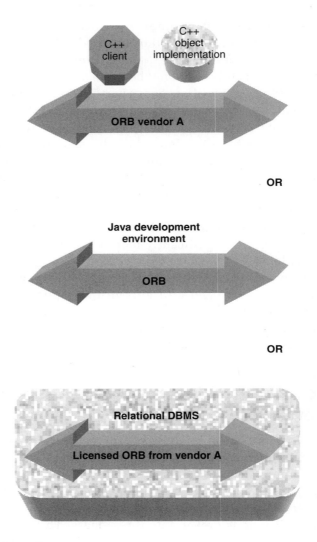

FIGURE 10.5   Scenario Stage One

1. The first might be through a single development project in which C++ is being employed. The developers in this case would be looking for a mechanism to provide connectivity between their client and server applications. They would begin to examine two possible alternatives: an all-Microsoft approach based on DCOM or a CORBA approach. In selecting a CORBA approach, they would buy an ORB from a product vendor. Other solutions they might select from are all proprietary in nature.

2. The second entry point would be through a Java development in which a distributed invocation is required. As discussed in Chapter 9, the choice would be an RMI over IIOP versus a Java IDL approach. While the selection process is similar in nature to the C++ example, it would be driven by a different set of decision points, since C++ users are not faced with the RMI option.

3. The final entry point would be through a new application development as the overall structure around which to architect the system. In this case, it might be brought in through a packaged application that embeds the ORB or it might be to support a C++ or Java development.

Most likely, these entry points will be single domains and interoperability will be a relatively minor concern. Most organizations are at this point with the technology. The particular choice does not appear important, and each project is essentially left to its own devices.

10.4.2 Stage 2: System Expansion

In stage 2, the technology begins to gain broader exposure due to initial success in stage 1. The second stage will most likely occur for one of two reasons, shown in Figure 10.6. The first is as an extension to the entry point, when a project had significant visibility and was successful. In this case, other developments would mimic the architecture of this project and ORBs would continue to penetrate. This would begin to form sequential domains.

The second reason is when an organization is integrating disparate systems into a new mission-critical application. As the organization begins to look at technology for integration, it will rapidly discover that there are four approaches:

- Messaging
- CORBA
- Proprietary
- Build it yourself

In Chapter 2, we went into detail on these approaches. CORBA is the only distributed object technology available for this activity. Furthermore, if C++ or Java is used for development, CORBA becomes an even more compelling choice. In this second situation, the organization will begin to feel a growing need to ensure interoperability. As applications begin to cross systems and lines of business, the creation of multiple domains begins to take hold. It is at this point that the system architect must begin to examine the nature of the distributed object technology that exists in the organization. When multiple proprietary solutions exist, finding ways to bring each of these systems into alignment

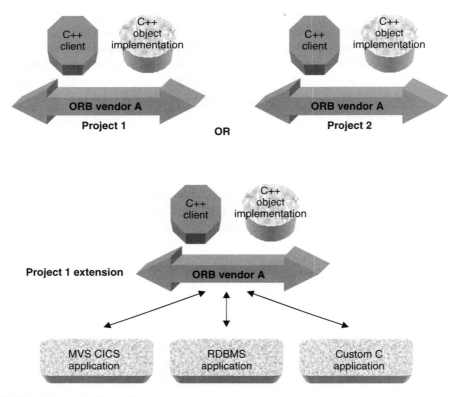

FIGURE 10.6   Scenario Stage Two

will become necessary. The only choice for interoperability becomes CORBA. Organizations are beginning to enter this stage in increasing numbers. When an organization has made too diverse a selection across projects, driving toward an interoperable solution becomes increasingly difficult.

10.4.3 Stage 3: Core Enterprise Technology

In stage 3, the technology becomes a core technology for all systems because the benefits have been proven out in stages 1 and 2. In the third stage, the organization commits to using distributed object technology on a corporate scale. This is depicted in Figure 10.7. Only a few organizations have reached this stage. It is at this stage that interoperability becomes a critical requirement. (It is interesting that an organization has the most control over interoperability when it has the shallowest of requirements for it.) At this point,

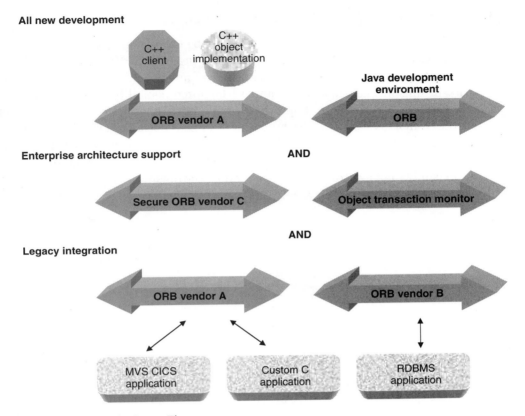

FIGURE 10.7   Scenario Stage Three

the organization must deal with legacy systems, religious fervor related to technology selection, and optimizing the selection for the total benefit of the organization. Most organizations reach this stage because they realized the large investment being made by individual projects. In addition, they view components as the most effective way to gain leverage from their information system investments and they are committed to Java or C++ development. Thus organizations commit significant resources toward making their legacy systems available through object interfaces. This allows the Java or C++ programmer access to components that were previously difficult to use due to their interface complexity. It is now that the system architect starts to deal with many domains, the demand for significant object services, and improved interoperability.

10.5 Summary of IIOP and Interoperability

Distributed object technology will most likely be brought into an organization in a slow, steady progression starting with small projects. Because interoperability will be less important in the early stages, developments will not always be able to work in unison later. IIOP is a standard for interoperability that, if applied as intended, can guarantee interoperability without hampering a software product vendor. If IIOP as well as CORBA continues to be the leading technology for distributed object technology, organizations will be able to obtain the level of interoperability they desire at the appropriate time. However, interoperability is the responsibility not only of the software vendor. The organization applying the technology must be aware of how to best select, apply, and manage the technology.

GIOP Messages

Version 1.1 GIOP Messages

Message Type	Issuer	Enum Value	GIOP Versions
Request	Client	0	1.0, 1.1
Reply	Server	1	1.0, 1.1
CancelRequest	Client	2	1.0, 1.1
LocateRequest	Client	3	1.0, 1.1
LocateReply	Server	4	1.0, 1.1
CloseConnection	Server	5	1.0, 1.1
MessageError	Both	6	1.0, 1.1
Fragment	Both	7	1.1

Version 1.2 GIOP Messages

Message Type	Issuer	Enum Value	GIOP Versions
Request	Both	0	1.2
Reply	Both	1	1.2
CancelRequest	Both	2	1.2
LocateRequest	Both	3	1.2
LocateReply	Both	4	1.2
CloseConnection	Both	5	1.2
MessageError	Both	6	1.2
Fragment	Both	7	1.2

GIOP Version 1.0 Message Header

```
module GIOP {
  struct Version {
    octet major;
    octet minor;
  };

enum MsgType_1_0 {
  // Renamed from MsgType
    Request, Reply, CancelRequest, LocateRequest, LocateReply,
    CloseConnection, MessageError
  };

struct MessageHeader_1_0 { // Renamed from MessageHeader
    char magic [4];
    Version GIOP_version;
    boolean byte_order;
    octet message_type;
    unsigned long message_size;
  };
};
```

GIOP Version 1.1 Message Header

```
module GIOP {
  struct Version {
    octet major;
    octet minor;
  };

enum MsgType_1_1 {
    Request, Reply, CancelRequest, LocateRequest, LocateReply,
    CloseConnection, MessageError, Fragment // GIOP 1.1 addition
  };
  #endif

struct MessageHeader_1_1 {
    char magic [4];
    Version GIOP_version;
    octet flags; // GIOP 1.1 change
    octet message_type;
    unsigned long message_size;
  };
};
```

GIOP Version 1.2 Message Header

```
typedef MessageHeader_1_1 MessageHeader_1_2;
```

IOP Service Context

```
module IOP { // IDL
  . . .
  typedef unsigned long ServiceId;

struct ServiceContext {
    ServiceId context_id;
    sequence <<octet> context_data;
  };

typedef sequence <ServiceContext>ServiceContextList;

const ServiceId TransactionService = 0;
  const ServiceId CodeSets = 1;
  . . .
};
```

GIOP Version 1.0 Request Header

```
struct RequestHeader_1_0 { // Renamed from RequestHeader
  IOP::ServiceContextList service_context;
  unsigned long request_id;
  boolean response_expected;
  sequence <octet> object_key;
  string operation;
  Principal requesting_principal;
  };
```

GIOP Version 1.1 Request Header

```
struct RequestHeader_1_1 {
  IOP::ServiceContextList service_context;
  unsigned long request_id;
  boolean response_expected;
  octet reserved[3]; // Added in GIOP 1.1
  sequence <octet> object_key;
  string operation;
  Principal requesting_principal;
};
```

GIOP Version 1.2 Request Header

```
typedef short         AddressingDisposition;
const short  KeyAddr = 0;
const short  ProfileAddr = 1;
const short  ReferenceAddr = 2;

struct IORAddressingInfo {
  unsigned long    selected_profile_index;
  IOP::IOR    ior;
};

union TargetAddress switch(AddressingDisposition) {
  case KeyAddr:              sequence<octet>object_key;
  case ProfileAddr: IOP::TaggedProfile profile;
  case ReferenceAddr:        IORAddressingInfo ior;
};

struct RequestHeader_1_2 {
  unsigned long request_id;
  octet response_flags;
  octet reserved[3];
  TargetAddress target;
  sequence<octet> object_key;
  string operation;
  IOP::ServiceContextList service_context;
};
```

GIOP Version 1.0 Reply Header

```
enum ReplyStatusType {
  NO_EXCEPTION,
  USER_EXCEPTION,
  SYSTEM_EXCEPTION,
  LOCATION_FORWARD
};

struct ReplyHeader_1_0 {
  IOP::ServiceContextList service_context;
  unsigned long request_id;
  ReplyStatusType reply_status;
};
```

GIOP Version 1.1 Reply Header

```
typedef ReplyHeader_1_0 ReplyHeader_1_1;
```

GIOP Version 1.2 Reply Header

```
enum ReplyStatusType {
  NO_EXCEPTION,
  USER_EXCEPTION,
  SYSTEM_EXCEPTION,
  LOCATION_FORWARD,
  LOCATION_FORWARD_PERM,
  LOCATION_FORWARD_MODE
};

struct ReplyHeader_1_2 {
  unsigned long request_id;
  ReplyStatusType_1_2 reply_status;
  IOP::ServiceContextList service_context;
};
```

GIOP Version 1.0 LocateRequest Header

```
struct LocateRequestHeader_1_0 {
  unsigned long request_id;
  sequence<octet> object_key;
};
```

GIOP Version 1.1 LocateRequest Header

```
typedef LocateRequestHeader_1_0 LocateRequestHeader_1_1;
```

GIOP Version 1.2 LocateRequest Header

```
struct LocateRequestHeader_1_2 {
  unsigned long request_id;
  TargetAddress target;
};
```

GIOP Version 1.0 LocateReply Header

```
enum LocateStatusType_1_0 {
  UNKNOWN_OBJECT,
  OBJECT_HERE,
  OBJECT_FORWARD
};

struct LocateReplyHeader_1_0 {
  unsigned long request_id;
  LocateStatusType locate_status;
};
```

GIOP Version 1.1 LocateReply Header

```
typedef LocateReplyHeader_1_0 LocateReplyHeader_1_1;
```

GIOP Version 1.2 LocateReply Header

```
enum LocateStatusType_1_2 {
  UNKNOWN_OBJECT,
  OBJECT_HERE,
  OBJECT_FORWARD,
  OBJECT_FORWARD_PERM,
  LOC_SYSTEM_EXCEPTION,
  LOC_NEEDS_ADDRESSING_MODE
};
struct LocateReplyHeader_1_2 {
  unsigned long request_id;
  LocateStatusType_1_2 locate_status;
};
```

GIOP Version 1.2 Fragment Header

```
struct FragmentHeader_1_2 {
    unsigned long request_id;
}
```

GIOP Version 1.x Exceptions

```
struct SystemExceptionReplyBody {
    string exception_id;
    unsigned long minor_code_value;
    unsigned long completion_status;
};
```

Standard CORBA Exceptions

Exceptions	Reason
BAD_CONTEXT	error processing the context object
BAD_INV_ORDER	routine invocations are out of order
BAD_PARAM	an invalid parameter was passed
BAD_OPERATION	invalid operation
BAD_TYPECODE	bad TypeCode
COMM_FAILURE	communication failure
DATA_CONVERSION	data conversion error
FREE_MEM	cannot free memory
IMP_LIMIT	violated implementation limit
INTERNAL_ORB	internal error
INITIALIZE_ORB	initialization failure
INTF_REPOS	error accessing interface repository
INV_IDENT	invalid identifier syntax
INV_FLAG	invalid flag was specified
INV_OBJREF	invalid object reference
INV_POLICY	invalid policy
INVALID_TRANSACTION	invalid transaction
MARSHAL	error marshaling a parameter or result
NO_IMPLEMENT	operation implementation unavailable
NO_MEMORY	dynamic memory allocation failure
NO_PERMISSION	no permission for attempted operation
NO_RESOURCES	insufficient resources for the request
NO_RESPONSE	response to the request is not yet available
OBJ_ADAPTER	failure detected by object adapter
OBJECT_NOT_EXIST	non-existent object delete reference
PERSIST_STORE	persistent storage failure
TRANSACTION_REQUIRED	a transaction is required
TRANSACTION_ROLLEDBACK	the transaction rolled back
TRANSIENT	transient failure - reissue request
UNKNOWN	the unknown exception

Vendor Minor Codeset IDs

System Exception	Code	Reason
BAD_PARAM	1	unable to register value factory
BAD_PARAM	2	RID already defined in IFR
BAD_PARAM	3	name already used in the context in IFR
BAD_PARAM	4	target is not a valid container
BAD_PARAM	5	name clash in inherited context
BAD_INV_ORDER	1	dependency exists in IFR preventing destruction of this object
BAD_INV_ORDER	2	attempts to destroy indestructible objects in IFR
MARSHAL	1	unable to locate value factory
NO_IMPLEMENT	1	missing local value implementation
NO_IMPLEMENT	2	incompatible value implementation version
OBJECT_NOT_EXIST	1	attempt to pass an unactivated (unregistered) value as an object reference

TypeCode Encoding

TCKind	Enum Value	Type	Parameters
tk_null	0	Empty	None
tk_void	1	Empty	None
tk_short	2	Empty	None
tk_long	3	Empty	None
tk_longlong	23	Empty	None
tk_ushort	4	Empty	None
tk_ulong	5	Empty	None
tk_ulonglong	24	Empty	None
tk_fixed	28	Simple	Ushort (digits), short (scale)
tk_float	6	Empty	None
tk_double	7	Empty	None
tk_longdouble	25	Empty	None
tk_boolean	8	Empty	None
tk_char	9	Empty	None
tk_wchar	26	Empty	None
tk_octet	10	Empty	None
tk_any	11	Empty	None

TCKind	Enum Value	Type	Parameters
tk_TypeCode	12	Empty	None
tk_principal	13	Empty	None
tk_objref	14	complex	String (repositoryID), string (name)
tk_struct	15	complex	String (repositoryID), string (name), ulong (count) {string (member name), TypeCode (member type)}
tk_union	16	complex	String (repositoryID), string(name), TypeCode (discriminant type), long (default used), ulong (count) discriminant type (label value), string (member name), TypeCode (member type)}
tk_enum	17	Complex	String (repositoryID), string (name), ulong (count) {string (member name)}
tk_string	18	Simple	Ulong (max length)
tk_wstring	27	Simple	Ulong (max length or zero if unbounded)
tk_sequence	19	Complex	TypeCode (element type), ulong (max length)
tk_array	20	Complex	TypeCode (element type), ulong (length)
tk_alias	21	Complex	String (repositoryID), string (name), TypeCode
tk_except	22	Complex	String (repositoryID), string (name), ulong (count) {string (member name), TypeCode (member type)}
tk_value	29	Complex	String (repositoryID), string (name), ulong (count) {string (member name), TypeCode (member type)}
tk_value_box	30	Complex	String (repositoryID), string (name), TypeCode
None	0xffffffff	Simple	Long (indirection)

Primitive Type Alignment

Primitive Type	Octet Alignment
char	1
wchar	1, 2, 4 depending on code set
octet	1
short	2
unsigned short	2
long	4
unsigned long	4
long long	8
unsigned long long	8
float	4
double	8
long double	8
boolean	1
enum	4

IIOP Specialization

IIOP Version 1.x IOR

```
module IOP {
  //
  // Standard Protocol Profile tag values
  //

  typedef unsigned long ProfileId;
  const ProfileId TAG_INTERNET_IOP = 0;
  const ProfileId TAG_MULTIPLE_COMPONENTS = 1;

  struct TaggedProfile {
    ProfileId tag;
    sequence <octet> profile_data;
  };

  //
  // an Interoperable Object Reference is a sequence of
  // object-specific protocol profiles, plus a type ID.
  //

  struct IOR {
    string type_id;
    sequence <<TaggedProfile> profiles;
  };

  //
  // Standard way of representing multicomponent profiles.
  // This would be encapsulated in a TaggedProfile.
  //
```

```
    typedef unsigned long ComponentId;

    struct TaggedComponent {
      ComponentId tag;
      sequence <octet> component_data;
};

typedef sequence <TaggedComponent> MultipleComponentProfile;
struct Version {
    octet major;
    octet minor;
  };

};
```

IIOP Version 1.0 Profile Body

```
module IIOP {

struct ProfileBody_1_0 { // renamed from ProfileBody
    Version iiop_version;
    string host;
    unsigned short port;
    sequence <octet> object_key;
  };

};
```

IIOP Version 1.0 Profile Body

```
module IIOP { // IDL extended for version 1.1

struct ProfileBody_1_1 {
    Version iiop_version;
    string host;
    unsigned short port;
    sequence <octet> object_key;
    // Added in 1.1
    sequence <IOP::TaggedComponent> components;
  };

};
```

Guide to On-line Resources

IIOP Related On-line Resources

www.omg.org
Object Management Group home page

www.omg.org/library/c2indx.html
Complete CORBA/IIOP 2.2 specification

www.cerfnet.com/~mpcline/Corba-FAQ/
CORBA Frequently Asked Questions (FAQ)

www.javasoft/com/pr/1997/june/statement970626-01.faq.html
RMI and IIOP in Java Frequently Asked Questions

adala.smith.cis.syr.edu/~hlwettac/cis700/Compare.html
On-line Article—Comparison of IIOP, RMI, and HTTP

www.blackmagic.com/people/gabe/iiop.html
On-line Article—IIOP Specification: A Closer Look

www.javasoft.com/products/jdk/idl/omgNews.html
Sun Microsystems public commitment to intergrating the Java 2 platform and CORBA

RMI Related On-line Resources

java.sun.com/products/jdk/rmi
Sun Microsystems RMI information

www.javasoft.com/marketing/coollateral/javarmi.html
Sun Microsystems Java RMI white paper

java.sun.com/products/jdk/1.1/docs/guide/rmi/index.html
Sun Microsystems RMI description

www.javasoft.com/products/jdk/1.1/docs/guide/rmi/spec/rmiTOC.doc.html
Sun Microsystems RMI specification

java.sun.com/products/jdk/1.1/docs/guide/rmi/spec/rmi-objmodel.doc.html
Sun Microsystems Java Distributed Object Model description

java.sun.com/products/jdk/1.1/docs/api/packages.html
Sun Microsystems Java platform core API specifications

www.javasoft.com/products/jdk/idl/docs/index.html
Sun Microsystems JavaIDL overview

HTTP-NG Related On-line Resources

www.w3.org/TR/1998/WD-http-ng-goals
World Wide Web Consortium HTTP-NG goals

www.w3.org/TR/WD-HTTP-NG-architecture
World Wide Web Consortium Architectural Model for HTTP-NG specification

www.w3.org/TR/WD-HTTP-NG-interfaces
World Wide Web Consortium Web interfaces for HTTP-NG specification

www.w3.org/TR/WD-HTTP-NG-wire
World Wide Web Consortium binary protocol for HTTP-NG specification

www.w3.org/Protocols/rfc2068/rfc2068
World Wide Web Consortium Hypertext Transport Protocol version 1.1 description

lists.w3.org/Archives/Public/www.http-ng-comments
World Wide Web Consortium Archives of HTTP-NG activities

DCOM Related On-line Resources

www.microsoft.com/com/default.asp
Microsoft Component Object Model information

www.microsoft.com/com/dcom.asp
Microsoft Distributed Component Object Model description

Bibliography

Clip, Paul, "IIOP: The Next HTTP?" *Byte Magazine,* January 1998.

Curtis, David, "Java, RMI and CORBA," *Distributed Object Computing,* October 1997.

Endrijonas, Janet, *Data Security:* How To Bulletproof Your Hardware and Software, Prima, Rocklin, Calif., 1995.

Fischer, Peter, "Meeting Business Challenges with Middlware," *Object Magazine,* October 1997.

Freier, A., P. Karlton, and P. Kocher, *The SSL Protocol Version 3.0,* Netscape Communications Corporation, Mountain View, Calif., 1996.

Gettys, Jim and Henrik F. Nielsen, "SMUX Protocol Specification, W3C, *http://www.w3.org/TR/1998/WD-ux-19980710,* Working Draft, W3C, July 10, 1998.

Harkey, Dan and Robert Orfali, "RMI Over IIOP: Everybody Wins," *Distributed Object Computing,* August/September 1997.

Iona Technologies, Orbix Knowledge Base, Dublin, Ireland, 1998.

Janssen, Bill, Henrik F. Nielsen, and Michael Spreitzer, "HTTP-NG Architecture Model, W3C Working Draft, W3C, *http://www.w3.org/TR/1998/ WD-HTTP-NG-architecture-19980710,* July 10, 1998.

Janssen, Bill, "HTTP-NG Binary Wire Protocol, W3C Working Draft, W3C, *http://www.w3.org/TR/1998/WD-HTTP-NG-wire-19880710,* July 10, 1998.

Kaliski, Burton S., Jr., *An Overview of the PKCS Standards,* RSA Laboratories, San Mateo, Calif., November 1, 1993.

Kaliski, B., M. Robshaw, and Y. Yin, *Answers to Frequently Asked Questions About Today's Cryptography Version 3.0,* RSA Laboratories, San Mateo, Calif., 1995.

Kalisky, Lorin David, "Java RMI/IIOP Interoperability," *Distributed Object Computing,* August/September 1997.

Laukien, Marc and Uwe Seimet, *OmniBroker Preview Release Version 2.0b4 Manual,* Object Oriented Concepts, Billerica, Mass., 1997.

Linthicum, David S., "Net Developer," *Distributed Objects Get New Plumbing,* January 1997, *http://www.dbmsmag.com/9701i04.html.*

Morgan, Bryan, "Corba Meets Java," *www.Javaworld.com/javaworld/jw-10-1997/jw-10-corbajava.html.*

Mowbray, T. Ruh, W., *Inside CORBA: Distributed Object Standards and Applications,* Addison-Wesley, Reading, Mass., 1997.

Nielsen, Henrik F. and Michael Spreitzer, Editors, "Short- and Long-Term Goals for the HTTP-NG Project," W3C Working Draft, W3C, *http://www.w3org/TR/1998/WD-http-ng-goals-19980327,* March 27, 1998.

Neumann, Peter G., *Computer Related Risks,* Addison-Wesley, Reading, Mass., 1995.

OMG, *The World Wide Web Security FAQ,* Lincoln D. Stein, *lstein@cshl.org,* Version 1.9.0, June 30, 1998.

CORBA Messaging—Joint Revised Submission with Errata, OMG TC Document orbos/98-05-06, May 18, 1998.

OMG, *Joint Revised Submission CORBA/Firewall Security + Errata,* OMG Document orbos/98-07-03, July 6, 1998.

OMG, *Objects By Value—Joint Revised Submission with Errata,* OMG TC Document orbos/98-01-18, January 1998.

OMG, *The Common Object Request Broker: Architecture and Specification,* OMGTC Document Formal 198-02-35, February 1998.

Orfali, Robert, Dan Harkey, and Jeri Edwards, *The Essential Distributed Objects Survival Guide,* New York, N.Y.: John Wiley & Sons, 1996.

Patterson, David A. and J. Hennessy, *Computer Architecture, A Quantitative Approach,* San Mateo, Calif.: Morgan Kaufmann Publishers, Inc., 1990.

Pfleeger, Charles P., Security *In Computing 2nd Edition,* Upper Saddle River, N. J.: Prentice Hall, 1997.

Pope, Alan, *The CORBA Reference Guide,* Reading, Mass.: Addison-Wesley, 1998.

Russell, D. and G. T. Gangemi, *Computer Security Basics,* O'Reilly and Associates, Inc., Sebastopol, Calif., 1991.

Spreitzer, Michael, "HTTP-Next Generation," Briefing at Internet PSIG meeting, June 8, 1998.

Stallings, William, *Data and Computer Communications,* Upper Saddle River, N. J.: Prentice Hall, 1994.

Stallings, William, *Network and Internetwork Security Principles and Practice,* Upper Saddle River, N.J.: Prentice Hall, 1995.

Stone, Chris, "IIOP: OMG's Internet Inter-ORB Protocol," *Distributed Object Computing,* June 1997.

Sun Microsystems, *Remote Method Invocation Specification,* Sun Microsystems, Inc., Mountain View, Calif., *http://java.sun.com/products/jdk/ 1.1/docs/guide/rmi/spec/rmiTOC.doc.html,* 1997.

Sun Microsystems, "RMI and IIOP in Java-FAQ," *The Source for Java Technology,* Sun Microsystems, Inc., *http://java.sun.com/pr/1997/june/ statement970626-01.faq.html,* May 8, 1998.

Sutherland, Doug, "RMI and JAVA™ Distributed Computing," *The Source For JAVA™ Distributed Computing,* Sun Microsystems, Inc., *http://www.javasoft.com/features/1997/nov/rmi.html,* November 1997.

Visigenic Software, Inc., *Visigenic Visibroker Programmer's Guide 3.0 for C++,* San Mateo, Calif., 1997.

Wettach, Heidi, "Comparison of IIOP, RMI, HTTP," Syracuse University, November 13, 1997, *http://adala.smith.cis.syr.edu/~hlwettac/cis700/ Compare.html.*

Acronyms

ACL	access control list
ANSI	American National Standards Institute
API	application programming interface
BOA	basic object adapter
CDR	common data representation
CICS	customer interface control system
COM	Component Object Model
CORBA	Common Object Request Broker Architecture
CSS	Common Secure Interoperability Specification
DCE	Distributed Computing Environment
DCE-CIOP	Distributed Computing Environment-Common Inter-ORB Protocol
DCOM	Distributed Component Object Model
DES	data encryption standard
DNA	Distributed Internet Architecture
DTP	distributed transaction processing
EOR	exportable object reference
ESIOP	Environment Specific Inter-ORB Protocol
GIOP	General Inter-ORB Protocol
GSS-API	Generic Security Service Application Programming Interface

GUID	globally unique identifier
HTTP	hypertext transport protocol
HTTP-NG	hypertext transport protocol-Next Generation
IETF	Internet Engineering Task Force
IDE	interactive development environment
IDL	interface definition language
IEEE	Institute of Electrical and Electronics Engineers
IIOP	Internet Inter-ORB Protocol
IOR	interoperable object references
IP	internet protocol
ISO	International Organization for Standardization
JRMP	Java remote method protocol
LAN	local area network
MAC	message authentication code
MIDL	Microsoft IDL
MOM	message-oriented middleware
MPEG	Motion Picture Expert Group
MTS	Microsoft Transaction Server
NDR	network data representation
OAD	object activation daemon
ODBC	Open Database Connectivity
OLE	object linking and embedding
OMA	Object Management Architecture
OMG	Object Management Group
ONC	open network computing
ORB	object request broker
ORPC	object remote procedure calling
OSF	Open Software Foundation
OSI	Open Systems Interconnection

OTS	Object Transaction Service
POOP	Plain Old Orbix Protocol
RAD	rapid application development
RFO	request forwarding options
RFP	Request for Proposal
RM	AP to RM interface
RMI	remote method invocation
RM	Resource Manager
RPC	remote procedure call
SECIOP	Secure Inter-ORB Protocol
SID	securityID
SNA	Systems Network Architecture
SPX	Sequenced Packet Exchange
SQL	standard query language
SSL	Secure Sockets Layer
TCP	transmission control protocol
TCWA	The Classic Web Application
TP	transaction processing
XML	eXtended Markup Language
XNS	Xerox Network Systems
UDP	user datagram protocol
UNO	Universal Networked Object
URL	Uniform Resource Locator
VM	virtual machine
VMCID	vendor minor codeset ID
WWW	World Wide Web
W3C	World Wide Web Consortium
XDR	External Data Representation
4GL	fourth generation language

Index

CORBA Distributed Objects

Using Orbix
Seán Baker

CORBA Distributed Objects is a practical guide to the CORBA standard. Orbix is used throughout to demonstrate the ease of use and power of CORBA. Drawn from personal experience of implementing and using the standard, this book demonstrates how CORBA can be used to write the components of a distributed software system. Its pragmatic, hands-on approach will make it an invaluable reference for experienced programmers and system developers with a working knowledge of C++—those looking to acquire either an overview or a full understanding of the CORBA specification.

0-201-92475-7 • Hardcover • 544 pages • ©1997

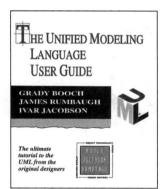

The Unified Modeling Language User Guide

Grady Booch, James Rumbaugh, and Ivar Jacobson
Addison-Wesley Object Technology Series

The Unified Modeling Language User Guide is a two-color introduction to the core eighty percent of the Unified Modeling Language, approaching it in a layered fashion and showing the application of the UML to modeling problems across a wide variety of application domains. This landmark book is suitable for developers unfamiliar with the UML or modeling in general, and will also be useful to experienced developers who wish to learn how to apply the UML to advanced problems.

0-201-57168-4 • Hardcover • 512 pages • ©1999

Doing Hard Time

Developing Real-Time Systems with UML, Objects, Frameworks, and Patterns
Bruce Powel Douglass
Addison-Wesley Object Technology Series

This book is written to facilitate the daunting process of real-time systems development. *Doing Hard Time* presents an embedded systems programming methodology that has been proven successful in practice. The process outlined in this book allows application developers to apply practical techniques, garnered from the more mainstream areas of object-oriented software development, to meet the demanding qualifications of real-time programming. The author offers ideas that are up-to-date with the latest concepts and trends in programming.

0-201-49837-5 • Hardcover with CD-ROM • 800 pages • ©1999

Real-Time UML
Developing Efficient Objects for Embedded Systems
Bruce Powel Douglass
Addison-Wesley Object Technology Series

The Unified Modeling Language is particularly suited to modeling real-time and embedded systems. *Real-Time UML* is the introduction that developers of real-time systems need to make the transition to object-oriented analysis and design with UML. The book covers the important features of UML and shows how to effectively use these features to model real-time systems. Special in-depth discussions of finite state machines, object identification strategies, and real-time design patterns are also included to help beginning and experienced developers alike.

0-201-32579-9 • Paperback • 400 pages • ©1998

UML Distilled
Applying the Standard Object Modeling Language
Martin Fowler with Kendall Scott
Foreword by Grady Booch, Ivar Jacobson, and James Rumbaugh
Addison-Wesley Object Technology Series

Recipient of *Software Development* magazine's 1997 Productivity Award, this concise overview introduces you to the Unified Modeling Language, high-lighting the key elements of its notation, semantics, and processes. Included is a brief explanation of UML's history, development, and rationale, as well as discussions on how UML can be integrated into the object-oriented development process. The book also profiles various modeling techniques associated with UML—use cases, CRC cards, design by contract, dynamic classification, interfaces, and abstract classes.

0-201-32563-2 • Paperback • 208 pages • ©1997

The Unified Software Development Process
Ivar Jacobson, Grady Booch, and James Rumbaugh
Addison-Wesley Object Technology Series

The Unified Software Development Process goes beyond other object-oriented analysis and design methods by detailing a family of processes that incorporate the complete lifecycle of software development. This new book, representing the collaboration of Ivar Jacobson, Grady Booch and James Rumbaugh, clearly describes the different higher-level constructs—notation as well as semantics—used in the models. Thus, stereotypes such as use cases and actors, packages, classes, stereotypes, interfaces, active classes, processes and threads, nodes, and most relations are described intuitively in the context of a model.

0-201-57169-2 • Hardcover • 512 pages • ©1999

Inside CORBA

Distributed Object Standards and Applications
Thomas J. Mowbray and William A. Ruh
Addison-Wesley Object Technology Series

Inside CORBA is a comprehensive, up-to-date, and authoritative guide to distributed object architecture, software development, and CORBA standards. It includes the latest coverage of the new CORBA IDL Language Mapping for the Java programming language and comprehensive coverage of the CORBA 2 standard and CORBA services. The authors outline essential lessons learned from experienced CORBA managers and architects to ensure successful adoption and migration to CORBA technology.

0-201-89540-4 • Paperback • 400 pages • ©1997

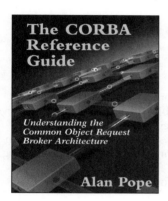

The CORBA Reference Guide

Understanding the Common Object Request Broker Architecture
Alan Pope

This book offers a clear explanation of CORBA as well as a complete reference to the standard. *The CORBA Reference Guide* provides a general background in distributed systems and explains the base architecture as well as the services and facilities that extend this architecture. Of particular note, it details the most sophisticated security framework that has been developed for any architecture to date and covers interoperability with other ORBs.

0-201-63386-8 • Paperback • 432 pages • ©1998

The Unified Modeling Language Reference Manual

James Rumbaugh, Ivar Jacobson, and Grady Booch
Addison-Wesley Object Technology Series

James Rumbaugh, Ivar Jacobson, and Grady Booch have created the definitive reference to the UML. This two-color book covers every aspect and detail of the UML and presents the modeling language in a useful reference format which serious software architects or programmers will need on their bookshelf. *The Unified Modeling Language Reference Manual* is organized by topic and designed for quick access. The authors also provide the necessary information to enable existing OMT, Booch, and OOSE notation users to make the transition to UML. A concise appendix provides an overview of the semantic foundation of the UML.

0-201-30998-X • Hardcover with CD-ROM • 576 pages • ©1999

Applying Use Cases
A Practical Guide
Geri Schneider and Jason P. Winters
Addison-Wesley Object Technology Series

Applying Use Cases provides a practical and clear introduction to developing use cases, demonstrating their use via a continuing case study. Using the Unified Software Development Process as a framework and the Unified Modeling Language as a notation, the authors lead the reader through the application of use cases in different phases of the process, focusing on where and how use cases are best applied. This book also offers insight into the common mistakes and pitfalls that can plague an object-oriented project.

0-201-30981-5 • Paperback • 208 pages • ©1998

Enterprise Computing with Objects
From Client/Server Environments to the Internet
Yen-Ping Shan and Ralph H. Earle
Addison-Wesley Object Technology Series

This book helps you place rapidly evolving technologies—such as the Internet, the World Wide Web, distributed computing, object technology, and client/server systems—in their appropriate contexts when preparing for the development, deployment, and maintenance of information systems. The authors distinguish what is essential from what is incidental, while imparting a clear understanding of how the underlying technologies fit together. The book examines essential topics, including data persistence, security, performance, scalability, and development tools.

0-201-32566-7 • Paperback • 448 pages • ©1998

The Object Constraint Language
Precise Modeling with UML
Jos Warmer and Anneke Kleppe
Addison-Wesley Object Technology Series

The Object Constraint Language is a new notational language, a subset of the Unified Modeling Language, that allows software developers to express a set of rules that govern very specific aspects of an object in object-oriented applications. With the OCL, developers are able to more easily express unique limitations and write the fine print that is often necessary in complex software designs. The authors' pragmatic approach and illustrative use of examples will help application developers to quickly get up-to-speed.

0-201-37940-6 • Paperback • 144 pages • ©1999